Cambridge University Library

Cambridge University Library is one of the world's great research libraries. This book is a celebration of the treasures of the library from the perspective of a group of eminent scholars who actively use the collections for research. Chapters have been selected to illustrate the vast range of the library's collections: from the fifth-century Codex Bezae to the archives of contemporary writers and politicians; from medieval manuscripts to the letters of Charles Darwin; on history, theology, politics, sociology, art history, biology, agriculture, mathematics and astronomy. Extensively illustrated with over two hundred photographs, many of them in colour and published for the first time, *Cambridge University Library: The Great Collections* offers a unique perspective on a remarkable institution.

Cambridge

EDITED BY PETER FOX

University Librarian, Fellow of Selwyn College, Cambridge

University Library

The Great Collections

CAMBRIDGE UNIVERSITY PRESS

PUBLISHED BY THE PRESS SYNDICATE OF THE UNIVERSITY OF CAMBRIDGE
The Pitt Building, Trumpington Street, Cambridge CB2 1RP, United Kingdom

CAMBRIDGE UNIVERSITY PRESS
The Edinburgh Building, Cambridge CB2 2RU, UK   http://www.cup.cam.ac.uk
40 West 20th Street, New York, NY 10011–4211, USA   http://www.cup.org
10 Stamford Road, Oakleigh, Melbourne 3166, Australia

First published 1998

Printed in Great Britain at the University Press, Cambridge

Designed by Rob Sawkins in Lexicon 9.45/14pt
(*from The Enschedé Font Foundry*) using QuarkXPress ™

A catalogue record for this book is available from the British Library

ISBN 0 521 62636 6 hardback
ISBN 0 521 62647 1 paperback

Contents

Contributors

Professor C. N. L. Brooke	Emeritus Dixie Professor of Ecclesiastical History University of Cambridge
Dr F. Burkhardt	Senior Editor, Charles Darwin Correspondence Project
The Reverend Professor W. O. Chadwick	Emeritus Regius Professor of Modern History University of Cambridge
Professor Sir Alan Cook	Emeritus Jacksonian Professor of Natural Philosophy University of Cambridge
P. K. Fox	University Librarian, University of Cambridge
Professor G. D. S. Henderson	Emeritus Professor of Medieval Art University of Cambridge
Dr P. Hutchinson	Lecturer in German, University of Cambridge
Dr P. F. Kornicki	Reader in Japanese History and Bibliography University of Cambridge, and Honorary Keeper of the Japanese Books, Cambridge University Library
Dr E. S. Leedham-Green	Deputy Keeper of the University Archives University of Cambridge
Professor J. M. Mackenzie	Professor of History, University of Lancaster
Dr D. J. McKitterick	Librarian, Trinity College Cambridge
The Reverend Dr D. C. Parker	Senior Lecturer in Theology, University of Birmingham
Dr S. C. Reif	Director of the Taylor-Schechter Genizah Research Unit Cambridge University Library
D. E. Rhodes	Formerly in the Department of Printed Books The British Library
J. S. Ringrose	Under-Librarian, Department of Manuscripts Cambridge University Library
Professor M. Twyman	Professor of Typography & Graphic Communication University of Reading

References in the text in square brackets are illustration numbers;
those set in bold, e.g. [**109**]*, are figures in the colour plate sections*

Introduction

PETER FOX

In November 1995 the Sunday newspaper, the *Observer,* described Cambridge University Library as 'the nearest thing to Paradise that this world has to offer ... the most accessible collection of literary treasure on this side of the Atlantic'. The following month a columnist in the *Sunday Telegraph* said that the Library was 'one of the most wonderful places I know, not for what it looks like but for what it contains ... Walking around its mile on mile of ... corridors, you know you are walking around the world mind.'

This book is a celebration of some of the collections that arouse such praise and enthusiasm the world over. It seeks to give a flavour of those collections, not just as artistic, literary or scientific treasures in their own right but as sources for the research and teaching which are central to the University's purpose. It makes no attempt to survey the collections in anything like a comprehensive way, nor to be a history of the Library – that has already been written, at least for the period up to the end of the nineteenth century.

In selecting topics for inclusion, the editorial committee have attempted to provide an impression of the range of the Library's collections: in terms of period, from the fifth-century Codex Bezae to the archive of the living writer Stefan Heym, which is still being created; in terms of geographical spread, from the British Isles, through continental Europe to the Middle East and on to Japan, with the Royal Commonwealth Society adding the global perspective of the Empire 'on which the sun never set'; in terms of subject matter, with history and theology represented in several chapters, but also studies of the worlds of literature, politics, sociology, art history, biology, agriculture, mathematics and astronomy. Aware that a comprehensive survey was impossible, even for those parts of the Library's holdings selected for inclusion, the editorial committee invited scholars with a deep knowledge of their subjects to adopt an approach which was not simply descriptive but would seek to demonstrate how the material in question serves as the raw material for research.

The illustrations have been carefully selected both to support the text of the chapters and also to provide an indication of a wider range of material in the Library than could be considered in detail.

It was clear that any book of this scope can do little more than scratch the surface of what is housed on the 160 kilometres or so of shelves in the University Library. The editorial committee have tried to maintain a balance in their selection of chapters but have done so acutely aware that almost every reader, on picking up the book for the first time, will ask why a chapter on ... was not included. A different editorial committee might well have selected a very different range of topics, and produced a book which is just as representative as the present one. This dilemma, however, illustrates the wide-ranging nature of the University Library's collections and the reason why it is so central to research in so many fields not just in Cambridge but on a national, indeed international, level.

What is it about the University Library that causes it to have such a powerful positive influence on its users? Obviously, much rests upon the size and range of the collections which, as David McKitterick indicates in his chapter on the history of the Library, have been built up by donation and purchase over a period of over 600 years, augmented in the last 300 by the legal deposit privilege. In terms of size, the collections do not match those of the British Library or the Bodleian in Oxford. What marks out the Cambridge library is the large proportion of material on open access, and thus immediately accessible to users, and the privilege of borrowing, which is extended to a wide range of readers. This lends the University Library a 'user-friendliness' unusual among major national libraries.

The Library's fundamental philosophy is that its collections are there to be used. But that use brings its own problems. Given that its readers are not just those of today but those of decades, even centuries hence, preservation plays a major role in the overall activities of the Library. Preservation activities range from the binding and repair of modern books and journals to the painstaking conservation of medieval manuscripts. In this way, the treasures illustrated in this book are being kept in a condition that ensures that they will be usable for centuries to come [1].

In many ways, though, manuscripts written on vellum, or books printed before about 1850 on rag paper, are remarkably resilient, provided they are kept in suitable storage conditions. It is the preservation of books and journals printed on wood-pulp paper since the middle of the nineteenth century which is causing librarians across the world the greatest concern. This paper is acidic and contains within itself the seeds of its own destruction. Good storage and low exposure to light and heat will slow down the process of decay, but inevitably books, journals, music – anything – printed

on this type of paper are at risk from what is known as the 'brittle-paper' syndrome. The quantity of material is so great, and the artefactual value of many of the items relatively low, that the normal preservation process is to microfilm, and thus preserve, the content, whilst accepting that the original might eventually disintegrate. Microfilm is generally disliked by readers, and so more and more now it is combined with digitization, so that the microfilm acts as the preservation medium and the digital image the version made available to users. Though much cheaper than hands-on conservation, this is, nevertheless, an expensive process, and the University Library is collaborating closely with other major research libraries in the British Isles, continental Europe and in north America, to ensure that the most cost-effective methods are used and that duplication of effort is reduced to a minimum.

The rapid growth of electronic publishing is bringing with it exciting new opportunities for access to information and is undoubtedly opening up new avenues for research. For a library which has to plan in terms of decades or centuries, the new media are bringing their own problems. One can put a book onto a shelf and be fairly confident that, in a hundred years' time, one's great-grandchild will be able to remove it and read it. Do the same with a CD-ROM and the chances are that your great-grandchildren will probably not even recognize what it is. Even if they do, the chances of their being able to read it are quite remote. Libraries are investing heavily in providing access to electronic information, and in the same way that it is the role of the great research libraries to preserve and share information in traditional printed form long after its original publisher has lost interest in it, so it will be their role in the future to ensure the preservation of, and access to, information originally published in electronic form. The difficulty and cost of achieving this, however, are such that no library can act independently, and Cambridge University Library is working closely with its partners in the Consortium of University Research Libraries and the North American Research Libraries Group to establish standards and procedures to ensure that important work in electronic form is preserved for the use of future generations.

During the 1980s there was much speculation about the death not only of the book, but of libraries. It seems clearer to us now that, for many years to come, the future of information and other library provision will be a hybrid one, with electronic information resources augmenting or replacing print in some subjects and for some purposes. This is likely to be par-

1. Conservation work in the University Library on a manuscript catalogue of the Vatican and other Italian libraries, dating from the mid sixteenth century. A number of leaves had been damaged due to the acidic nature of the iron-gall ink, and the original binding had deteriorated. The manuscript has now been stabilized and rebound; the original binding has been preserved and boxed with the conserved manuscript.

ticularly so for journals in rapidly developing fields such as many of the sciences, for publications which need to be regularly updated such as reference tools, and for providing means of access and searching which are simply impossible with print. On the other hand, the human mind has not yet developed the capacity to work through a concentrated argument or to read comfortably a lengthy work of literature on a screen.

For many purposes the codex is, and will remain, the most effective information medium. It can also be a very beautiful object in itself, as can be seen from many of the illustrations in this book. The sense of tactile pleasure gained from opening a book, whether it be a brand new one, a well-loved copy, or one that has been sitting on the Library's shelves waiting patiently for its time to come, is something which will never be achieved by turning on a computer.

The publication of this book coincides with the opening of a new exhibition centre, in which, for the first time in its 600-year history, the University Library will be able to show to the general public some of its treasures in a way which displays them to their best advantage whilst at the same time providing appropriate environmental conditions.

The editor acknowledges with gratitude the assistance of many people in preparing this book, both inside the Library and outside: the contributors, for the time and effort they have put into writing their chapters, selecting illustrations and dealing with editorial queries; colleagues in the Special Collections Division of the Library, particularly Brian Jenkins and Patrick Zutshi, who have worked through the chapters and organized the photography; staff of the Library's Photographic Department, especially Mark Scudder, the magnificent results of whose work can be seen on almost every page; other Library colleagues who have selected illustrations or made helpful suggestions – Richard Andrewes, Charles Aylmer, Terry Barringer, Jill Butterworth, Roger Fairclough, David Hall, Steve Hills, Craig Jamieson, Alan Jesson, Stephen Lees, Mark Nicholls, Adam Perkins, Nicola Thwaite, Jonathan Topham, Roy Welbourn, John Wells; Sally-Anne Buckle for countless hours of editorial support; members of the Library Syndicate, especially its Chairman, Anthony Edwards, for advice and assistance and for permission to reproduce the illustrations; and finally, our colleagues at Cambridge University Press, especially Andrew Brown.

Chapter 1

History of the Library

Dᴀᴠɪᴅ McKɪᴛᴛᴇʀɪᴄᴋ

Tʜᴇʀᴇ ɪs ᴏɴᴇ simple lesson to be learned from studying library history. Those administering, and those using, libraries have almost invariably faced a growth of knowledge, reflected in increasing numbers of books, that threatens to engulf each succeeding generation. In 1627, Gabriel Naudé was only one among many librarians and others across Europe in the early seventeenth century who expressed their concern at the multitudes of publications falling from the press. The efforts to order knowledge made then and subsequently, as well as by earlier generations, are the direct fore-runners of our present concerns with how best to exploit computing resources to avoid losing what we already have. In the last hundred years, Cambridge University Library has become known world-wide as one of the most efficient to use, most effectively run, and best-stocked libraries in the world. That reputation has held good for readers of modern books, of rare books, of manuscripts or of other special collections. Some understanding of the history of the collections and their organization, why there are particular strengths and particular weaknesses, helps enormously in using the Library as a reader today.

2. The University Library seen from Memorial Court, Clare College, before building of the new college library began in 1984.

3. Registrum librorum per varios benefactores communi librarie universitatis Cantebrigiensis collatorum. The Library's first catalogue, 1424 – c. 1440. (University Archives)

All new members of the University of Cambridge quickly learn one fact about its libraries: that they are divided into three kinds. Largest, and most obvious on the skyline, is the University Library, its seventeen-floor tower visible from many miles away [2]. In addition to this, there are faculty and departmental libraries run by the University, mostly identified according to their subjects, varying very greatly in size. Some incorporate important historical or other research collections, and others are much smaller, serving the everyday needs of departments with fewer people. Then, to complete the trio, there are the college libraries, again varying profoundly in their character and holding many a surprising treasure for the unwary. Altogether there are over a hundred libraries in the University.

Of all these, the libraries with the longest documented history are those of the colleges. The oldest departmental library, that for botany, was established in 1765; most date from the twentieth century. But of the colleges, Peterhouse is known to have possessed a library within a few years of its foundation in 1284. The library of Trinity College, now the largest of the college libraries, and second only to the University Library in its holdings of manuscripts and early printed books, includes several volumes that belonged to two of the smaller houses from which the college was cast by Henry VIII in 1534: King's Hall and Michaelhouse.

The date of the foundation of the University Library is not known. It is probable that it began, like so many other libraries, almost by accident, when books were deposited as securities against loans. However, it is clear that by the second half of the fourteenth century there were enough books in the possession of the University for it to be reasonable for it to be bequeathed further ones; the Library's first catalogue, begun in 1424 and continued to about 1440, lists 122 volumes [3]. The names of many of the early benefactors are known; but only a handful of their gifts have survived and most of them are noticeably plain to look at. They include, however, a finely decorated copy of Chaucer's translation of Boethius, *De consolatione philosophiae*, given by John Croucher of Gonville Hall [48]. Other volumes have fallen victim to theft, religious intolerance, educational reform and, perhaps most damaging of all in a library, sheer neglect – especially, but by no means exclusively, in the upheavals of the sixteenth century.

By 1473, the date of the Library's second catalogue, the space occupied by the old library (on the site now known as the Old Schools) was inadequate; and, in the figure of Thomas Rotherham, then Chancellor of the University and from 1480 Archbishop of York, the Library found a benefactor of imagination as well as wealth. He not only gave books (no contemporary list survives, but they numbered probably over ninety), but also provided for a new room to be built as the upper room of the east range of the Schools. This new room, to which access seems to have been restricted, was designated the *nova bibliotheca*, so as to distinguish it from the old.

The first printed books to enter the Library were present by the mid-1480s, though the celebrated copy of Cicero, *De officiis*, printed at Mainz in

1466, referred to by Dennis Rhodes on page 65, arrived only in 1715, with the books of John Moore. Rhodes also alludes to the Greek books presented by Cuthbert Tunstall, Bishop of Durham, in 1529, which lent a new air of modernity to the Library as a whole.

Though the political and religious upheavals of the mid-sixteenth century brought much to an end in Cambridge, a surprising amount survived from its libraries [49]. There still remain in their colleges' possession, for example, large portions of the medieval libraries of Gonville Hall (later Gonville and Caius College), Pembroke College and Peterhouse. The danger was neglect, or the more positive decision that, as some books were no longer of value, they could be recycled – either as waste paper or vellum or as materials for the bookbinder. By the 1570s the University was sufficiently settled for a major effort to restore and improve the Library [50]. Under the guidance of Andrew Perne, Master of Peterhouse, five times Vice-Chancellor, and by the time of his death in 1589 owner of easily the largest library in the University – not excluding the colleges or the University Library – a group of donors combined in 1574 to provide many of the core texts of Protestant theology, of history, of the sciences and of ancient literature. These men were Matthew Parker (Archbishop of Canterbury), Robert Horne (Bishop of Winchester), Sir Nicholas Bacon (Lord Keeper) and James Pilkington (Bishop of Durham) [51, 52]. Parker's gift included several Anglo-Saxon manuscripts from his own shelves, which thus did not figure in his bequest to Corpus Christi College a few months later. Eight years after this affirmation of faith in the Library's and the University's secure future, Théodore de Bèze entrusted the University with the fifth-century manuscript of the Gospels and Acts that bears his name (see chapter 2).

In the mid seventeenth century, when the Library was under the care of Abraham Whelock, learned alike in Anglo-Saxon and in oriental studies,

4. The central section of an early seventeenth-century panorama of Cambridge from the Backs. The panorama runs from Castle Hill to Queens' College.

the University Library gained and then lost an entire library. The Lambeth Palace Library was temporarily removed from London to Cambridge, and then back again [53]. During its sojourn in the University, it was meticulously catalogued; but any disappointment that may have been felt at its return on the Restoration of Charles II in 1660 was soon modified by a protracted lawsuit that resulted in the University's receiving the large and diverse library of Richard Holdsworth, Master of Emmanuel College, who had died in 1649 leaving his books to Emmanuel, or else to the University 'provided that it please God within five years to make a resettlement of the Church', and provided the University returned the Lambeth books to their home. He was far from alone in making such provision, for in the same year, 1649, Anne Sadleir, daughter of Sir Edward Coke, had expressed similar hopes in leaving to Trinity College her great thirteenth-century illuminated Apocalypse: 'God in his good time restore her [Cambridge] with her sister Oxford to there [*sic*] pristine happines, the Vulgar People to there former obedience, and God bless and restore Charles the Second'. It is thanks to Holdsworth that the University Library acquired not only its first books printed by Caxton but also, among several English medieval manuscripts, a volume (now MS Gg.4.27) dating from the second quarter of the fifteenth century, in which an early attempt was made to assemble all of Chaucer's major poetry [54].

The so-called Royal Library, gathered by John Moore, member of Clare College, and Bishop successively of Norwich and of Ely, is the subject of a separate chapter by Jayne Ringrose (see pages 78–89). In the eighteenth century, and thanks especially to Conyers Middleton, who in 1721 was appointed to care for Moore's books, increasing emphasis was placed on the care and study of the early printed books. Middleton owed his post more to those who wished to spite Richard Bentley, Master of Trinity (his own college), than to any latent bibliothecarial skills. But in 1735 he published a perceptive study of Caxton and other early English printing. In doing so he was to prove to be at the beginning of a tradition of Librarians among whom Henry Bradshaw, Librarian from 1867 until his death in 1886, has never been surpassed.

In the sixteenth century it was sufficient for the Library to have books in Latin, Greek and Hebrew; there were none in English or other foreign languages until the 1580s, save for some medieval manuscripts. By the nineteenth century, led by missionary and commercial interests (the two could seem indistinguishable), it was assumed that a major library would spread

Dialogue. A huict. Premier cœur.

5. An initial from Orlande de Lassus, *Livre de chansons nouvelles* (Paris, 1571), one of an important set of partbooks of motets and madrigals bought in 1995 from the library of the Comtesse de Chambure.

its interests worldwide. In the first years of the century, manuscripts and printed books from India were given by Claudius Buchanan, a zealous advocate of Christianity there. As the century wore on, the Library took on much of its present shape. Serious efforts were made to buy in order to fill in gaps and extend the collections. In John Lodge, self-effacing but widely esteemed, the University had, between 1828 and 1845, a highly effective Librarian. Later on, the music and maps were at last organized as collections in their own right [5, **55**]. The century also witnessed the arrival of a succession of collections of oriental manuscripts, some as gifts and others bought [**56–9**]. J. L. Burckhardt's Arabic manuscripts from north Africa and the Middle East came after his death, in 1817. In the second half of the nineteenth century considerable effort was put into cataloguing these and other related collections.

As the commitments of the University as a whole expanded into new subjects, new posts were established, new courses were taught and new laboratories were built, so the University Library found its own interests extended. The study of Sanskrit was underpinned by a succession of gifts and purchases by, among others, Cecil Bendall, professor of the subject from 1903 [**60**]. The gift in 1886 by Sir Thomas Wade, subsequently the first Professor of Chinese, of over 4,000 books in Chinese and Manchu [7] was followed within a generation by the purchase of more than twice that number of Japanese books from the executors of W. G. Aston, Secretary to the British Legation in Tokyo. These and other smaller collections established the Library as a centre for oriental studies [8–10, **61**]. None could compare with the crates of fragments preserved from the Cairo Genizah, given to the Library at the end of the century and requiring skills that were to be developed only over the next 90 years: this collection is discussed by Stefan Reif in a separate chapter on pages 54–64.

It was only, however, in the twentieth century that there seriously began to accumulate the kinds of archival collections from the west, printed or manuscript, that are now so familiar a part of large libraries. During the First World War, the Librarian Francis Jenkinson devoted his energies less to directing the Library than to importuning friends and acquaintances for

6. An example of American pro-German propaganda: Richard M. McCann, *The fable of the stuffed lion. How he conspired with the frog and the bear to rob the Prussian eagle* (New York, 1915). (First World War Collection)

MANY years ago a majestic Eagle made his home in the north central portion of the European continent.

From his Eyrie he could espy the British Lion in the West, the Russian Bear on the East and nearer to the westward the great French Frog that had stolen from the Eyrie the gems called Alsace and Lorraine.

But the Prussian Eagle did not interfere with any of these and was content to live in peace and freedom. He grew so glorious

SEIT vielen, vielen Jahren bewohnte ein maechtiger Adler sein Felsenheim im mittleren Nord-Europa.

Von seinem hohen Horst konnte er den britischen Loewen im ferneren Westen erspaehen, den russischen Baer im Osten, und naeher im Westen den grossen fraenkischen Frosch, welcher frueher einmal jene zwei Edelsteine, genannt "Elsass" und "Lothringen," vom Adlerhorst weggestohlen hatte.

Aber der preussische Adler kuemmerte sich nicht weiter um jene, war er doch zufrieden in Freiheit und Frieden zu leben.

Jedoch sein Ruhm verbreitete sich, so dass sogar ein Land, genannt Spanien, das Er-

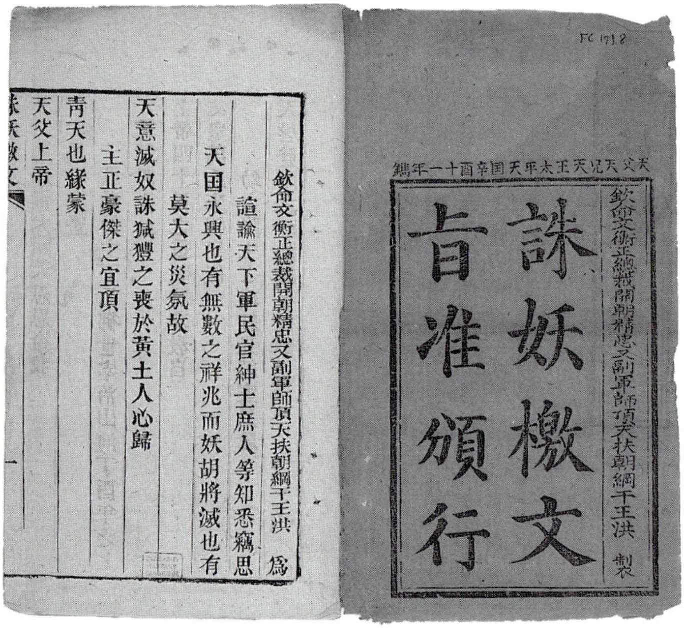

7. The Taiping Rebellion (1850–64), based on a messianic cult of Christian inspiration, cost over 10 million lives and was probably the most destructive civil war in history before the twentieth century. Most of the literature of the insurgents has survived only in collections outside China, including that of Sir Thomas Francis Wade, which he donated to the University Library in 1886. The anti-Manchu publication shown here, *Chu yao hsi wen* (A proclamation on the extermination of demons), a xylograph dated 1861, is the only known copy.

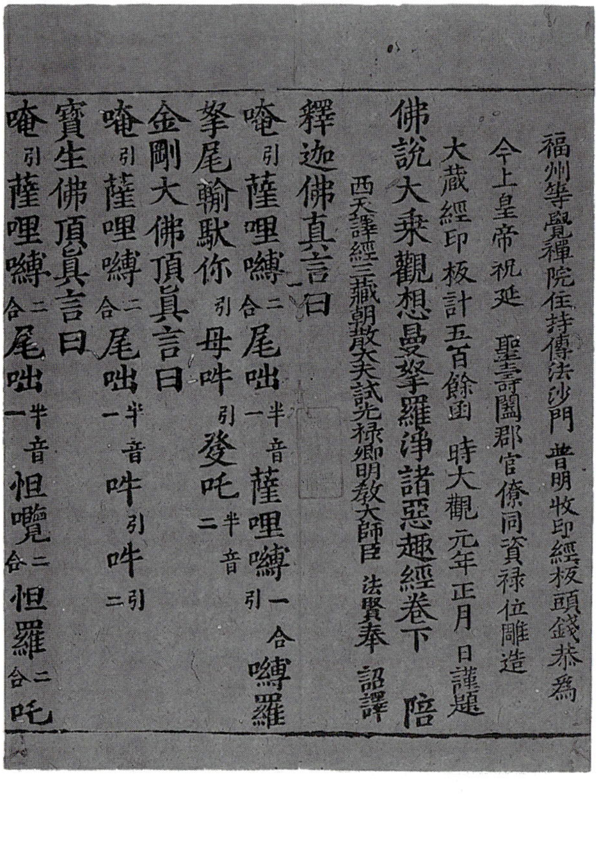

8. Paper has been used in China at least 1,000 years, and printing began at least 500 years, earlier than in Europe. The first printed books were mostly religious, reproduced for devotional purposes. The example shown here, *Fo shuo ta ch'eng kuan hsiang man na lo ching chu o ch'ü ching* (*Buddhabhāṣita-mahāyāna-dhyāna-saṃjñāna-maṇḍala-sarvadurbhāva-prasādaka-sūtra*), is a xylograph dated 1107. It is a Buddhist text, translated into Chinese from Sanskrit by Fa-hsien (died 1001). The book is printed from engraved wood-blocks and made up of sheets of paper pasted together and folded in 'concertina' fashion. This is the oldest printed book in the Library.

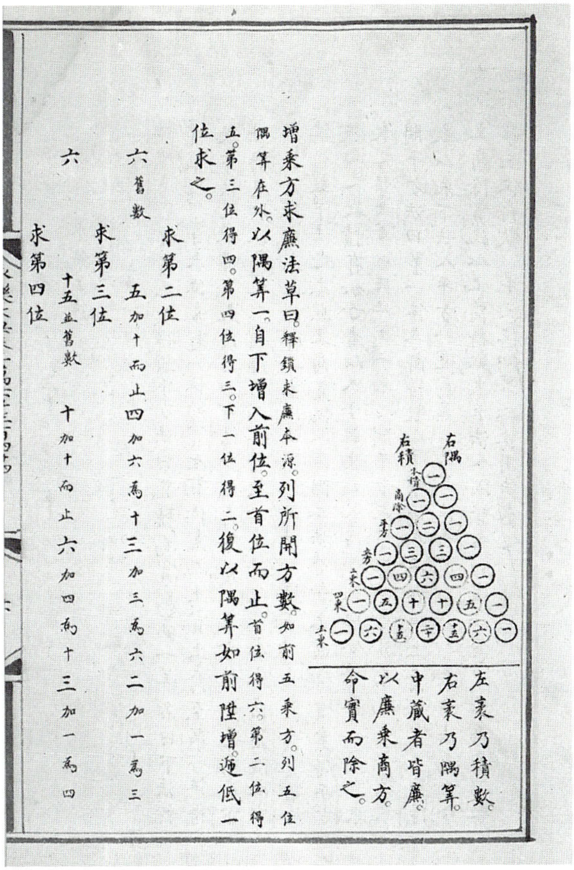
左衺乃積數。
右衺乃隅筭。
中藏者皆廉。
以廉乘商方。
命實而除之。
增乘方求廉法草曰。釋鎖求廉本源。列所開方數。如前五乘方。列五位
隅筭在外。以隅筭一。自下增入前位。至首位而止。首位得六。第二位得
五。第三位得四。第四位得三。下一位得二。復以隅筭如前陞增。遞低一
位求之。
求第二位
六舊數 五加十而止 四加六為十 三加三為六 二加一為三
求第三位
六 十五並舊數 十加十而止 六加四為十 三加一為四
求第四位

9. 'Pascal's Triangle' – the arithmetical triangle of binomial coefficients – has roots in Chinese, Hindu, Arabic and Greek mathematics, and is the most important number pattern in the whole of mathematics. In 1654 Pascal wrote the *Traité du triangle arithmétique* about its properties, of which the University Library possesses two copies. Pascal's Triangle played a major part in the development of the calculus by Leibniz and Newton. The illustration shows one of the oldest extant representations of Pascal's Triangle, from the manuscript 'Yung-lo ta tien' (Great encyclopaedia compiled in the reign of the Yung-lo Emperor), compiled between 1403 and 1407.

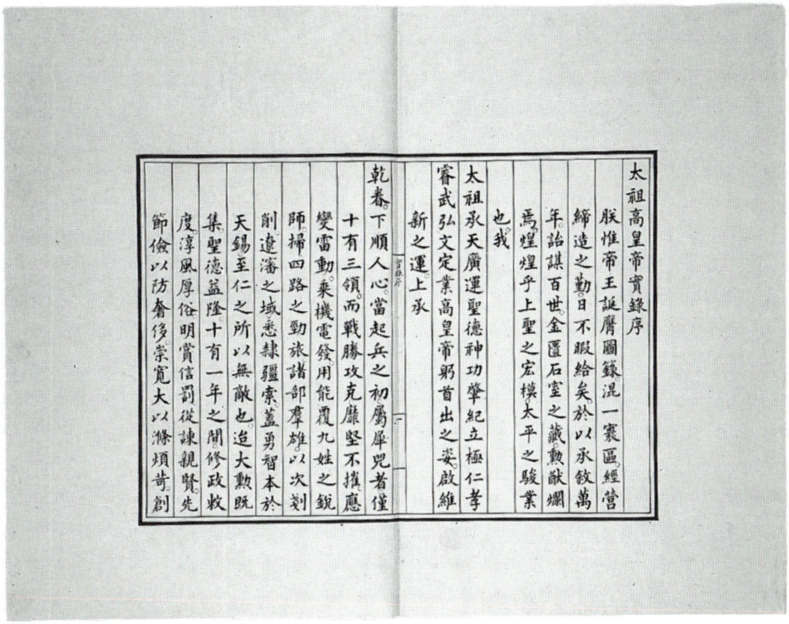
太祖高皇帝實錄序
朕惟帝王誕膺圖籙混一寰區經營
締造之勤日不暇給矣於以承欽萬
年詒謀百世金匱石室之藏勳猷爛
焉煌煌乎上聖之宏模太平之駿業
也我
太祖承天廣運聖德神功肇紀立極仁孝
睿武弘文定業高皇帝躬首出之姿啟維
新之運上承
乾眷下順人心當起兵之初屬犀兕者僅
十有三領而戰勝攻克靡堅不摧應
變雷動乘機電發用能覆九姓之銳
師掃四路之勁旅諸部羣雄以次剗
削邊藩之域悉隸疆索蓋勇智本於
天錫至仁之所以無敵也迨大勳既
集聖德益隆十有一年之間修政敕
度淳風厚俗明賞信罰從諫親賢先
節儉以防奢侈崇寬大以滌煩苛創

10. 'Ta Ch'ing T'ai-tsu Kao huang ti shih lu' (The veritable records of the Emperor T'ai-tsu), manuscript, dated 1686. These 'Veritable records' contain details of the life of Nurhaci (1559–1626), founder of the Ch'ing Dynasty (1644–1911), and were intended to be used as source material for the official Dynastic History. Apart from its documentary value, this is also a fine specimen of standard Chinese calligraphy.

the ephemera of war, and as a result accumulated an archive of unique value [6, **62**]. Most of Sir Isaac Newton's mathematical and other scientific papers were given by the Earl of Portsmouth in the 1870s and were a foretaste of things to come [11]. The real expansion in the collection of western manuscripts began in 1901, with the papers of the Buxton family, of Norfolk, dating back to the thirteenth century. Again, two of the largest such collections now in the Library are discussed elsewhere in this book: the papers, books and offprints of Charles Darwin on pages 118–35, and the archive of the Royal Greenwich Observatory, deposited in 1990, on pages 185–96 [12]. Major accessions of political papers have included those of Sir Robert Walpole [13], Spencer Perceval [14], Viscount Templewood [15], and Stanley Baldwin [16]. Business papers, whose significance has been recognized only comparatively recently, include the enormous paper and photographic archive of Vickers Plc, once the largest armaments company in the world [17,18]. More familiarly, the papers of the philosopher, and for many in Cambridge their inspiration, G. E. Moore, were acquired in two tranches in 1980 and 1991 [19,20].

Beside the numerous collections of nineteenth- and twentieth-century papers now housed in the University Library, readers in Cambridge have to

11. Newton's discovery of the general binomial theorem: the manuscript shows Newton's workings in the winter of 1664–5 as he extended Pascal's Triangle (now arranged in columns rather than a triangular array of rows) by interpolating intermediate values, leading to his discovery of the binomial theorem for fractional and negative indices, a vital step in the development of modern mathematics. In the upper table Newton simply calculates the numbers in Pascal's Triangle by the addition rule, but in the lower table he makes the crucial extension of adding intermediate values, including those below the original boundary. (Newton Papers)

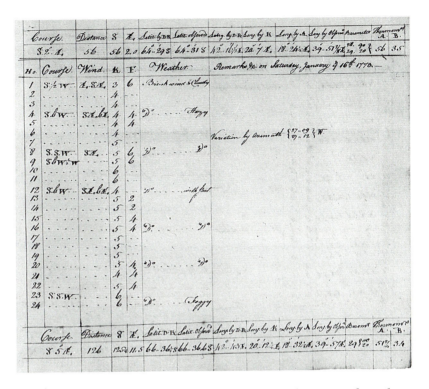

12. 'Log book of HM Sloop *Resolution* bound on discoveries towards the South Pole'. William Wales sailed with James Cook as the astronomer on HMS *Resolution* and kept a log of the voyage. The entry for 16 January 1773 shows the *Resolution*'s latitude of 66° 36½' south, shortly after he accomplished the first crossing of the Antarctic circle in recorded history. (Royal Greenwich Observatory Archives)

set the collections that have come to colleges, such as the papers of members of the Bloomsbury Group at King's, the political and scientific papers at Churchill College, or the mixture of literary, political and scientific papers at Trinity. Two manuscripts of this country's best known poems, held in the University Library, are illustrated in [21] and [22]. Out of this diversity of collections and responsibilities has grown much of the strength of the University as a whole.

It was several centuries before the University Library was accorded its present pre-eminence in the minds of observers or visitors. In 1600, Baron Waldstein, visiting Cambridge from Moravia, remarked on the libraries of Peterhouse, 'the most famous of all the college libraries'; of Emmanuel College; and of King's College, housed (as it still was until the nineteenth century) in four vestries of the college chapel. His diary does not mention the University Library, just a few yards away. Though seventeenth- and eighteenth-century tourists were taken to view the University Library, few of them seem to have been as impressed by it as by other libraries in Cambridge – and not surprisingly so. The books given by King George I lay around in heaps, uncatalogued and pilfered for a generation, while attempts to build a new library, schools and offices (including at one stage a new university press) on and adjacent to the ancient site foundered in arguments and lack of money. The University Library had treasures, to be sure, headed always by the Codex Bezae; but in the eyes of tourists searching for grandeur its buildings were unimpressive. Instead, visitors remarked upon Sir Christopher Wren's new library at Trinity College, completed in 1693, or the library at King's, or the library of St John's, built in the 1620s – all of them notable buildings. The library of Samuel Pepys, at Magdalene College, was less visited at this time because it was treated as a part of the Master of the College's personal fiefdom.

So, too, those who considered bequeathing their collections tended – not unnaturally – to think first of their colleges, rather than of the University Library. In the seventeenth century, the University Library had received three large benefactions: those of Richard Holdsworth, of Henry Lucas (Member of Parliament for the University) and of John Hacket (Bishop of Lichfield) [63]. In the next century – apart from the wholly exceptional gift of Moore's library, and a much smaller collection of orien-

13. An archivist's nightmare: this letter from Jonas Rolfe to Britain's first Prime Minister, Sir Robert Walpole, describes the destruction wreaked by his 'thousand ungratefull companions', the mice infesting Walpole's study at Houghton. (Cholmondeley (Houghton) Papers)

14. In the autumn of 1810, King George III lapsed into insanity. A team of doctors attended the stricken monarch, keeping the Prime Minister, Spencer Perceval, informed by means of regular, written reports. The one shown is for 31 October. (Spencer Perceval Papers)

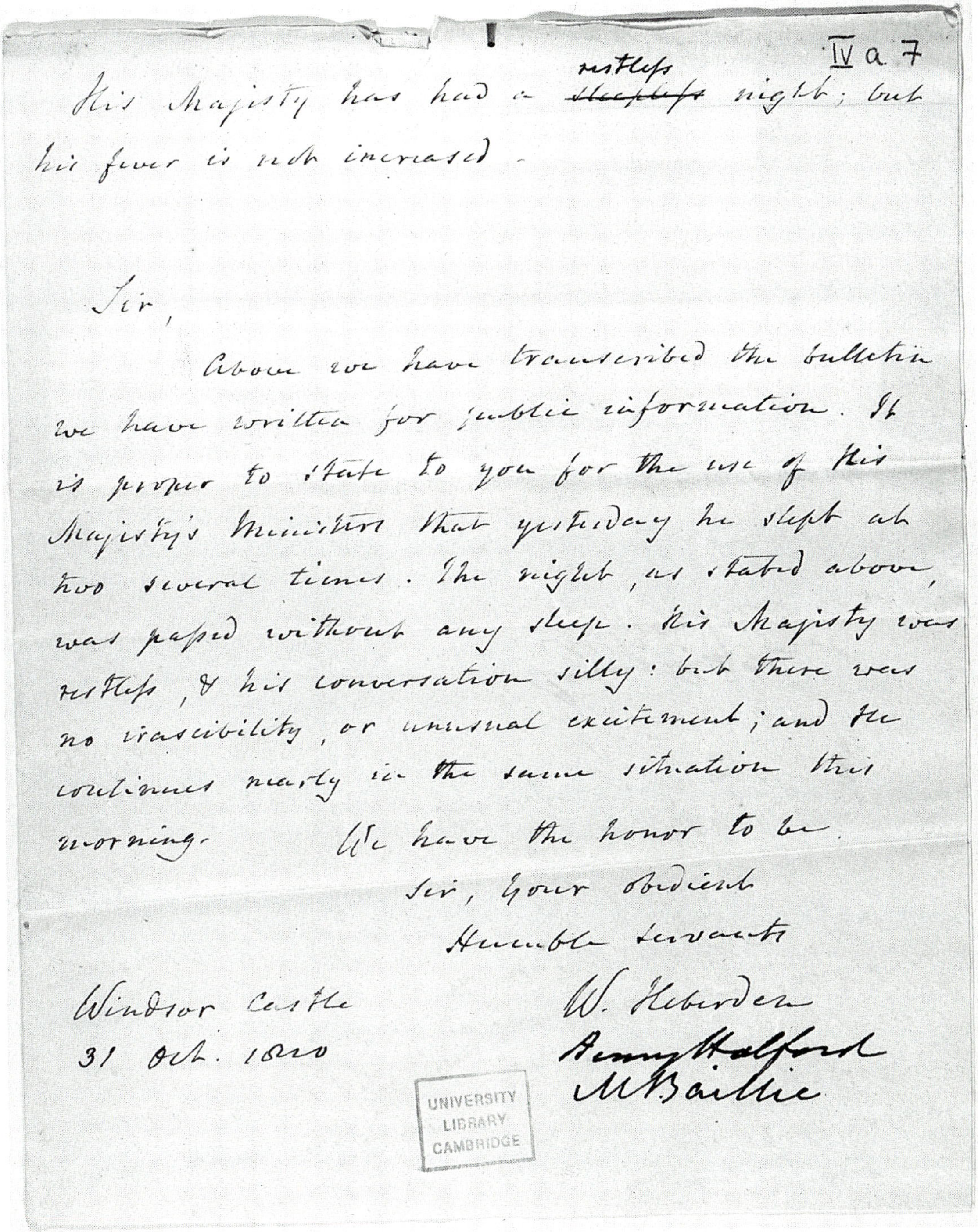

restless

His Majesty has had a ~~sleepless~~ night; but his fever is not increased –

Sir,

Above we have transcribed the bulletin we have written for public information. It is proper to state to you for the use of His Majesty's Ministers that yesterday he slept at two several times. The night, as stated above, was passed without any sleep. His Majesty was restless, & his conversation silly: but there was no irascibility, or unusual excitement; and he continues nearly in the same situation this morning. We have the honor to be.

Sir, Your obedient

Humble Servants

W. Heberden

Henry Halford

M Baillie

Windsor Castle
31 Oct. 1810

$\overline{\text{IV}}$ a 7

WINDSOR CASTLE

We live under very trying conditions, nowadays, since the direct attack on Buck.ᵐ Pal. we have to live here as we have no glass windows. We were there & saw & felt the explosions of the bombs in the quadrangle. An experience not to have repeated, but we had no ill effects. We all live underground to sleep now, & we are getting used to it.

15. Among the approximately 40,000 documents that form the Templewood Papers is a small collection of personal letters from King George VI. Written in October 1940, when Sir Samuel Hoare was ambassador to Spain, this example illustrates vividly the life of the monarch during the Blitz.

tal manuscripts assembled by George Lewis, chaplain to the East India Company in Fort St George between 1692 and 1714 – there were no gifts to compare with these. Instead, books were given or bequeathed to college libraries. Among such gifts to colleges, the more important include the library of Henry Puckering (including many books from the shelves of Henry, Prince of Wales and son of King James I), given to Trinity at the beginning of the century, and the outstanding collection of early editions of Shakespeare assembled by Edward Capell, again to Trinity, in 1779; the Hebrew books of Humphrey Prideaux (d. 1724) to Clare; and the library of Thomas Baker, rich in history and early printing, to St John's in 1740. All of these would have enhanced the University Library. The same remained true in the early nineteenth century. Isaac Milner, President of Queens', Professor of Natural Experimental Philosophy and then of Mathematics, and a notable figure both in the religious affairs of the University and in the administration of the University Press, left his books to his college, which promptly arranged for them to be recorded in a printed catalogue. In 1816, the bequest to the University by Richard, Viscount Fitzwilliam, including his books, manuscripts and music as well as his other works of art, led to the opening in 1848 of the Fitzwilliam Museum which has in turn attracted its own further benefactors.

The decision by Samuel Sandars (d. 1894), a member of Trinity College, to leave the best of his books (including notable groups of medieval manuscripts and early printed books) to the University Library is all the more important in the Library's history [**64–6**]. He had been wooed by two University Librarians, Henry Bradshaw and Francis Jenkinson; and much of his collecting taste had been moulded by their advice. In also providing for annual lectures in bibliography, he further emphasized his bibliophile instincts, while encouraging the more analytical approach that characterized the work of Bradshaw and Jenkinson. Bradshaw had been in the habit of giving books to the Library for most of his adult life, and others came after his death in 1886. Most of them were incunabula and books printed in or relating to Ireland; but the Library also bought from his estate one of his most percipient and surprising purchases, the collection of about 30,000 printed street ballads assembled by Sir Frederic Madden, Keeper of Manuscripts in the British Museum [23, 24].

Where Sandars led, others followed. Lord Acton's great library, a working collection built on such a scale that it inevitably contained many treasures of early printing, is the subject of a separate chapter by Owen Chadwick (see pages 136–52). In the next fifty years, the University Library received major gifts of early printed books from, among others, J. W. Clark (University Registrary), John Venn (Gonville and Caius), John Charrington (Trinity) [25, **112**], A. W. Young (Trinity) [**113**], and Sir Stephen Gaselee (King's). A tradition had been established at last, and many more names might be added to this list.

The years since the Second World War have seen major donations to colleges, such as the Rothschild collection of eighteenth-century English literature and the Sraffa collection in the history of economics given to Trinity, John Maynard Keynes's and John Hayward's bequests to King's, Susan Skilliter's bequest of her Ottoman collection to Newnham, or Graham Watson's gift of his colour-plate books to Emmanuel.

Meanwhile, and in this context, the University Library has come into its own – partly by gift and partly by a book budget that for the first time has acknowledged its position as a national library. The acquisition of the library of eighteenth-century French literature belonging to Ralph Leigh (d. 1987) and the library of Geoffrey Keynes (d. 1982), with its exemplary author collections ranging from John Donne and Sir Thomas Browne to William Blake and Jane Austen, Siegfried Sassoon and Rupert Brooke – quite apart from its scientific and medical sections exemplified in Boyle, Willis and Harvey – each in their ways placed the University Library at the head in their respective interests [26, 114, 115]. It is difficult, in a small space, to choose among the collections that have come in the last forty or so years; but some have, either by their prominence or by their nature, directly influenced the direction of work in the University. In 1952, a bequest of a large group of Chinese oracle bones added a new dimension to the Library's collections, and their importance is still being explored [116]. In 1968, the gift by Sir Allen Lane, founder of Penguin Books, of the library of the typographer and historian of printing Stanley Morison (quickly followed by his papers) prompted the arrival of other collections that further document the revolution in printing in the latter part of the twentieth century. The collection of colour printing still being added to by Norman Waddleton [190–3], the Hunter-McAlpine collection on the history of psychiatry [27], and the Restoration drama assembled by John Brett-Smith and his father all likewise demand further investigation. The implications of the acquisition in 1993 of the largest collection of all, the library of the Royal Commonwealth Society, discussed on pages 166–84, have still to be absorbed, and developed.

Just as the manuscripts drawn from the libraries of the monasteries given by Matthew Parker to Corpus Christi College had reflected institutional change in the sixteenth century, so the twentieth century has seen a re-examination – admittedly less draconian, though drastic nonetheless – of other institutional collections, both ecclesiastical and secular. In this way, parish libraries established in the eighteenth century have found a

16. From one Prime Minister to another: Winston Churchill writes to Stanley Baldwin, less than a month into his premiership, and just after the evacuation of the British Expeditionary Force from Dunkirk. The prospect of a long, forbidding struggle causes him to temper his optimism: 'I feel quite sure that better days will come: though whether we shall live to see them is more doubtful.' (Baldwin Papers)

4, June 1940
10, Downing Street,
Whitehall.

My dear SB,

I have not till now found a moment ~~have~~ ~~been able~~ to thank you for yr kind letter & good wishes wh reached me . I am ashamed to say — nearl a fortnight ago.

We are going through hard times & I expect worse to come : but I feel quite sure that better days will come! Though whether we shall live to see them is more doubtful.

I do not feel the burden weigh too heavily, but I cannot say that I have enjoyed being Prime Minister so much so far.

Yours sincerely
Winston S. Churchill

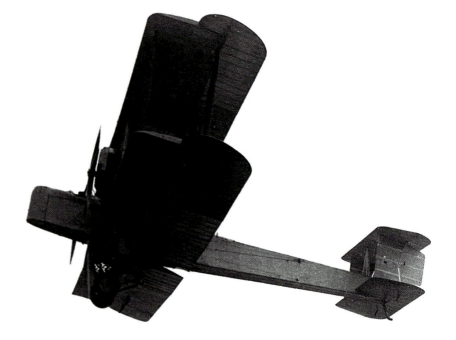

17 and 18. At 4 p.m. on 14 June 1919 two former RAF officers, Captain John Alcock and Lieutenant Arthur Whitten Brown, set off from St John's, Newfoundland, in a Vickers Vimy, a converted First World War bomber. Some 16 hours and 1,900 miles later they crash-landed in an Irish bog, having completed the first non-stop transatlantic flight. Below; the second page of Brown's navigation log for the flight. (Vickers Archives)

home on the shelves of the University Library; and much of the library of Ely Cathedral was given by the Dean and Chapter in 1970. Other collections have been placed on long-term deposit, such as the library of Peterborough Cathedral and books from the grammar school at Bury St Edmunds, founded by King Edward VI. The deposit by the British and Foreign Bible Society of its library and archive in 1984 was a reminder of the crucial part that members of the University had played in the Society's foundation in 1804, as well as of its links – longer than with any other printer – with the University Press [28, **117**].

Such a roll-call of names reveals comparatively little of contents, or of the myriad ways in which these recent arrivals complement and strengthen the existing collections. It does stress the importance of repositories such as the University Library as places both of preservation and of study. Yet the recitation of major collections is a distraction from the Library's greatest strength of all, one that it shares with the British Library, the Bodleian Library, the National Libraries of Scotland and of Wales, and with Trinity College Dublin, and which distinguishes these from libraries formed, however successfully, on a basis of purchase and donation. Next to these glamorous (and often more obviously valuable) gifts or special acquisitions, there is another side to the Library. It is no less vital to remember also to appreciate the gradual accretion, week by week, year by year, of the legal-deposit intake [**118, 119**]. In France, the idea that new books should be

19. A letter from the philosopher Ludwig Wittgenstein to the Professor of Philosophy, G. E. Moore, discussing the cost of duplicating lectures that he was dictating to his class in the academic year 1933–4. A few copies were mimeographed and circulated, and became known as *The blue book*. (Moore Papers)

deposited in the Royal Library, without direct charge, dated from the mid sixteenth century. In England, the same concept was embodied in the Licensing Act in 1665, whereby the Royal Library and the libraries of the then two English universities were entitled to a copy of each book that was published. The same provision has been embodied in successive legislation ever since, and there are now six so-called copyright or legal-deposit libraries in the British Isles. For many generations it was a mixed success. Only a tiny minority of what was published was sent in by the trade; and the libraries did not always desire what in practice arrived. As one consequence, novels, popular science, plays, poems, books on domestic economy and thousands of pamphlets were disregarded. For many years the University Library – like the other privileged libraries – took little advantage of the law. Faced with books whose numbers threatened to engulf the shelves, by the early nineteenth century it was in the habit of selling off those deemed to be of no importance to an academic library. Much slipped away of what we now value most highly as reflecting English history and the interests of the reading public in the eighteenth and early nineteenth centuries.

The history of the University Library in the nineteenth century is, not least, a history of attempts to improve this situation. Amidst arguments, conducted elsewhere in the country (and largely in London) as well as in Cambridge itself, concerning the function of legal deposit, and the obligations thereby laid upon the receiving institutions, the mood gradually changed. In London, Panizzi's efforts to oblige publishers to deliver up copies of their publications to the British Museum had a direct effect on Cambridge, the Bodleian and the other libraries. By the late nineteenth century, the University Library was established in the leading position it has occupied ever since. The legal-deposit privileges were confirmed in 1911 after a difficult passage through Parliament, in which Francis Jenkinson, the then University Librarian, was to the fore as a lobbyist in pressing the libraries' needs. This legislation has survived little altered until today, though with the advent first of microfilm publication and more recently of publication in electronic formats it has become increasingly unsatisfactory. At the time of writing, a proposal to extend the legislation to other media is under discussion.

The names of benefactors and of special collections inspire admiration and gratitude of a particular kind. Each year, in the University Church or in

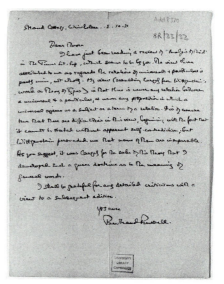

20. A letter from Bertrand Russell to fellow-philosopher G. E. Moore, elaborating on a point raised by Moore's review of Russell's book *The analysis of mind*. The two men were near-contemporaries at Cambridge, and followed each other's work with critical interest. (Moore Papers)

21. A page from Alfred Tennyson's manuscript of *The princess*, presented to the Library in 1921 by the poet's son Hallam, 2nd Lord Tennyson.

O tell her, swallow, thou that knowest each,
That bright & fierce & fickle is the South,
And dark & true & tender is the North.

O swallow, swallow, if I could follow, & light
Upon her lattice, I would pipe & trill,
And cheep & twitter twenty million loves.

O were I thou that she might take me in
And lay me on her bosom & her heart
Would rock the snowy cradle till I died.

Why lingereth she to clothe her heart with love
Delaying as the tender ash delays
To clothe herself when all the woods are green.

O tell her, swallow, that thy brood is flown
Say to her I do but wanton in the South
But in the North long since my nest is made.

O tell her brief is life but love is long
And brief the sun of summer in the North
And brief the moon of beauty in the South.

O swallow, flying from the golden woods,
Fly to her & pipe & woo her & make her mine,
And tell her, tell her, that I follow thee.'
      I ceased & all the ladies, each at each,
Like the Ithacensian suitors in old time
Stared with great eyes, & laugh'd with alien lips
And knew not what they meant; for still my voice
Rang false: but smiling Not for thee she said
O Bulbul any rose of Gulistan

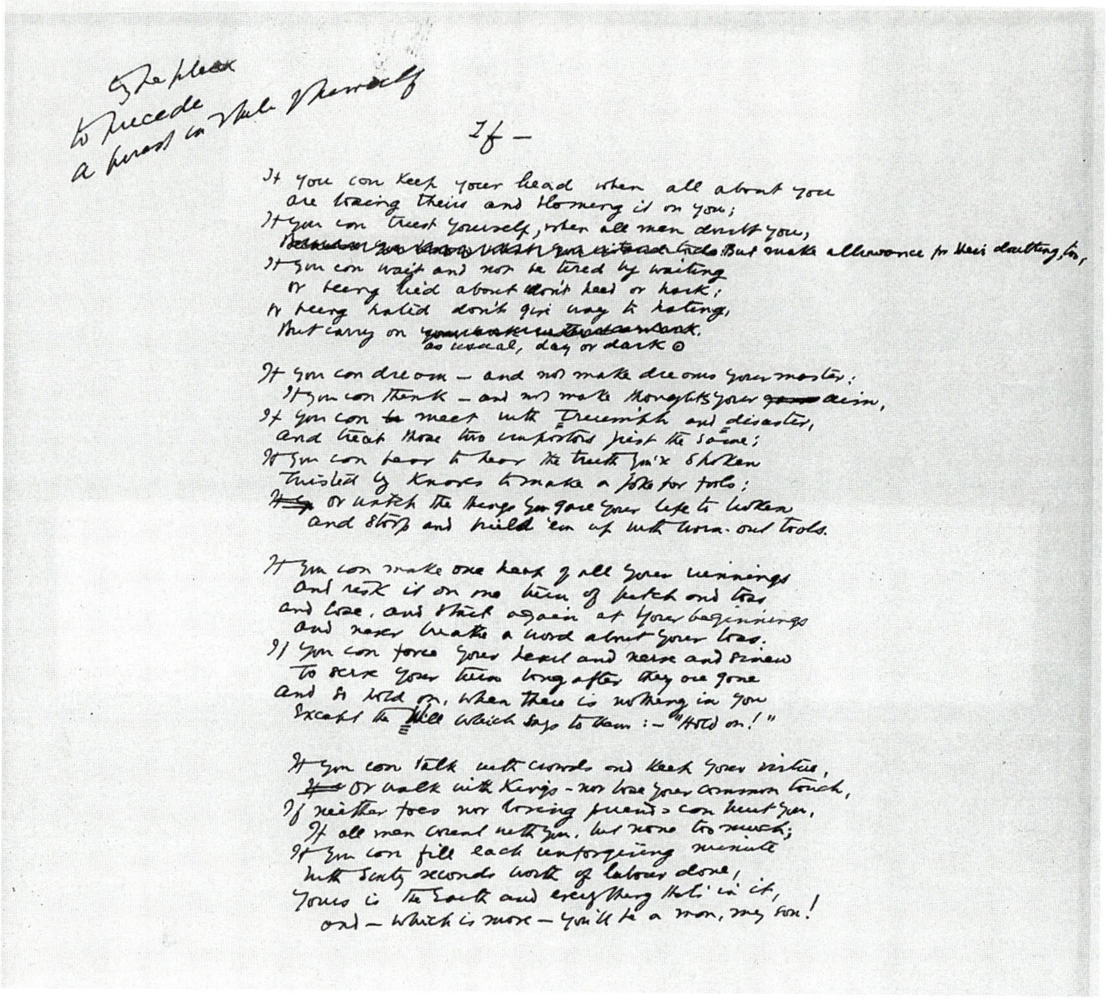

If—

If you can keep your head when all about you
Are losing theirs and blaming it on you;
If you can trust yourself, when all men doubt you,
But make allowance for their doubting too;
If you can wait and not be tired by waiting,
Or being lied about don't deal in lies;
Or being hated don't give way to hating,
But carry on as usual, day or dark.

If you can dream—and not make dreams your master;
If you can think—and not make thoughts your aim,
If you can meet with Triumph and disaster,
And treat those two impostors just the same;
If you can bear to hear the truth you've spoken
Twisted by knaves to make a joke for fools;
Or watch the things you gave your life to broken
And stoop and build 'em up with worn-out tools.

If you can make one heap of all your winnings
And risk it on one turn of pitch and toss,
And lose, and start again at your beginnings
And never breathe a word about your loss.
If you can force your heart and nerve and sinew
To serve your turn long after they are gone
And so hold on, when there is nothing in you
Except the Will which says to them:—"Hold on!"

If you can talk with crowds and keep your virtue,
Or walk with Kings—nor lose your common touch,
If neither foes nor loving friends can hurt you,
If all men count with you, but none too much;
If you can fill each unforgiving minute
With sixty seconds worth of labour done,
Yours is the Earth and everything that's in it,
And—which is more—you'll be a man, my son!

college chapels, as appropriate, the various parts of the University have long been in the custom of commemorating these and other benefactors. The everyday humdrum activities of keeping abreast with current publications for deposit, and of discovering and ordering books (usually published abroad) that will sit beside the output of the British press, are the largest sources of the University Library's strengths as a working collection. Until 1666, when Tobias Rustat provided for the purchase of land, with instructions that its rents were to be used for the purchase of books, the University Library had no book fund. Such a situation was not uncommon: Harvard University, for example, whose early members included so many people from Cambridge, had no regular book fund until 1764. In this it was unlike the new University of Leiden, which in the 1590s quickly built up its collections, very largely by purchase. It was also unlike many of the colleges, whose buying (admittedly rather intermittent) complemented gifts

22. 'The Nation's Most Popular Poem': *If*, from Rudyard Kipling's autograph of *Rewards and fairies*, presented to the Library by the author in 1926. *If* received most votes in a nationwide poll for Britain's favourite poem, run in conjunction with National Poetry Day, in 1995.

from their members. The Rustat Fund, whose bookplate graces innumerable books especially in historical subjects, remained a separate account into the twentieth century, reminder of assumptions of an earlier age [120].

In two key respects, the Library has become especially valued to the University: in its open stacks, and in allowing books to be borrowed. When in 1583 a new catalogue of the Library was compiled, following the gifts of Beza, Parker and others, the resulting list not only revealed a library shelved partly by subject and partly by donor (the latter as much to show off the latest acquisitions as to avoid the need for recataloguing the existing collection in new locations), but also a part of the library that was locked away, 'in the cupboard'. This reserved portion consisted mainly of manuscripts, including the Codex Bezae and the Anglo-Saxon manuscripts

23. A handbill issued during the election contest for County Down in 1805 between Viscount Castlereagh (supporting the Union) and Colonel the Hon. John Meade, who was elected. (Bradshaw Collection of Irish Books)

AS some misapprehension may have arisen on the present occasion, with regard to the part I mean to take in the present Election, I feel it incumbent on me, under such delicate circumstances as I stand in, to declare that it is my intention to support LORD VISCOUNT CASTLEREAGH, and I wish my Tenantry may do so likewise.

ROBERT WARD.

DOWNPATRICK,
Saturday, July 27, 1805.

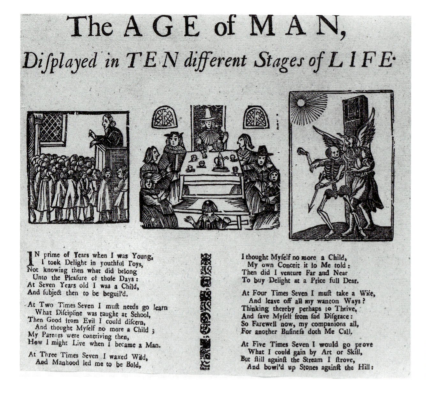

The AGE of MAN,
Displayed in TEN different Stages of LIFE.

IN prime of Years when I was Young,
   I took Delight in youthful Toys,
Not knowing then what did belong
Unto the Pleasure of those Days:
At Seven Years old I was a Child,
And subject then to be beguil'd.

At Two Times Seven I must needs go learn
   What Discipline was taught at School,
Then Good from Evil I could discern,
   And thought Myself no more a Child ;
My Parents were contriving then,
How I might Live when I became a Man.

At Three Times Seven I waxed Wild,
   And Manhood led me to be Bold,

I thought Myself no more a Child,
   My own Conceit it so Me told :
Then did I venture Far and Near
To buy Delight at a Price full Dear.

At Four Times Seven I must take a Wife,
   And leave off all my wanton Ways ?
Thinking thereby perhaps to Thrive,
And save Myself from sad Disgrace :
So Farewell now, my companions all,
For another Business doth Me Call.

At Five Times Seven I would go prove
   What I could gain by Art or Skill,
But still against the Stream I strove,
And bowl'd up Stones against the Hill :

24. Part of a single-sheet garland
from the Aldermary Churchyard
press, Bow Lane, London, c. 1750.
(Madden Collection of Broadside
Ballads)

given by Parker. It also included Parker's magnificently coloured copy of
the *Nuremberg chronicle* (1493) [51]. From this period may be traced the beginning of a tradition in modern times that has always placed as many books as
possible on open access. In this, the University Library is unlike both the
British Library and the Bodleian Library, and also most research libraries
on the European continent. Over the centuries, books have of course been
reclassified many times, but innumerable traces of the early collections
remain. Much of the Library as it stood in the seventeenth century still
stands together today, in the so-called 'stars' classes, named thus because of
the small printed stars that were affixed to the paper spine labels when the
cataloguing of the Royal Library produced a second, parallel, series of
books likewise identified by letters of the alphabet and numbers denoting
their locations. Similarly, much of the Royal Library still stands together. In
the broad subject classification of these parts of the Library may be perceived
not only the prominence accorded to theology, but also contemporary per-
ceptions of, for example, historical disciplines, of mathematics, of medicine, and of natural philosophy.

tabulata collocentur crates ex tenuibus uirgis creberrime texta. Ma-
ximeq; recentibus: percrudis cotiisq; duplicibus consutis fultis al-
ga: aut paleis in aceto maceratis circumcirca tegatur machina tota:
ut a plagarum ictibus: & incendiorum impetu tuta sit.

NON mihi etiam uidetur alienum de testudine: quam hector by-
zantius fecit: quibus rationibus sit facta exponere: Frons eius erat
quemadmodum anguli trigoniorum uti a muro tela cum in eos mit-
tantur non planis frontibus excipiant plagas: ut hic.

25. Robertus Valturius, *De re
militari* (Verona, Johannes Nicolai,
1472). The woodcuts, depicting
military operations and weapons,
were among the first printed
illustrations of technical or
scientific subjects. (Given by
John Charrington, 1916)

To the Sunne.
Busie olde foole, vnrulie sunne,
Why, doost thou thus,
Through windowes and through Curtaines call on vs?
Must to thy, motions, loues seasons runne?
Sawcie pedantique wreth goe chide
Late schooleboyes, and sower prentices,
Goe tell Court huntsmen, that the K: will ride,
Call Countrie Ants, to harvest offices,
Loue all alike, no season knowes, nor clyme,
Nor howers, daies, months, which are the raggs of time.

26. From a manuscript collection
of John Donne's poems, probably
written for his friend Henry
Percy, Earl of Northumberland
(1564–1632), formerly in the
Leconfield Library, Petworth
House, Sussex. (From the library
of Sir Geoffrey Keynes)

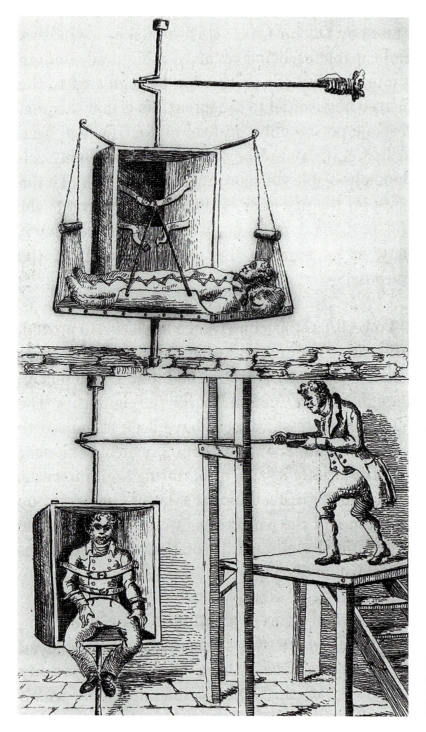

27. The 'circulating swing' used by William Saunders Hallaran, physician to the Cork Lunatic Asylum, as depicted in his *Practical observations on insanity* (Cork, 1818). (Hunter-McAlpine Collection)

28. First page of St John's Gospel, 1847, in Western Cree, the first book of the Bible printed in any Cree language. It was translated by William Mason, whose annotation at the top of the page includes instructions for the printer. (Bible Society collections)

It was not until the end of the nineteenth century that a serious attempt was made to provide a general classification scheme for virtually all the new books (other than oriental) acquired by the Library. With this, the 'three-figure' scheme which remains basically the same today, adapted to and compromised by changes in scientific and humanistic knowledge alike, books were classified for the first time according to other books in their subject, rather than by the space available in a particular designated part of the Library. Fixed locations became a thing of the past. This vital aid for readers added immeasurably to the value of open access, since it made informed browsing a realistic proposition. But it was also applied, in a modified form, to a large part of the books that were not placed on the open shelves, so that by means of the shelf-lists further subject access was possible. It must be a matter of regret that in recent years, thanks to an acute lack of shelves, desperate measures have had to be taken to save space, and books that would once have been shelved by subject are now placed simply in order of acquisition. The so-called subject access offered by a sophisticated online catalogue is no substitute for the human eye and enquiring mind seeking inspiration rather than merely following predetermined vocabularies.

No library historian contemplating the development of the University Library collections over the last hundred years can fail to be astounded at the diversity, as well as the scale, of their growth. In contemplating how those books are disposed, and hence how they are used, a further feature is soon apparent. As Christopher Brooke remarks on page 223, until 1954 the Royal Library was on the open shelves. Until the late 1960s, there were many books on the open shelves dating from the early sixteenth century. When, following trends in other major libraries, a Rare Books Department was established in 1972, it was made responsible for virtually all books printed before 1800, besides special collections. Since then, the department's brief has spread to 1850, and in some subjects more recent books still have been withdrawn from open access. This process will continue, complicated further by the poor materials employed in the manufacture of books, especially since the mid nineteenth century, and by the unprecedentedly heavy use to which the Library is now subject. The result of such withdrawals is increased (and very necessary) security for the collections; but this is achieved at a price. Thanks to rearranged provision for access, and to the considerable additions in recent years to the collections of early books, the number of books designated for use in the Munby Rare Books Reading Room has easily doubled since the early 1970s. The room is now over-full with readers; there are many more books to be fetched by a staff already under pressure from dwindling resources; and readers have, unavoidably, less ready access to the older collections.

So we should stand back a little. Programmes for digitization of early printed books will never replace the widespread first-hand experience to which readers, until only a generation ago, were accustomed; and in any case the cost of creating, storing, 'refreshing' and delivering electronic images makes general application of such a medium unlikely. More generally, and as many libraries and readers are learning to their cost, pressure on space, and the emphasis on under-developed or under-capitalized computer resources, may actually destroy or withdraw accumulated knowledge. The effects on learning of these recent changes are mostly unpredictable, but the old concept of a library as an organization of knowledge has taken on a new meaning.[1]

1. Essential reading: J. C. T. Oates, *Cambridge University Library; a history. From the beginnings to the Copyright Act of Queen Anne* (Cambridge, 1986); David McKitterick, *Cambridge University Library; a history. The eighteenth and nineteenth centuries* (Cambridge, 1986); E. Leedham-Green and D. McKitterick, 'A catalogue of Cambridge University Library in 1583', in *Books and collectors, 1200–1700: essays presented to Andrew Watson*, ed. J. P. Carley and C. Tite (London, 1997), pp. 153–235; annual reports of the University Library Syndicate, published in the *Cambridge University Reporter*.

Chapter 2

Codex Bezae

David Parker

Some manuscripts are famed for the beauty of the hand in which they are written; others because they reproduce an outstandingly pure text; others because they are the oldest or the only copy of that text; others even by association with the author. For none of these reasons could the Codex Bezae Cantabrigiensis commend itself to us. Its copyist, while writing in a regular and professional hand, cannot have been famed for his calligraphy. While much can be said about the text of the Gospels and Acts which it contains, even most of those who consider it to be valuable confess that it is by no means pure. Nor could Codex Bezae, today at least, be regarded as of remarkable antiquity. Certainly, a century ago it would have been among the dozen or so oldest known copies of the Greek New Testament. Today, however, it is a full two and a half centuries younger than the oldest such manuscript. As to uniqueness, it is one among thousands of witnesses to the text of those books it contains. Yet, even though it has no claim to eminence on any of these scores, there can be few other manuscripts in existence about which more has been written. No other New Testament witness could even begin to rival its bibliography of monographs, articles and editions. In what lies its fascination?

Before attempting to answer that question by calling for the two dark green boxes in which the manuscript is kept, let us order to our desk in the Manuscripts Reading Room a few of the other New Testament manuscripts kept in the University Library, and see whether a comparison will help us to understand. There are 46 Greek New Testament witnesses (if we include ones that belong to other institutions but are held in the Library). Just over half of them were, as one might expect, copied in the period 1000–1300. Although a small collection by some standards (there are about 370 each in Paris and Rome, and the world's largest concentration, on Mount Athos, contains 900), it is still the fourteenth largest collection of Greek New Testament manuscripts, and more than makes up in variety and interest for what it lacks in bulk. Time restricts us, so we must sample carefully.

We begin with the oldest, the fragmentary remains of a papyrus codex of Romans (Add. 7211, numbered P[27] in the listing of Greek New Testament manuscripts) [29]. Containing verses from chapters 8 and 9, it was copied in the course of the third century, and thus predates Codex Bezae by over a century. There is one other papyrus witness in the library (Add. 5893, P17), a fourth-century witness containing parts of eight verses of Hebrews 9. Compared to these tiny papyrus remains, Codex Bezae is extensive, containing as it does, on the 406 out of its original 534 parchment leaves, most of the four Gospels and Acts. Its only extensive gaps are 67 folios between the Gospels and Acts (which perhaps contained Revelation and the Johannine Epistles), and the last six chapters of Acts. P17 and P27 are the only two biblical manuscripts in the University Library older than Codex Bezae. Four more approach it in age. The first is a palimpsest manuscript, containing fragments of the first eleven chapters of Luke's Gospel (BFBS MSS 213, 040 in the listing of New Testament Greek manuscripts). Called Codex Zacynthius, because it was found on the Ionian isle of Zante, it is given a letter as well as a number: Ξ, 040 [30]. The use of letters for majuscule manuscripts of the New Testament predates the use of numeral indicators. Codex Bezae is known as D (a demonstration that it was one of the first majuscules known). Although generally dated to the sixth century, Codex Zacynthius is, in this writer's judgement, of the seventh. This manuscript is of great interest, because it contains an excellent text, because it has the same division into chapters as the famous Codex Vaticanus (along with at the most two other witnesses), and because it is the oldest witness to contain a commentary (in the form of a catena of patristic comments) as well as the text. It is a matter of great regret to modern scholarship that it was re-used in the thirteenth century to make a lectionary text of the Gospels (l299). The other three manuscripts are of the sixth century. The first of them (MS Add. 1875; l1354) is a lectionary [31]. More notably, it is bilingual: it contains the readings in Greek and Coptic. In this respect it is like Codex Bezae, which is a Greek–Latin bilingual, one of only four surviving from the early church. Bilingual manuscripts are not uncommon. There are two others in the Library, also lectionaries: one (MS Add. 1879.13; l311) is four pages of a Graeco-Arabic witness, of the twelfth century; the other (Or. 1699; l1575) consists of two leaves of a ninth-century Graeco-Coptic witness. Other leaves of the same manuscript survive in Vienna, Paris and London. The other two sixth-century witnesses belong with Codex Bezae as codices written on parchment in majuscule (also known as uncial) letters, containing the continuous text. They are a Cairo Genizah manuscript, T-S 12, 189.208 (093), a palimpsest of two leaves of Acts and

29. MS Add. 7211 (P27), the oldest Greek New Testament manuscript in the Library, dating from the third century.

30. Codex Zacynthius. The underwriting is seventh-century majuscule, of Luke 3.7–8 with commentary; the upper writing thirteenth-century minuscule, of Matthew 26.39–51, part of the lection for Holy Thursday.

31. MS Add. 1875 (*l*1354), a sixth-century majuscule lectionary.

1 Peter, which were re-used to copy a Hebrew text; and 0246: the property of Westminster College, Cambridge, this is a fragment of the Epistle of James. The page was later scraped for re-writing, but never used.

We have now looked at eight manuscripts; three of them palimpsests, all extremely fragmentary. This indicates how fortunate we are that any manuscripts so extensive as Codex Bezae should have survived from Antiquity.

Now the time has come to return this large pile of manuscripts to the long-suffering counter staff, and beg for a sight of one of the most intriguing manuscripts of Antiquity. We will not be allowed to see it unless we have good reason; and rightly so, for the metallic based ink which the scribes used has released an acid which has slowly eaten through the fine parchment, weakening it. Animal skin is a strong and durable substance, but it cannot be expected to survive for 1600 years unscathed. The very fine thicknesses achieved here lead to the pages curling very sharply as soon as the pressure that keeps the volumes closed in their boxes is released. The codex was rebound 30 years ago by Douglas Cockerill of Grantchester, in a vellum binding similar to that which he employed for the Codex Sinaiticus. It has been bound into two volumes, matching the two of the facsimile edition.

I have anticipated much of what is before us when we open a volume at random: written in majuscule letters in about the year 400, we see a page of the four Gospels and Acts. The parchment is fine and pale in colour, the ink an attractive olive-brown. Each page is 26 cm high and 21.5 cm across. On the left page (verso) is the Greek text, and on the right (recto) a Latin version of it. The lines are uneven in length, written in units of sense (or at least meant to be). There is quite a generous margin, and a running title at the top of each page. What is the history of this 1600-year-old bundle of skins [32, **121**]?

We begin in uncertainty. Debate about the area in which it was produced continues. I have argued that it was made in Berytus (modern Beirut) by a Latin copyist who spent most of his time turning out legal texts and documents. There are two lines of argument, the one palaeographical, the other based on the early history of the manuscript. Other suggestions recently canvassed include Jerusalem, Egypt and the Rhône valley.[1]

The manuscript was frequently corrected and annotated. There is a sequence of about eighteen hands, of whom the most important worked in the first hundred years or so. Nearly half of all corrections are to the text of Acts, and every corrector but the earliest one worked principally on the

1. D. C. Parker, *Codex Bezae: an early Christian manuscript and its text*, (Cambridge, 1992); J. N. Birdsall, 'The geographical and cultural origin of the Codex Bezae Cantabrigiensis: a survey of the *Status Quaestionis*, mainly from the palaeographical standpoint', in *Studien zum Text und zur Ethik des Neuen Testaments*, ed. W. Schrage (Berlin/New York, 1986), 102–14.

32. Codex Bezae, folios 139v–140r. This opening is as it was when the scribe finished it, not having been touched by any later hand (except for the modern folio numbering in the top right-hand corner of the recto).

Greek text. Some of the most unexpected secondary material is the addition in the margin (sometime between 550 and 650) of sentences for use in fortune telling [34]. An example is 'If you lie, they will condemn you.' The manuscript is not unique in containing them. There is a similar set in a later manuscript from St Gall, and there is a whole group of papyrus manuscripts of John in which each page shows a short passage from the Gospel followed by such a sentence. By my reconstruction of events, all this happened in Berytus, or at least in Syria. We now move on to surer ground, for without doubt we find the manuscript in Lyons in the middle of the ninth century. Some pages were replaced at that time, and the proof is found in the replacement pages. They contain blue ink and a particular form of interrogation mark. Both features are *lyonnaise* [33, **122**]. Further evidence is that some of the New Testament citations of a writer from Lyons called Ado show close similarities to the text of Codex Bezae. In addition, I have recently proposed that the restored leaves were copied from a surviving *lyonnaise* manuscript (Lyons, Bibliothèque Municipale 431). The thesis has been advanced that the leaves were penned by the famous Florus of Lyons. This is, however, hard to sustain; but that his was the inspiration behind the manuscript's restoration, only one of many marks of respect to Antiquity with which early medieval Lyons is associated, can hardly be doubted.

33. Codex Bezae, folio 172*r, showing the distinctively *lyonnaise* question mark (line 8 from the bottom).

For the next 600 years there is – silence; then, in the sixteenth century, renewed interest. The manuscript is cited in 1546 at the Council of Trent as witness to a reading at the end of John's Gospel. It is collated for Cardinal Sirleto (1514–85). In 1550 it features as one of the fifteen witnesses cited in the first Greek New Testament to contain variant readings. In 1562 Lyons was sacked during a religious war, and the manu-

34. Codex Bezae, folio 302v, foot, showing one of the lots (sentences for fortune-telling).

35. Beza's letter presenting Codex Bezae to the University of Cambridge, written from Geneva and dated 6 December 1581.

script was removed from the Monastery of St Irenaeus to Geneva, where it passed into the possession of the Reformer Théodore de Bèze (latinized as Beza). Although Beza produced a number of editions of the Greek New Testament, only in the first did he make any use of his venerable possession. Indeed, thereafter he rated it very low, so low that when he gave it the University of Cambridge in 1581, he took some of the generosity out of the deed in his accompanying letter, saying that it was 'better hidden than published', and that he suspected that its corruption was the work of ancient heretics. The University's gracious acceptance of the gift avoided any comment on the gift itself [35].

If Beza thought that this dubious manuscript would be safely lost to view in its new home, however, he was mistaken. From within fifty years of its removal to Cambridge, it was the frequent object of study. Such famous scholars as Mill, Wettstein and Tischendorf collated it. In 1793 Thomas Kipling published a transcript of the manuscript, and in 1864 F. H. A. Scrivener produced another extremely accurate one, which contained lists of the corrections. A facsimile was printed in 1899.

Such is the history of the manuscript. A Greek–Latin bilingual, with its numerous early correctors and annotators, its flourishing in the ninth-century renaissance of Lyons, and its re-appearance in the Renaissance of the sixteenth century, it almost provides a history in miniature of the dealings between Greek-speaking and Latin-speaking Christendom.[2] But even the interest of the history of the manuscript pales before the fascination of its text, and it is an attempt to illuminate its unique significance in early Christianity that will occupy our remaining space. The best approach is to take a passage as illustration. The text of the Revised Standard Version (RSV) (with a few changes to bring out the underlying Greek text more clearly) and the Greek text of Codex Bezae (I have made my own translation for the occasion) are set in parallel columns (opposite). Where the latter contains additions, they are given in bold type; where one word is substituted for another, it is in italics. Changes in word order in the Greek are indicated by underlining (with double underlining where there are minor changes in order within a larger re-ordering of material). Words found in the RSV and omitted in Codex Bezae have a line through them in the former. The passage is the beginning of Luke 6 [36].

There are three ways in which the text of Codex Bezae is distinctive. Generally, it may be seen that there are numerous small changes which, tiny in themselves, together constitute a re-writing of the text. Of the 172 words of Codex Bezae that we have printed, only 53 are in ordinary Roman type. Secondly and most evidently, there is the length. The RSV passage

2. *Codex Bezae: papers from the Lunel Colloquium*, ed. D. C. Parker and C.-B. Amphoux (Leiden, 1996).

36. Codex Bezae, folios 205v–206r, the opening containing Luke 6.1–9. The hole on the left is a flaw in the skin, already there when the scribe wrote the page.

RSV	CODEX BEZAE
¹And it came to pass on a sabbath, that he was going through the grainfields, and his disciples plucked and ate some heads of grain, rubbing them in their hands.	¹*And* it came to pass on a **second-first** sabbath that he was going through the grainfields, *and* his disciples **began to** pluck the heads of grain and rubbing them in their hands ate.
²But some of the Pharisees said, 'Why are you doing what is not lawful to do on the sabbath?'	²But some of the Pharisees *said* **to him** '**See** *what your disciples* do on the sabbath which is not lawful.'
³And Jesus answering them said …(⁴) and also gave it to those with him?'	³*But* Jesus answering them *said* …(⁴) and also gave it to those with him?'
⁵And he said to them, 'The Son of man is lord of the sabbath.'	
	The same day, seeing someone working on the sabbath, he said to him, 'Man, if indeed you know what you are doing then you are blessed But if you do not know, then you are accursed and a transgressor of the law.'
⁶On another sabbath, when he entered the synagogue ~~and taught~~, a man was there whose right hand was withered.	⁶*And when he entered again* into the synagogue on a sabbath, *in which there was* a man *who had a withered hand,*
⁷~~And~~ the scribes and the Pharisees watched him …(¹⁰) and his hand was restored.	⁷the scribes and the Pharisees watched him …(¹⁰) and his hand was restored **so as to be like the other one.**
	⁵And he said to them **that** 'The son of man is lord **even** of the sabbath'.
¹¹But they were filled with fury …	¹¹But they were filled with fury …

contains 108 words against Codex Bezae's 172. Besides minor additions, a whole passage has been added: the story of the man working on the sabbath, dubbed by Dr Ernst Bammel the *pericope cantabrigiensis*.[3] Found in no other source, it is an event in the life of Jesus which some scholars (mostly notably Joachim Jeremias) have claimed to be authentic.[4] Thirdly, the simple act of placing verse 5 after verse 10 makes a triplet of stories on the theme 'The son of man is lord of the sabbath', and thus radically revises Luke's structure.

I have chosen the passage, of course, because its divergences are so marked. It is universally agreed, however, that Codex Bezae offers a separate edition of the Gospels, even though its text of Matthew and John is less evidently distinctive than that of Luke and Mark. As for Acts, its text is even more markedly different. Considerably longer than that of the other early majuscule manuscripts such as the codices Sinaiticus and Vaticanus, it has long been recognized that it constitutes a separate edition of Luke's second book. Recent study has demonstrated that although Codex Bezae is a principal witness to the longer text, it contains a form of it that has undergone further development. Some scholars have suggested that both texts come from Luke's pen. A few have argued in favour of the authenticity of the longer text. The majority have favoured the shorter version.[5]

In writing of addition and revision in the passage from Luke 6, I am, of course, assuming that Codex Bezae does not present the original text. But the question must be raised whether it in fact *is* authentic, and that it is most other manuscripts that are wrong. There are, and long have been, scholars who maintain that Codex Bezae provides the authentic text. They have always been in a minority. There are a number of possible positions:

1 Codex Bezae presents us with a hopelessly corrupt text of the Gospels and Acts.
2 Although Codex Bezae is largely corrupt, it does on occasion preserve the original text. This is the majority position.
3 Codex Bezae is a corrupt representative of one of the earliest types of text. This is not incompatible with (2).
4 Codex Bezae preserves the original text.
5 The original text cannot be recovered, but Codex Bezae is the oldest and best text available to us, dating from the second century.
6 Codex Bezae is a late example of a way of copying the text that felt quite free as regards the precise wording.

3. E. Bammel, 'The Cambridge pericope: the addition to Luke 6.4 in Codex Bezae', *New Testament Studies* 32 (1986), 404–26.
4. J. Jeremias, *Unknown sayings of Jesus* (London, 1957), pp. 49–54.

5. W. Strange, *The problem of the text of Acts* (Cambridge, 1992).

It is the last alternative that the present writer favours. I have argued that the manuscript is a late survivor of the period when the precise letter was of less value to Christians than the spirit of the tradition. Thus, stories could be added from oral tradition before they were lost, and a Gospel could be subtly revised to bring out the evident meaning, the moral pointed and the tale adorned. Such revision is similar to the ways in which the earliest Gospel (Mark) was altered by its successors, Matthew and Luke.

This is not to say that the manuscript's text is altogether a late creation. In the Gospels, Codex Bezae's Greek text is close to the earliest (late second- or third-century) translations of the Gospels into Syriac and Latin. Its Latin text shows signs of being influenced by two third- and fourth-century traditions of Latin translation: the African and the European. The Greek text has, moreover, close affinities to the texts of second-century writers (where we can recover them).

While the majority of its readings are not original, and although its text continued to be freely altered, Codex Bezae is a key witness to the most widely used text of the second century. Apart from the age of the text, the manuscript's value rests in its character. For it manifests that freedom in copying which typified the early Christian attempt to honour not the wording of the tradition but its spirit.

Chapter 3

Illuminated medieval manuscripts

GEORGE HENDERSON

IT IS A POPULAR axiom (and a rather patronizing one at that) that all medieval illuminated manuscripts are 'beautiful'. Some of the illuminated manuscripts in Cambridge University Library are indeed beautiful, judged by the highest standards of painting or of graphic art, as I shall argue below, but every one of them, at their different levels of competence, has a place in the history of book-manufacture and design. They arrived haphazardly in different donations at different times, the earliest arrivals very directly refugees from the cultural revolution known as the Reformation. Each manuscript was necessarily a hand-crafted, one-off production.

By the late sixteenth century, when the empty shelves of the University Library were gradually starting to be stocked, the technology of the medieval book, invented in late Antiquity, was for practical purposes out-of-date, just as the printed book, then in its first flush, is getting out-of-date today. The University of Cambridge, although very much part of the new post-Reformation establishment, retained a healthy appetite for books as historic documents, as records of facts and ideas, and as transmitters of well-respected texts.

The medieval books which concern us here presented, emphasized and interpreted their verbal contents by visual means, decorative or pictorial. Since few illuminated medieval manuscripts came to the University Library on the 'beauty' ticket (at least until comparatively recent times), the collection here has an objective quality particularly valuable to the modern student of medieval books, who rightly regards visual art as an integral part of the whole book, on a par with the script, the preparation of the parchment, and the binding, if that happily survives, each of which may comprise evidence of the manuscript's origin, status and date.

Today, the integrity of the book is crucial. Just how little that mattered in the late sixteenth century can be judged from the University Library's MS Kk.1.24, a once handsomely decorated Gospel Book written in Northumbria in, or not long after, the lifetime of Bede, which reached the safe haven of the University Library in the 1580s in a drastically mutilated condition.[1] Its first half, containing the text of Matthew and Mark, is

1. See N. R. Ker, *Catalogue of manuscripts containing Anglo-Saxon* (Oxford, 1957), no. 22, pp. 35–6; E. A. Lowe, *Codices antiquiores latini*, 2nd edn (Oxford, 1972), no. 138, p. 7; G. Henderson, *Losses and lacunae in early Insular art*, Garmonsway Memorial Lecture 1975 (York, 1982), pp. 29–31.

37. MS Kk.1.24: eighth-century Gospel Book, showing the faint impression of a lost initial letter.

38. Initial letter 'D' from MS Ff.1.23 (Psalms).

missing. From the remaining portion a new, busy, post-Reformation breed of Anglo-Saxonists had excised, for research purposes, legal documents in Old English (these survive in various collections elsewhere) which, in the tenth century, the owners of the Gospel Book, the monks of Ely, had transcribed on to blank leaves *on pysse crystes bec*. In unknown circumstances, knives had been out also to cut away various forms of Anglo-Saxon decoration, notably the large initial 'I' at the beginning of St John's Gospel. By lucky chance, the next surviving leaf bears the faint impression of the lost initial, as it was firmly drawn by the eighth-century designer. The initial ran from top to bottom of the page, curling round at the base to terminate in a dog's head with snub nose and open mouth, displaying fangs and a protruding tongue, a lively example of the naturalistic animal style which was made current in Northumbria, and far beyond, by the designer of the famous Lindisfarne Gospels [37].

Thus, right from the start, Anglo-Saxon designers concentrated on initial letters, to give grace, and focus, to the sacred texts of which they were custodians and purveyors. This traditional point of emphasis was exploited by the scribe of MS Ff.1.23, a copy of the Psalms, in two interlinear versions, Latin and Old English, made in the south of England sometime in the second quarter of the eleventh century.[2] The manuscript owes its preservation (by Queen Elizabeth Tudor's Archbishop of Canterbury, together with her Lord Keeper of the Great Seal) to its Old-English-language component, not to its devotional function and certainly not to its art. Today, however, it is admired for the cleverly varied forms of the letters – C's or D's, L's or S's – with which it starts each new Psalm. Drawn in dark sepia ink with infilling in bright orange and green, the initials are mostly made up of short sprays of coiling acanthus leaves, interspersed with occasional lion or dragon heads. They are sturdily constructed, as if their designer was used to the feel of cast-metal strap ends or sword pommels. Two of the initials terminate in a fine hairline interlace, characteristic of much earlier, Northumbrian art, and in four or five cases the artist weaves acrobatic human figures into his letters, a trick he must have learned ultimately from the most sumptuous of the early Insular Gospel Books, the Book of Kells. His art style is not only well versed and retrospective, however; many times his acanthus fronds lie flat in parallel bands, closely meshed in a specific new decorative idiom which, thanks to England's political ties with Denmark and Norway in the first half of the eleventh century, later helped to shape Scandinavian 'national' styles [38, 39, 40].

2. See F. Wormald, *English drawings of the tenth and eleventh centuries* (London, 1952), no. 2, p. 59; S. H. Fuglesang, *Some aspects of the Ringerike Style: a phase of 11th century Scandinavian art* (Odense, 1980), pp. 70–2, 198; E. Temple, *Anglo-Saxon manuscripts 900–1066*, A Survey of Manuscripts Illuminated in the British Isles 2, general editor J. J. G. Alexander (London, 1976), no. 80, pp. 97–8.

The Normans who took over the government of England in the second half of the century also adopted Anglo-Saxon ways of designing books. The initial letters which open the chapters in the University Library's copy of Josephus's 'Jewish Antiquities', MS Dd.1.4, written around 1130 in Christ Church, Canterbury, employ the familiar shaggy acanthus scrolls, grotesque beasts and acrobatic humans, piling them all up together on a truly portentous scale, typical of the Europe-wide twelfth-century Romanesque style.[3] The combat in which men and beasts are locked has become a rather tiresome decorative device, without inner drive or meaning [41].

Much more subtle in its debt to Anglo-Saxon exemplars, and exploratory, in its own right, of the meeting-point of art and theology is the initial to Book I of Boethius's treatise 'On Music', in the Library's MS Ii.3.12, also from Christ Church, made about the same time, and bequeathed to the Library in 1664.[4] Playing with Boethius's words 'concordance is pleasing, discordance is hateful', the artist has lifted the idea of harmony to its highest level, visualising it in the persons of Christ and his bride, Holy Church, seated side-by-side and finally triumphing over the old enemy, Satan. On the left and right of the initial are personifications of the sun and moon. The moon's torch is extinguished, to evoke literally the prophecy of Psalm 71 that, in Christ the Saviour's reign, there shall be 'abundance of peace, till the moon be taken away' [42].

An initial inhabited in this way by figures interpreting a theme or story is described as 'historiated'. The historiated initial was invented by the Anglo-Saxons in the eighth century and through their influence spread to the rest of Europe. Visually the most powerful and majestic historiated initials are those in a series of great Anglo-Norman Bibles made for Bury, Winchester and elsewhere, fully painted in brilliant enamel-like colours set off by smoothly polished gold backgrounds. A late example of such a Bible in which the monumentality of the Romanesque is giving way to the lighter more fluent 'Gothic' style is MS Dd.8.12.[5] The initial 'I' to the Book of Genesis encapsulates the story of creation in a sequence of medallions which lie like a broad jewelled belt down one half of the page. The Bible scenes are quite conventional in their iconography, as becomes a book designed for formal institutional use [43].

Much more flighty, elliptical, sometimes positively abstruse, is the pictorial imagery provided for the edification of the lay owner of a Psalter made in Paris around the mid thirteenth century, MS Ee.4.24.[6] Whereas the Anglo-Saxon Psalter, MS Ff.1.23, made for monastic use, features only

39. Initial letter 'C' from MS Ff.1.23 (Psalms).

40. Initial letter 'C' from MS Ff.1.23 (Psalms).

3. See C. M. Kauffmann, *Romanesque manuscripts 1066–1190*, A Survey of Manuscripts Illuminated in the British Isles 3, ed. Alexander (London, 1975), no. 43, p. 80.
4. See Kauffmann, *Romanesque manuscripts 1066–1190*, no. 41, p. 79.
5. See P. Brieger, *English art 1216–1307*, (Oxford, 1957), p. 80; N. Morgan, *Early Gothic manuscripts 1190–1250*, A Survey of Manuscripts Illuminated in the British Isles 4, ed. Alexander (London/Oxford, 1982), vol. I, no. 44, p. 92.
6. See G. Henderson, 'Narrative illustration and theological exposition in medieval art', in *Religion and humanism*, ed. K. Robbins (Oxford, 1981), pp. 20–3; T. Alfillé, 'The Psalms in the thirteenth-century Bible moralisée: a study in text and image' (University of London Ph.D. thesis [unpublished], 1991).

41. Initial letter 'A' from Josephus's 'Jewish Antiquities'.

42. Initial letter 'O' from Boethius's treatise 'On Music'.

43. (far right) Initial 'I' to the Book of Genesis in MS Dd.8.12.

one true historiated initial, the *agnus dei* placed in the initial 'D' of Psalm 6, the Paris Psalter's initials are historiated throughout. They draw inspiration from a new, continental, phase of Bible illustration, the great scholastic enterprise, the *Bible moralisée*, where literal illustration and learned allegorization march hand in hand through the entire biblical canon. In MS Ee.4.24 visual literalness, of a kind, and much allegorization are present, for example in the historiated initial to Psalm 47. It shows a crowned king and another man demolishing a boat with axes [**123**]. Psalm 47 at verse 8 reads 'You break the ships of Tarshish with a strong wind' or 'in an angry spirit'. Another Psalm, 71, refers to the Kings of Tarshish bringing gifts, and these kings had long been thought of by biblical commentators as the three Magi of St Luke's Gospel, chapter 3. So it is King Herod who angrily breaks up the Magi's means of escape, when he hears that they have fled without reporting the whereabouts of the newly born Saviour. Exactly the same picturesque addition to the Gospel narrative is carved among the splendid medallions illustrating the Nativity story on the Virgin's Portal of Amiens Cathedral, of around 1230.

In the medieval illuminated book, art is not used only to enhance individual letters of the text. From the fourth century onwards luxury books produced for discerning patrons might contain drawings or fully painted pictures, either inset in the text or taking over entire pages. The four Gospels were regularly so treated, throughout the Christian world from the Bosphorus to the Irish Sea. Two celebrated manuscripts in the University Library, the late eighth- or early ninth-century Book of Cerne, MS Ll.1.10, and the late ninth-century Book of Deer, MS Ii.6.32, without being themselves in the highest rank artistically, at least stand within a venerable tradition of Gospel illustration, the conventions of which they signal, even if in a modified or shorthand form.

The text of the Book of Cerne consists mainly of prayers compiled from various sources, designed for personal use by a Bishop Aedelvaldus (either an earlier Bishop of Lindisfarne or a later Bishop of Lichfield) whose name is spelled out in an acrostic poem, written in polychrome lettering, which, surely for apotropaic purposes, is inserted at the precise centre of the section of text copied from the four Gospel accounts of the Passion of Christ. It is this section that is accompanied by four full-page pictures representing in turn each Evangelist and his symbol. The rather clumsy top-heavy articulation of the Lion of St Mark suggests that the artist, like the compiler of the prayers, has drawn on diverse sources [**125**]. Though technically amateurish, the images are, however, markedly intellectual. All four picture pages place the portrait of the Evangelist in a medallion at the top, and the symbol of the Evangelist below, and eye-catching inscriptions emphasize the difference of the humanity of the one from the symbolic animal nature of the other. This unusual lay-out has its origin, I believe, in the commentary on the Old Testament vision of Ezekiel written by St Gregory the Great (revered by the English as their Apostle), in which humanity in the person of Christ is seen to be raised up to the highest place in the heavenly hierarchy, above the winged servants and messengers of God, the angels. The bold and rather fancifully formed capital letters of the inscriptions have a number of significantly close parallels in the art and epigraphy of this period, the turn of the eighth to the ninth century. The name of St John the Evangelist is similarly written on a wonderful little gold plaque, fallen from a lost book cover or altar cross and found by chance in 1978 at a site at Brandon in Suffolk, not far from Cambridge. Similar lettering is displayed on the splendid pages surviving from a once massive copy of the Bible which, around 1600, was in the hands of John, Lord Lumley, a donor of eighty-four books to Cambridge University Library. Lord Lumley's Bible pages, unfortunately, did not come to the Library. They are remarkable for being coloured deep crimson all over, evoking the fabled purple codices of late Antiquity. In Cambridge the Book of Cerne is, as it happens, their nearest kin in this taste for royal purple. The initials to the four Passion narratives use a strikingly grand combination of purple and granular gold. The shade of purple, especially in St John's Gospel, agrees with that of Tyrian purple and might even be made from the glands of shellfish.[7]

The Book of Deer contains parts of the Gospels of Matthew, Mark and Luke, and the whole of John. Like the Book of Cerne it was acquired by the University Library in the royal donation of 1715 of Bishop Moore of Norwich's collection. Since the 1860s, when the manuscript was 'discovered' by the then University Librarian, the 'lynx-eyed' Henry Bradshaw, the importance of Gaelic notes added to the book in the north-east of Scotland in the twelfth century has been widely recognized. The fame of the Book of Deer in linguistic and social history has, though, been offset by artistic infamy. Only a quarter of a century ago an editor of the Gaelic notes castigated the illuminated pages as being 'of the most grotesque and barbarous crudeness'. This is merely visual illiteracy.[8] The illuminations belong to a well-defined Insular tradition of schematic figurative art, to be related to ornament and calligraphy, not to some supposititious norm of classical naturalism. The small scale of the Book of Deer (it measures 15.4 cm by 10.7 cm) and the inclusion after St Mark of a litany for the visitation of the sick

7. A. B. Kuypers, *The Book of Cerne*, (Cambridge, 1902); D. N. Dumville, 'A re-examination of the origin and contents of the ninth-century section of the Book of Cerne', *Journal of Theological Studies*, n.s. 23 (1972) 374–406; J. J. G. Alexander, *Insular manuscripts 6th to the 9th century*, A Survey of Manuscripts Illuminated in the British Isles 1, ed. Alexander (London, 1978), no. 66, p. 84; M. Brown, *The Book of Cerne: prayer, patronage and power in ninth-century England* (London, 1996).

8. K. Jackson, *The Gaelic notes in the Book of Deer* (Cambridge, 1972); Alexander, *Insular manuscripts*, no. 72, p. 87.

associate it firmly with an interesting Irish series of private pocket Gospel Books. Small as it is, it contains no fewer than seven full-page miniatures, one half-page miniature and five framed initial pages. For a volume of only forty-three folios this is an ambitious programme. The ingenuity of its quiring shows sophisticated knowledge of book construction, appropriate to full-scale complete altar Gospel Books. It is reasonable to suspect that the Book of Deer reflects richly decorated Insular Gospel Books, of around 800, now lost to us. Although the basic pattern of decoration is conventional enough, the figures prefacing the Gospels have attributes and gestures consistent with new narrative and symbolic tendencies at work in Insular art. The Book of Deer is now at long last being made the subject of the inter-disciplinary study it deserves [124].

Book illumination was not confined to the major liturgical types of manuscript. From around 1200 a gradually expanding market for books, among lay people as well as clerics, brought about a diversification of illus-trative matter and at the same time a rational refinement of style. Henry III (1216–72) was the first King of England since the Norman Conquest to embrace patronage of the visual arts as a positive tool of the state. Two of the University Library's manuscripts display impressive examples of royal iconography, made by London artists, one dating from the youth, and one from the maturity, of Henry III. MS Kk.4.25 is a Bestiary, an illustrated book of animal lore, but it also contains a miscellany of other texts.[9] One of these, the so-called letter of Alexander the Great to Aristotle, about his Indian expedition, is enlivened by a drawing of Alexander as an ideal medieval king: youthful, crowned, sitting bolt upright on a broad bench-like throne, over which his mantle is spread out in beautiful jabbing undulating folds. In its bright hopeful look, the image has much in common with that of Henry III in his first Great Seal of 1218, but an extra element of drama and panache is introduced by the vigorous twist of the right hand holding the sceptre and particularly by the right leg, bent and lifted high up over the left knee [126]. This dynamic pose was much used in the twelfth and thir-teenth centuries to signify an exotic despot, a Herod, or a Diocletian; in this sense it even survived into the nineteenth century, in the portrayal of Nasir ad-Din, Shah of Persia, by the political cartoonist 'Spy'.

For the author of the Life of St Edward the Confessor, *La estoire de Seint Aedward le rei*, MS Ee.3.59, Alexander the Great was a paradigm of the vanity of earthly power, whereas the chaste and charitable St Edward was a model king, Christ's true vice-regent on earth.[10] At his death he earned the crown

9. Brieger, *English art 1216–1307*, pp. 149–50; Morgan, *Early Gothic manuscripts 1190–1250*, no. 53, pp. 100–1.

10. M. R. James, *La estoire de Seint Aedward le rei* (Oxford, 1920); *La estoire de Seint Aedward le Rei*, ed. K. Y. Wallace, Anglo-Norman Text Society 41 (London, 1983); P. Binski, 'Reflections on *La estoire de Seint Aedward le rei*; hagiography and kingship in thirteenth-century England', *Journal of Medieval History*, 16 (1990) 333–50.

of immortality in heaven. The tenderly refined tinted drawing on folio 29, showing Edward's presentation by the Apostles Peter and John to Christ, is one of the earliest to tackle such a theme, familiar in later medieval and Renaissance portraits of a donor with supporting saints. It is also remarkable for its new realization of pictorial space. The image of Christ in majesty, enthroned between the four beasts (Evangelist symbols) of the Book of Revelation, is not here laid out in its familiar flat frontal position but is turned round to face the kneeling Edward, so that we, the readers, get a side view of it [127]. A shimmering finesse in the draughtsmanship and colour-washes makes the picture cycle in the Cambridge *Estoire* fit for a queen. Its original owners/readers very likely were two successive queens of England, Eleanor of Provence and Eleanor of Castile. The impulse behind the making of *Estoire* was the same as that which raised the new choir and transepts of Westminster Abbey, as the setting for the spectacular new shrine of the royal saint, on whose exaggerated virtues and credentials the ruling dynasty hoped to rely. On folio 30 the manuscript preserves an important archaeological record of the shrine itself, inaugurated in 1269 and destroyed at the Reformation. The gold *chasse* is seen gable-end on, and the high platform on which it is raised is echoed by two slender shafts, on which stand elegant statues illustrating the legend of the meeting of St Edward and St John the Evangelist in the guise of a poor pilgrim [128]. The idea of placing these statues beside the shrine might have come to King Henry from the sight or report of the half-life-sized gold statues of saints Peter and Paul which had stood from Merovingian times on Antique porphyry columns beside the shrine of St Denis, north of Paris. The true-to-nature leaves and fruits of the oak and the vine, which are a novel feature of the illustrations in *Estoire* can be paralleled by the botanically accurate foliage sculpted in the 1240s at the royal chapel in Paris, the Sainte-Chapelle, but are also paralleled on Antique vases and cameos newly fallen into acquisitive Western hands after the sack of Constantinople.

One of the pages of *Estoire* carries in the margin a spray of naturalistic vine leaves and grapes. On another page the artist, picking up a pious reference in the text to St Edward's conquest of the flesh, inserts in the margin his visual comment, ambivalent in tone: the vice for the virtue – the profile heads of a man and a woman, pressed together in a clearly lecherous kiss. Here we are witnessing the very first tentative step towards the creation of pictorial marginalia, which by the first half of the fourteenth century, notably in East Anglian illuminators' workshops, were to anticipate

Chaucer in their breadth of allusion and lack of inhibitions. The manuscript of *Estoire* entered Cambridge University Library with the royal donation in 1715. Neither then, nor in the seventeenth or sixteenth century, is it
likely to have been admired for its pictorial and narrative skill. It was its
Anglo-Saxon subject matter that saved it. Its first leaves carry the names,
and motto, of pioneer Saxonists of the sixteenth century, William Lombard
and Lawrence Nowell. The latter is the man who helped preserve an even
more precious manuscript for posterity, the sole surviving copy of the Old
English heroic poem *Beowulf*.

Another kneeling figure of a pious intercessor appears on folio 1ᵛ of MS
Dd.4.17, a private prayer book, a Book of Hours, prefaced by twelve full-
page miniatures, examples of an eloquent and gracious style of drawing
and painting which flourished, probably in London, during the two
decades 1310–30, of which the key monument is the famous Queen Mary
Psalter, now British Library Royal MS 2 B vii. Entries in the litany and
calendar of Cambridge's MS Dd.4.17 have been recognized as providing
important pointers to solving vexed problems regarding the Queen Mary
Psalter style, a style which binds together what has been described as 'the
largest most cohesive' group of fourteenth-century English manuscripts.
In itself, MS Dd.4.17 presents many puzzles.[11] The unknown intended
owner kneels in prayer before a bishop–saint, perhaps St Hugh of Lincoln
or St Thomas Cantilupe, canonized in 1320; but within a very few years her
mantle had been redesigned heraldically to give her the identity of Alice of
Reymes, of Wherstead in Suffolk, and at the same time the bishop–saint
was upgraded to archbishop [**129**, **130**]. The text of the Hours in Alice of
Reymes's book is decorated in a different, East Anglian, manner.
Manuscript workshop practice, and the role of patrons in this period, are
still wide open for research. But it is generally true that there was in the
fourteenth and fifteenth centuries a steadily expanding international
market for illuminated books, books which served both as directives of
intense inner spiritual life and as visible symbols of social status.

Another Book of Hours in the University Library, MS Ii.6.2, another
royal contribution, from the former Bishop Moore's collection, typifies in
its *ad hoc* construction the marketing techniques prevalent in Bruges, a
major centre of book production, around the year 1400. The sacred images
of God and his saints, and of the life of Christ, were painted independently
of any text, but could be bound up with appropriate texts according to the
wishes of the purchaser. The sweet style of the miniatures was one which

11. L. F. Sandler, *Gothic manuscripts
1285–1385*, A Survey of Manuscripts
Illuminated in the British Isles 5, ed.
Alexander (Oxford, 1986), vol. II, no.
67, pp. 75–6.

12. N. Rogers, 'Books of hours produced in the Low Countries for the English market in the fifteenth century' (University of Cambridge M. Litt. thesis [unpublished], 1982), pp. 307–10; A. Arnould and J. M. Massing, *Splendours of Flanders: late medieval art in Cambridge collections*, Catalogue of Exhibition, Fitzwilliam Museum, Cambridge, 1993 (Cambridge, 1993), no. 32, p. 114.

13. Arnould and Massing, *Splendours of Flanders*, no. 42, p. 134.

14. Arnould and Massing, *Splendours of Flanders*, no. 61, p. 174.

was popular at that time all across Europe, from England to Bohemia, with fresh faces, aristocratically accoutred figures, heavily swathed in blanket-like draperies, in narrow claustrophobic spaces under a heavy architectural canopy, represented as half in shadow [131]. The manuscript was evidently destined for use by a family in Suffolk, and received its specifically English devotional slant after it left Flanders. Recent research, and a major exhibition of Flemish manuscripts in Cambridge, have notably advanced knowledge of this aspect of late-medieval international culture.[12]

Even as early as Alice of Reymes's Book of Hours, conventions borrowed from panel painting had begun to infiltrate book design, the arrangement of the pictures in symmetrical pairs, like diptychs, and architectural cusped arches over the pictures, imitating their carpentry exemplars. The powerful detailed realism developed by the great Netherlandish panel painters, such as Van der Weyden, Van der Goes and Gerard David, came to be the norm also in late-medieval book painting, for example MS Nn.4.1, a Benedictional made in the 1520s for the use of an abbot of a wealthy Cistercian monastery in Bruges.[13] Its lavish pages are elaborately personalized, ornamented with the abbot's coat of arms, his motto and his initials. Each picture is like a window into an idealized but strictly contemporary scene, even if the events depicted are those narrated in the Gospels [132].

A thousand years earlier, in late Antiquity, when the Christian illuminated book had newly been created, the artists' careful scrutiny of nature, supported by *epinoia*, power of thought, was similarly esteemed. In the Middle Ages proper, book art tended to take a more abstract symbolic form which kept text and image in a better balance. In this regard the Cambridge *Estoire* is among the most accomplished of medieval books, experimental yet essentially maintaining the unity of the flat page, perfectly consonant in the layout and colouring of script and illustrations, cleverly orchestrating the levels of communication of both word and image. But an insatiable love of life, representing in miniature all aspects of the physical world, gets control of the medieval book in its last centuries. Even when paper and printing were well on their way in, it took patrons and book manufacturers a long time to shake off the fascinating habit of having books lavishly illuminated by hand. The elaborately decorated copy in the University Library of the treatise on the Latin language by the fifteenth-century Italian humanist Laurentius Valla (SSS.40.16) is a splendid example of this kind of fastidious and painstaking anachronism.[14]

Chapter 4

The Genizah fragments: a unique archive?

Stefan C. Reif

THE GENIZAH collection in the University Library represents a unique archive in content and research value, and the story of its acquisition and library fate is that of a special set of circumstances. In including this collection in a celebration of the Library's treasures, I hope to stimulate the reader's interest by offering a treatment that will attempt to be fresh as well as instructional, of general as well as scholarly interest, as attractive to those intrigued by literary resources as it might be to others in search of the human story behind the tedious text. To that end, the first part of this chapter will be concerned with how such a wealth of medieval Mediterranean material came to be amassed in Cairo and transferred to Cambridge. This will be followed by insights into its astonishing variety of content and a summary of the manner in which it has excited, and continues to excite, the attention of the professional historian, whilst firing the imagination of the enthusiastic amateur. The second half of the chapter will tell a tale of curatorship. It will trace the process of conservation and description within the University Library and provide a brief account of the collection's somewhat chequered history among the outstanding research resources of a remarkable centre of learning.

If an archive is a cache of documents carefully and conscientiously preserved by an earlier generation for the edification, or perhaps entertainment, of a later one, the Genizah collection, in common with many such literary finds, may make no such claim to the title. It was assembled for religious rather than historical reasons and its growth over the centuries was the result of an unusual, even unique, set of circumstances. By the time that the congregants of the Ben Ezra Synagogue were erecting their new building close to the Christian places of worship of their fellow minorities in early eleventh-century Fustat (or Old Cairo), they were the inheritors of a highly literate culture. Scrolls and codices, texts and annotations, as well as scribes and libraries were well-established phenomena, particularly as a result of the wider Jewish adoption of the written medium to encompass what had previously been a predominantly oral rabbinic tradition. When such written material was of a sacred nature and, through wear-and-tear or damage, could no longer perform its ritual function, the synagogal officials followed the widespread Jewish custom of not destroying texts on which the name of God or sections of Scripture were recorded by consigning them to a genizah, or storage place, where they would disintegrate through natural forces or from which they could be taken for burial in a communal cemetery [44].[1]

Happily for the historian and the collector, however, these officials did not limit themselves to the requirements of the rule-book. Apparently fearing that all written items might contain some element of the sacred, or convinced that Hebrew and Jewish scripts themselves had an innate sanctity, they established the practice of preserving a wide variety of mundane texts. In the course of doing this, on a site that they were destined to occupy for the unusually lengthy period (in Jewish historical terms) of 800 years, generations of communal functionaries created a rich web of information about their ancestors that lacks any parallel in general, as well as Jewish, history. Add to these facts the considerations that the Cairo community was one of medieval Jewry's most socially and economically active centres, and that the dry climate of Egypt is particularly suited to the long-term survival of antiquities, and you have a recipe for the emergence of an archive as impressive as that of the 'Cairo Genizah'. What is more, the Egyptian capital served at different times as a haven for persecuted Jews from a number of countries, including twelfth-century Crusader Palestine and Almohadic North Africa, as well as Inquisition Spain in 1492. It thereby attracted to itself, and preserved for posterity, historical and theological records that would, but for its famous depository, inevitably have been lost to humanity's inquisitive eye.

That eye was particularly well exercised by western *savants* on eastern pilgrimages during the nineteenth century. Travellers and explorers inspired missionaries and traders; missions and trading posts required military protection; and the existence of such security encouraged scholars to transform bookish interests into the practical search for primary research materials. Hence the appearance in Egypt, as elsewhere at that time, of dealers anxious to bring success to that search, and the growth of an awareness on the part of Cairene synagogal officials that what to them was no more than a heap of worn and torn scraps might deftly be transformed into a lucrative source of additional income. As a result of these developments,

44. A diorama representing synagogal officials depositing texts in the Genizah in the Middle Ages. (*Beth Hatefutsoth – Visual Documentation Center, Tel Aviv*)

1. S. C. Reif, 'Aspects of mediaeval Jewish literacy', in *The uses of literacy in early mediaeval Europe*, ed. R. McKitterick (Cambridge, 1990), pp. 134–55.

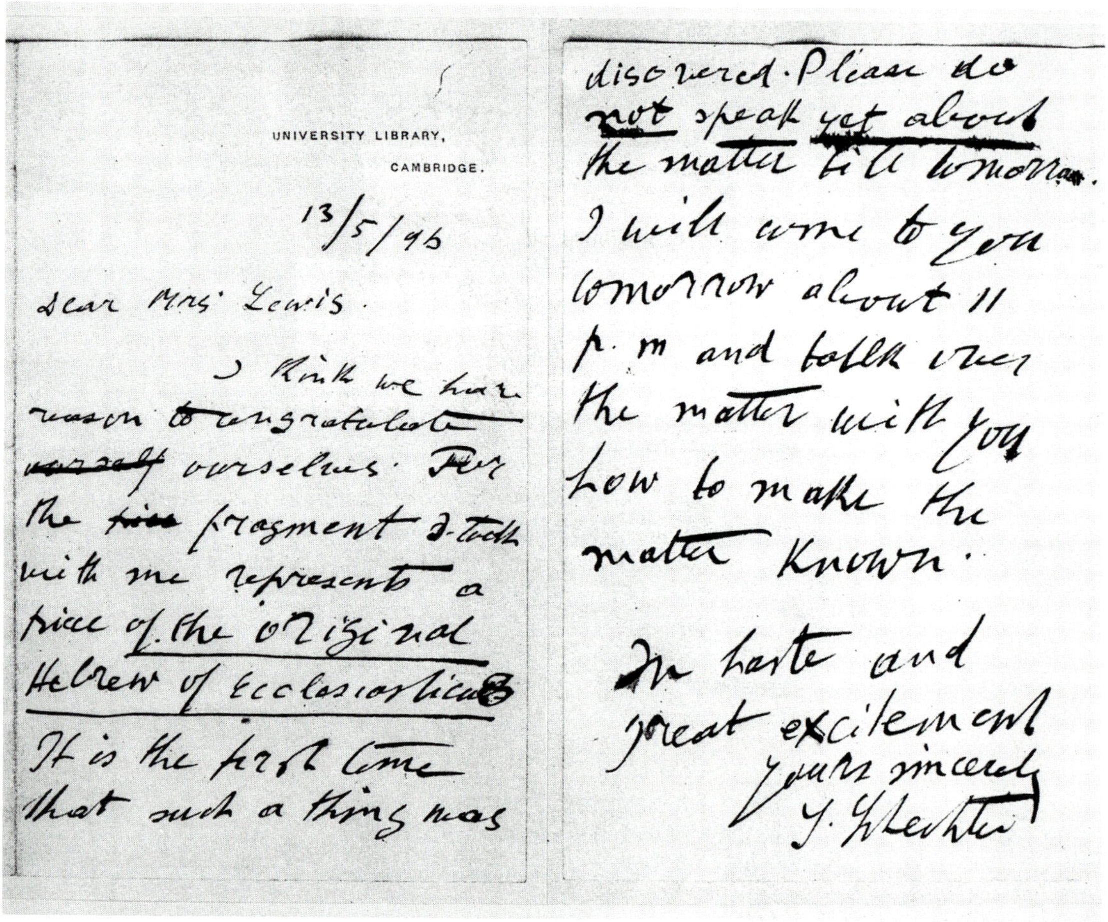

UNIVERSITY LIBRARY,
CAMBRIDGE.

13/5/96

Dear Mrs Lewis.

I think we have
reason to congratulate
ourselves. For
the fragment I took
with me represents a
piece of the original
Hebrew of Ecclesiasticus

It is the first time
that such a thing was

discovered. Please do
not speak yet about
the matter till tomorrow.
I will come to you
tomorrow about 11
p.m. and talk over
the matter with you
how to make the
matter known.

In haste and
great excitement
yours sincerely
S. Schechter

45. A letter from Solomon Schechter to Agnes Lewis written in Cambridge in 1896.

and especially due to the efforts of Rabbi Solomon Aaron Wertheimer in Jerusalem, Archimandrite Antonin of the Russian Orthodox Church in the Holy City, and the Reverend Greville Chester, an Anglican (and Oxonian) clergyman with Egyptological interests, medieval Hebrew and Jewish fragments made their appearance in western institutions during the final fifteen years of the Victorian epoch, but with no widespread awareness of their previous provenance. Among British libraries that offered accommodation to such early and unusual items were the British Museum (as it then was), the Bodleian in Oxford, and Cambridge University Library, while the English lawyer Elkan Nathan Adler, son of one Chief Rabbi and brother of another, acquired his own private collection directly from the Ben Ezra Synagogue.[2]

2. P. Lambert, ed., *Fortifications and the Synagogue: the Fortress of Babylon and the Ben Ezra Synagogue, Cairo* (London, 1994).

It was when the widowed twin Scottish sisters, Mrs Agnes Lewis and Mrs Margaret Gibson, showed some purchased fragments to Solomon Schechter in May 1896 that the matter took on a greater degree of urgency and attracted a more intensive form of attention [45]. As a teacher of tal-mudic literature at the University of Cambridge, and an expert in the editing of medieval rabbinic texts, Schechter recognized an exciting bibliographical discovery when he saw one and recalled that both Adler and some of the fragments already in Cambridge had indicated that Cairo was the place for further exploration. Encouraged, recommended and financed by the Master of St John's College, Charles Taylor (himself no mean hebraist), Schechter spent the winter of 1896–7 in the Egyptian capital and, by dint of spending many coffee-drinking and cigarette-smoking sessions with its Chief Rabbi, Aaron Raphael Ben-Shim'on, obtained communal permission to examine, and then to remove to Cambridge, the literary remains of the thousand-year-old centre of Jewish religious activity. Despite the receipt of bountiful 'baksheesh' from Schechter, the local beadles were not averse to diverting some of his spoils to their own commercial contacts, thereby forcing him to repurchase them before he could pack the whole collection for transport to England. Such financial self-interest made the

46. Solomon Schechter at work on the Genizah fragments in Cambridge University Library, about 1898.

Cambridge rabbinic scholar very indignant but it had prepared the way for the transformation of a pile of synagogal detritus into a hoard of scholarly riches [46].[3]

The varied content of such riches is nothing short of astonishing, matching, if not indeed eclipsing, the literary discoveries made at the Dead Sea, and similarly continuing to excite the attention and imagination of scholars many decades after the initial revelations. Each piece of information teased out of the texts is intriguing but the historical questions that remain unanswered even after the literary evidence has emerged are themselves no less beguiling. On the subject of the Dead Sea Scrolls, for instance, it is not widely appreciated that the first and fullest text of one of the sect's major religious tracts, the Damascus Document (or Zadokite Fragment) [47], came to light among the Genizah finds fifty years before the contents of the Qumran caves made their sensational impact on Jewish and Christian history. Nor indeed would it have been possible for the long-lost Hebrew text of the Wisdom of Ben Sira, written in the second pre-Christian century, to have been reconstructed without extensive input from the fragments found in the Ben Ezra Synagogue. But in which context did these two works continue to circulate in the intervening centuries and who copied them, and for what purpose, in Fatimid Cairo? The oldest Genizah texts are undoubtedly the palimpsests that preserve, beneath their tenth-century Hebrew overwriting, remnants of Greek Bible versions that predate the Muslim conquest of the Near East. Was it Jews or Christians who were using such versions in the sixth century and how did they come to be consigned to the Genizah?[4]

What that source has clarified is the manner in which the Jews transmitted, translated, annotated and expounded the biblical books from the tenth until the thirteenth century. Hitherto unknown works by unsung authors, in the field of rabbinic midrash no less than in that of literal and philosophical exegesis, are constantly coming to light and stand testimony to contemporary controversies about how best to interpret Scripture. Also documented are the efforts of

3. S. C. Reif, *A guide to the Taylor–Schechter Genizah Collection*, 2nd edn (Cambridge, 1979).

4. S. C. Reif, 'The Cairo Genizah and its treasures, with special reference to biblical studies', in *The Aramaic Bible*, ed. D. R. G. Beattie and M. J. McNamara (Sheffield, 1994), pp. 30–50; S. C. Reif, *Published material from the Cambridge Genizah Collections: a bibliography 1896–1980* (Cambridge, 1988).

47. The Damascus Document (CD), containing part of the religious ideology of the Dead Sea sect, as found in the Genizah. (T-S. 10K6)

48. Boethius, *De consolatione philosphiae*, with the English translation by Geoffrey Chaucer. Written *c.* 1400 and presented before 1424 by John Croucher, later Dean of Chichester.

49. More picturesque than accurate, Braun and Hogenberg's map of 1575 shows the houses and colleges of Cambridge confined together within the very small crowded historic town. Sheep graze near where the modern University Library now stands.

Within the illustration:

ARMA CANTEBR

AREA Scholar. Long 70
Cantebrigienfium. Lati 47

A. Bibliotheca Achademię.
B. Scholę paruę Achademie.

C. Sacell: Regemiū non regen dom̄ long 67. lati 28.
D. Schola. Theolog: long 67. Hebreica latitudo 28.

E. Scholaz Guilis. long 68. Greca. Rhetorica lati 24 Ped 10 vn
F. Schola. Logica. long itudo 68. lati 24.
G. Schola. Theolog Regis long 67.
H. Schola. Philolophica lati 25.

Altitudo XXXI
Ped

Altitudo XVI led III vnc

Altitudo xxii Ped iii vnc

Fenestra Orientalis Schole H.
Fenestra Orien Schole D.
Porte latit.do VII ped II vnc
Porte longi.do XI ped

50. The Schools Quadrangle, showing Rotherham's eastern front, with library above. From Matthew Parker's presentation copy to the University Chancellor, Lord Burleigh, of his *Catalogus cancellariorum*, 1574. (Royal Library)

51. A coloured copy of Hartmann Schedel's *Nuremberg chronicle* (Anton Koberger, 12 July 1493), one of a hundred books and manuscripts presented by Matthew Parker, Archbishop of Canterbury, in 1574. Parker's *Catalogus cancellariorum* lists these – the first printed list of donations to an English library.

dera est. inde zuccarū de madera. Inuenit ꝛ alias insulas ꜹplures ꝙs habitari baptizariꝙ noibus fecit vt
insulā seti Georiÿ fayal de pico ꝙruynā hoibus almanis ex flandria habitandā concessit.ferace trictici.An/
nis vo posterioribus vt anno dñi.1483.iohānes scōs portugalie rex altissimi vir cordis certas galeas oi/
bus ad victū necessarijs instruxit easꝗ vltra colūnas herculis ad meridiē versus ethiopiā inuestigaturos
misit. Prefecit aūt his patronos duos Iacobū canū portugalensem ꝛ martinū bohemū homine germa/
nū ex nurmberga superioris germanie de bona bohemorū familia natū. boiem inꝗ in cognoscendo situ ter/
re peritissimū marisꝗ pacientissimū. Quicꝗ pholomei lōgitudines ꝛ latitudines in occidente ad vnguē ex
perimēto.lōgeuaꝗ nauigatione nouit.Ӈÿ duo bono ꝺeorū auspicio mare meridionale sultantes a littore
nō longe euagantes supato circulo eꝗnoxiali in alterū ozbem excepti sunt. vbi ipis stantibus oziēteversus
vmbza ad meridiē,ꝛ dextrā proiciebaꝉ . Aperuere igiꝛ sua industria aliū ozbem bacten⁹ nobis incognitū ꝛ
multis annis a nullis ꝗ ianuensibus licet frustra temptatū.Peracta aūt hmōi nauigatione vicesimo sexto
mense reuersi sunt portugaliā pluribus ob calidissimi aeris patientiā moztuis. Insignū aūt poztauere pip
grana padisi.multaꝗ alia ꝗ longū esset recensere. Aperto illo ozbe magna piperis ꝗztitas flandriā versus
vehiꝛ.ꝛ licet nō sit adeo rugosum vt oziētale tñ acumen fozmā ꝛ oīa vtverū pip ꝑ se ferꝉ.Multa ea ꝺe re seri
benda fozent ꝗ ne tedij agrauar bono respectu oiisi.

Italia

Vltimis europe finibus pagratis ꝛ ꝗztī ꝓpositi nostri fuit septētrione ꝺecurso in patriā tandē reuersus
nouitates italie cū iā referende occurraꝉ.ab ea nimirū ozbe incipiendū esse arbitroz cuius creberrimas
mutationes ꝛ oziens simul ꝛ occidens admiraꝉ.Ea est genua ligurū dña ac regina ꝗ ciuilibus agitata di/
scozdijs memozia nͬa impiū maris amisit. In ea cū excluso philippo maria ꝡediolanensiū duce,eius ꝓtoze
opicio elzaco necato auctoze francisco spinula.vij. libertatis capitanei creati essent.eisꝗ paulopost subla
ta libertate exactis Suardus Smarde⁹ ducatū accepisset annos supza.lxx.natus auctoze thoma frigoso ꝗ
ꝛ ipe olim añ philippi ꝺominū ducali honoze functꝰ fuerat. Cū hō gzadeñ⁹ ad gubernatione inutilis vider eꝉ

MEDIOCRIA ★ FIRMA ·

N. Bacon eques auratus & magni
sigilli Angliae Custos librum hunc bi-
bliothecae Cantabrig. dicauit.
1574·

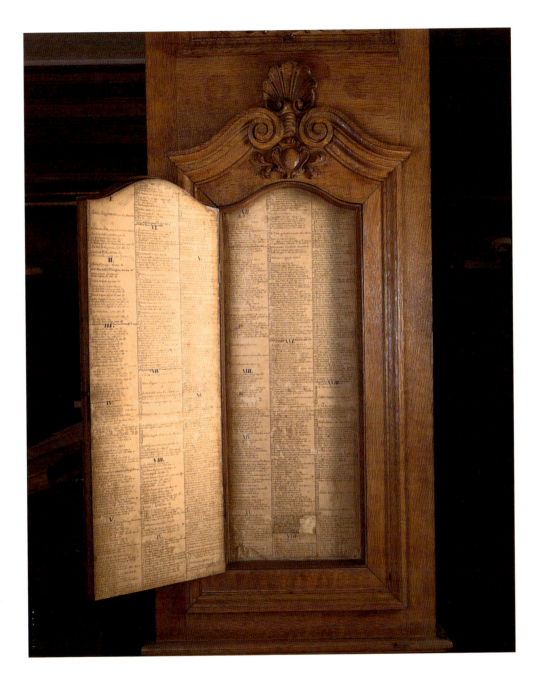

52. Nicholas Bacon's woodcut gift-plate, showing his arms, crest and motto, the earliest English example of its kind.

53. One of the bookcases built to house Archbishop Bancroft's Lambeth Palace library, which came to the University Library in 1649. The end of the case is open to show the original list of its contents.

54. The Manciple, from the *Canterbury Tales*. From a manuscript of Chaucer's poems written in the early fifteenth century, possibly in East Anglia.

55. Queen Elizabeth I is portrayed on this map of Cheshire by John Speed, engraved about 1603, the year of her death. Only two copies are known to exist.

56. Kṛṣṇa mandala from a lavishly
illustrated 'Kalāpustaka'. Two of
seventy-two folios of brilliantly
painted handmade paper glued
together in the fashion of a
concertina so that the complete
manuscript can be unfolded to be
viewed in its entire length. Each
folio is painted on both sides, and
therefore the manuscript needs to
be reversed to view the second run
of illustrations.

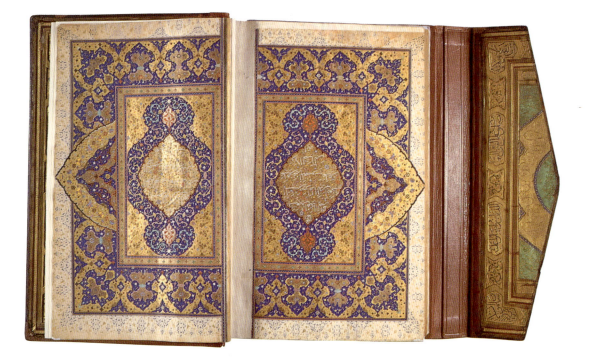

57. The opening *surah* of the Qur'an: a magnificent copy, probably *c*. 1600.

58. The combat of Afrasiyab and KayKhusraw, from the sixteenth- or early seventeenth-century Persian manuscript 'Shahnamah' (Book of Kings) of Firdawsi.

59. Alexander visiting the
wise man in the cave from the
'Sikandar-namah' in the *Khamsah*
(Five poems) of Nizami. Persian,
probably sixteenth-century.

60. The historical Buddha from the Aṣṭasāhasrikā Prajñāpāramitā (The perfection of wisdom in 8,000 verses) – the earliest known dated Indian illustrated manuscript, dated in the fifth year of Mahāpīpāla (c. 995 – 1043).

61. Jade books were reserved for the exclusive use of the Emperor of China. The illustration shows the colophon (an exquisitely incised Imperial five-clawed dragon) from Yü pi Pai-t'a shan wu chi (Five views of White Dagoba Hill), a description of a scenic spot within the precincts of the Imperial Palace in Peking, composed by the Emperor Kao-tsung (1711–99). A facsimile of the Emperor's manuscript, dated 1773, is engraved in gilt intaglio on 10 dark green jade plaques.

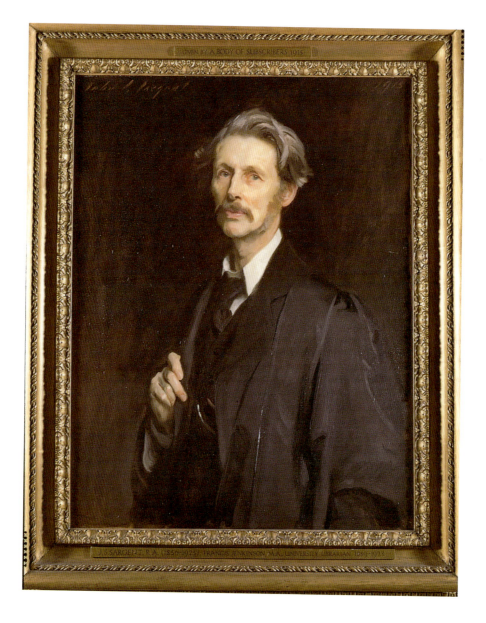

62. Francis Jenkinson, University
Librarian, 1889–1923. Portrait by
J. S. Sargent.

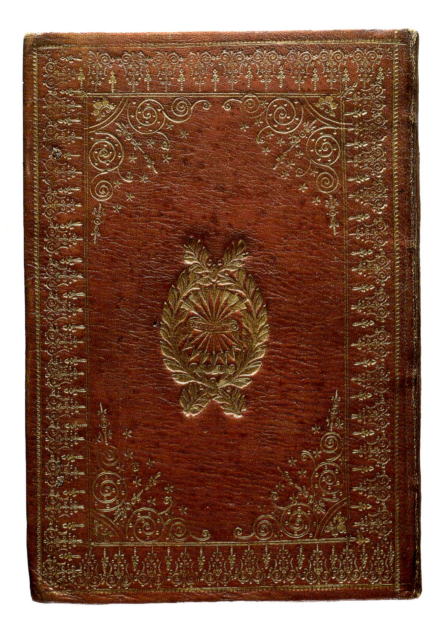

63. A seventeenth-century gift to the Library: Lord Herbert of Cherbury's presentation copy of the French translation of his *De veritate* (Paris? 1639). Red morocco gilt, with Herbert's crest.

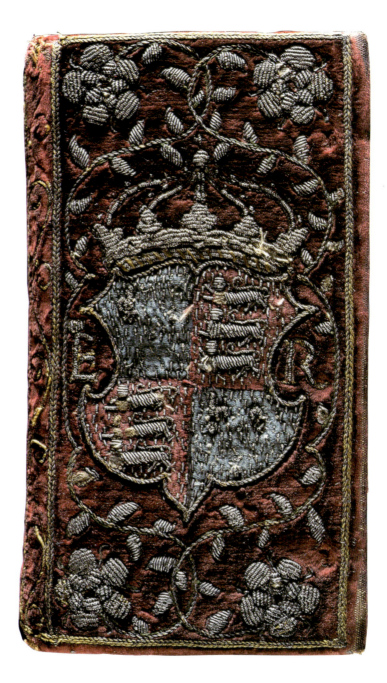

64. Sisto Poncello da Caravonica,
Le sacre historie del'Antico Testamento
(Padua, 1569). Dedication copy to
Cosimo de Medici (1519–74), Grand
Duke of Tuscany, whose arms –
featuring the ducal crown and the
collar of the Order of the Golden
Fleece – are painted on the black
morocco binding. (Bequeathed
by Samuel Sandars, 1894)

65. John Udall, *Certain sermons*
(London, 1596). Contemporary
crimson velvet binding,
embroidered in silver thread and
silks with the arms of Elizabeth I.
(Bequeathed by Samuel Sandars,
1894)

66. Aristotle, *De rhetorica* (London,
1619). Presentation copy from the
editor, Theodorus Goulston, to
Prince Charles, afterwards Charles I.
Olive-brown morocco with elaborate
gold tooling. (Bequeathed by Samuel
Sandars, 1894)

those who headed the rabbinic academies of Abbasid Iraq, and of their devotees, to establish the Babylonian Talmud as the authoritative source of Jewish religious law by mastering its intricacies, summarizing its ideas and codifying its decisions. The rulings issued by such leaders and the correspondence that they conducted with areas as distant from them as Spain testify afresh to the ideological clashes then current not only between Jews, Muslims and Christians, but also between different sects of Jews. Some Genizah fragments reflect the views of the Rabbanites, who saw the Talmud as authoritative for their beliefs and practices, while others provide evidence of the power once wielded in Jewish religious matters by the Karaites, who based themselves entirely on biblical precedent. If, as I myself have argued, the Jewish adoption of the codex in about the eighth century was the trigger for an explosion of Jewish literacy, it is not surprising to find that the medium of prayer took on a less fluid form and that the Genizah is making it possible to identify and compare the varying liturgical texts and customs that held sway, in the land of Israel and its north Mediterranean satellites on the one hand and in the diasporas of Mesopotamia, Arabia, North Africa and Spain on the other. New names (at least one of them feminine) have been added to the lists of medieval Hebrew poets, and the Holy Land's contribution to this genre of Jewish literature is now seen to have been of major significance before the Crusaders suspended Jewish communal and cultural activity in the homeland for the best part of a century.[5]

That period of persecution is only one among a number that are illuminated by our fragments and a variety of specific incidents of anti-Jewish behaviour are poignantly described. A community complains that the local Muslims are denying Jews access to the water well; a rabbi desperately seeks a visa to enable him to escape to a safer city; funds are sought to ransom a group of captives; and the leader of the Jews in Toulouse is obliged to bring the Jewish poll tax to his Christian masters on Good Friday and to suffer the indignity of a powerful blow on the head. Famous personalities also appear among the tattered texts, not just as distinguished authors but as writers of personal letters [67], creditors requesting the payment of debts, and travellers waiting

5. G. Khan, 'Twenty years of Genizah research', in *Encyclopaedia Judaica Year Book 1983/85* (Jerusalem, 1985), pp. 163–70; J. Blau and S. C. Reif, *Genizah research after ninety years: the case of Judaeo-Arabic* (Cambridge, 1992); S. C. Reif, 'Codicological aspects of Jewish liturgical history', *Bulletin of the John Rylands University Library of Manchester*, 75 (1993) 117–31.

67. A Judaeo-Arabic letter of recommendation, in autograph, written for a friend by Moses Maimonides (1138–1204), a leading figure of the medieval Jewish world. (T-S.12.192)

for a fair wind to begin a voyage. What is perhaps most exciting is the opportunity of entering the daily lives of ordinary families who lived so many centuries ago. Personal documents provide insights into their social, educational, professional and commercial activities, and new chapters are being written about medicine, magic, art and music, as they understood them. Medieval source material is always welcome but a collection containing over 140,000 items, ranging over every aspect of life, covering thirteen centuries and written in about a dozen languages and dialects deserves to be greeted in the warmest of scholarly fashions [133, 134, 178].[6]

Sometimes it has been. Solomon Schechter and the University Librarian of his day, Francis Jenkinson, differed greatly in both personality and background but enjoyed a common purpose in wishing to see the Genizah collection sorted, described and preserved, especially after it had been enlarged by the arrival of another batch of similar fragments from the same source, purchased from the bookseller W. S. Raffalovich. A room, predictably enough called the 'Cairo Room', was set aside in the University Library on the site that it then occupied between the Senate House and Clare College, and work was commenced. It was a distinguished and dedicated group that joined the Reader in Talmudic and the University Librarian in tackling the mammoth task. Charles Taylor, who had, with Schechter, formally presented the collection to the University in 1898, edited the Ben Sira texts jointly with him. He also co-operated with Francis Burkitt, soon to become University Lecturer in Palaeography and later Norrisian Professor of Divinity, in preparing the Greek palimpsests for publication. The redoubtable Mrs Lewis and Mrs Gibson studied the Christian items in Palestinian Syriac and produced an edition of 34 of these. In addition to setting aside some scholarly 'plums' for his own specific research, Schechter chose some 30,000 fragments that were among the clearest, largest and most promising, and sorted them under a variety of headings. As students of major archival collections know, no research is possible without such extensive scholarly groundwork and the credit for this belongs not only to Schechter but also to three other individuals who deserve special mention here.

Herman Leonard Pass was a graduate of Jews' College, the Orthodox London seminary, who continued his studies at Cambridge and, having there converted to Christianity (not an uncommon route to establishment recognition and acceptance at the time), was later ordained as an Anglican priest. Pass prepared an excellent summary of the biblical content of the

6. S. D. Goitein (with P. Sanders), *A Mediterranean society: the Jewish communities of the Arab world as portrayed in the documents of the Cairo Geniza*, 6 vols. (Los Angeles, 1967–93).

collection while another Jews' College contribution was made by its lecturer in Arabic and Syriac, Hartwig Hirschfeld, who produced a preliminary but most useful survey of the Arabic and Judaeo-Arabic manuscripts. Perhaps even more important were the foundations laid by a former bookshop salesman for the later reconstruction of Mediterranean Jewish history on the basis of these Judaeo-Arabic pieces. Ernest Worman continued Hirschfeld's work and his development of an impressive expertise in this area was recognized by his appointment in 1908 as Curator in Oriental Literature. His full-time efforts, together with those of the binder, Andrew Baldrey, who was responsible for what we would now call the conservation effort, and the overall supervision supplied by Jenkinson, ensured that Schechter's chosen 30,000 fragments were cleaned, repaired and flattened. In due course they were also stored between glass, bound up in volumes or placed loose in boxes, between papers.[7]

7. S. C. Reif, 'Jenkinson and Schechter at Cambridge: an expanded and updated assessment', *Transactions of the Jewish Historical Society of England*, 32 (1992) 279–316.

The curse of the mummy apparently had its equivalent in the Cairo Genizah. Schechter departed in 1902 for warmer religious climes in the form of the Jewish Theological Seminary in New York. The long-standing bachelor and devoted college man, Taylor, took a wife late in life and after a few months of marital bliss died in 1908. Worman barely reached middle age, succumbing to a brief but fatal illness one year after Taylor's death, and Schechter's successors in his talmudic post were less enthused by the Genizah than he had been. The First World War and the Depression brought the Library serious financial and staffing problems that left it little opportunity for attending to such specialized needs as those of the Genizah collection. By the time that Jenkinson's successor, A. F. Scholfield, was imposing a more authoritarian regime and calling for higher degrees of bureaucratic efficiency in the late 1920s, only Baldrey, who was not even able to read Hebrew, could recall the halcyon days of the Genizah pioneers, and another Library assistant hazarded the view that it was only Jenkinson's stubborn conservatism that had prevented the consignment to flames of the remaining (110,000!) fragments long before. Library success was, however, achieved on at least one front. After a protracted correspondence over a number of years, the University Librarian succeeded in obtaining from the Jewish Theological Seminary the return of most of the fragments that Schechter had borrowed by special arrangement ('Loan Collection' = T–S Misc.35 and 36) on his departure, but a lesson was learnt about the dangers of making loans of manuscripts without clear stipulations and controls, since the remainder were not returned until 1969.

Compensation for the Library's waning interest – even perhaps a certain degree of impatience – in the years between the World Wars was to be found in the major achievements of a number of individual researchers who either visited Cambridge or pored over photographs of Genizah items sent to them by the Library. A team at the Research Institute for Hebrew Poetry, founded by Salman Schocken in Berlin in 1929 and (not surprisingly) transferred to Jerusalem in 1934, located hundreds of secular as well as liturgical poems, identified forgotten authors and produced critical editions. Similar work was done on the texts and pointing systems of the Hebrew Bible fragments; on the eagerly examined versions of the long-neglected Palestinian Talmud; on the controversial exchanges between rabbinic leaders in the post-talmudic period; and on the sources of Jewish political, communal and intellectual history in the early Middle Ages.

Once the Second World War was over and the establishment of the State of Israel had inaugurated a period of more concentrated and vibrant Jewish scholarship, the expansion of oriental studies at Cambridge, in both library and faculty contexts, was bound to take fresh account of the Genizah treasures. The immediate motivation for some change of heart came about when Professor Shelomo Dov Goitein, then of the Hebrew University of Jerusalem, was conducting research on the documentary material among the 30,000 fragments sorted many decades earlier. He was shown by the University Librarian, H. R. Creswick, a huge crate containing the remainder of the collection, and asked whether it had any value for scholarship or could be discarded. Goitein's realization that these manuscript remnants, though smaller, more fragmentary and less easily deciphered, were the stuff of future scholarship led to the establishment of the 'New Series' and a rekindling of interest on the part of the University Library, the Faculty of Oriental Studies, and visiting scholars. In the 1960s, particularly at the urging of the Lecturer in Rabbinics, Dr J. L. Teicher, committees were set up by the University to look into the future of the collection and it was proposed that a programme of sorting, identification, scholarly description and bibliographical recording be initiated and that a senior scholar be appointed as curator to take responsibility for this. Various considerations ultimately led to a scaling-down of the original proposals and Dr Henry Knopf, already dealing with the Library's Hebrew printed books, was appointed to deal with queries regarding the Genizah collection, visitors to it, and the cataloguing of its biblical fragments. By the time that he left for an appointment in Israel in 1972, important progress had been made on aspects of that cataloguing, a significant proportion of the collection had been microfilmed, and a project to conserve the fragments, using the latest and most efficient techniques, was well under way. A new generation of scholars, both contemporaries of Goitein and students of his, were wending their way to Cambridge and expanding the range and number of Genizah publications.

On the appointment of the present author to be responsible for the collection in 1973, it was clear that any expansion of the Library's programme would be dependent on the attraction of external funding, and obvious that, at the rate of progress then being maintained, substantial achievements would take at least half a century. There was nothing for it but to set about the task of fund-raising, and an essential element in this process was of course a public relations campaign that would demonstrate to the wider world how significant the collection was for medieval history and how much more it could still contribute to our understanding of the Mediterranean area, as it evolved from the Middle Ages into the modern world. Fortunately, a number of foundations, philanthropists and academic bodies appreciated the significance of the project, a Genizah Research Unit was set up, with joint University Library and Oriental Faculty sponsorship, and a systematic and comprehensive set of aims was drawn up. The most urgent of these were the conservation of the entire collection and the microfilming of each conserved fragment. A suitably trained team was engaged on these tasks and by early 1982 they were successfully concluded, in a period of a little over eight years rather than the original estimate of fifty.[8]

8. S. C. Reif, 'One hundred years of Genizah research at Cambridge', *Jewish Book Annual*, 53 (1995–6) 7–28.

Meanwhile, a third and final part of the collection, the 'Additional Series', had also been separately sorted and conserved and the whole collection was therefore available for scholarly description. The special nature of Genizah material makes such description a challenging scholarly task that requires expertise, patience, wide knowledge and a degree of imagination. One is often confronted with what may amount to no more than part of one folio of an unknown work by an unidentified author with only limited clues as to content, written in a difficult hand, and in an unusual language or dialect. The only way of proceeding is to bring together a team of experts to prepare hand-lists in their own fields, and to hope that they will work in harmony and co-operatively tackle the particularly stubborn items that appear to defy decipherment and identification. Since the 1970s, fourteen visiting scholars in the Unit have functioned in this way and ten younger researchers have been trained how to respond to the Genizah collection's special challenges. Such specialists have compiled various scholarly catalogues and have also contributed to the preparation of similar reference works at other centres of learning. As a result, well over half of the Cambridge Genizah collection now has some form of detailed description. A Genizah Series of publications has been established, published by Cambridge University Press for Cambridge University Library, and ten volumes have appeared, with another six volumes at advanced stages of preparation. A serious attempt has been made, through a regular newsletter, *Genizah Fragments* – and various other publications, and through the media – to bring the results of Genizah research to a wider public, and exhibitions of Hebraica around the world have often included Cambridge Genizah items. Over £1 million has been raised from outside sources in support of the project. Perhaps most exciting, given present interests, is the plan to make use of the latest computer technology not only to describe the collection and prepare such descriptions for publication but also to permit online computer access to individual manuscripts, together with basic information about them, from all over the world [68]. There is no doubt that the progress made in recent years at Cambridge University Library has contributed to an intensification of Genizah research throughout the field of Jewish studies, so that it is no longer possible even to attempt to list the hundreds of scholars whose work is heavily dependent on the material that Schechter brought from Cairo and that the Library has made available for almost a century.

68. The preparation of digitized images of Genizah fragments in the Genizah Research Unit, 1995.

The intention of this chapter was, as noted at the outset, to indicate the degree to which the Genizah collection and its story, in both Cairo and Cambridge, constitute unique phenomena. Those who have worked closely with these torn and stained testimonies to bygone ages, while fully aware of the characteristics that they share with many other archives and their diverse fates, are in no doubt that they represent an unrivalled resource for students of intellectual history, worthy of being counted among the world's greatest literary treasures, housed in one of its finest research libraries.

Chapter 5

Printed books 1450–1550

DENNIS E. RHODES

Incunabula

1. P. Needham, 'A Gutenberg Bible used as printer's copy by Heinrich Eggestein in Strassburg, ca. 1469', *Transactions of the Cambridge Bibliographical Society*, 9 (1986) 36–75.

AT THE BEGINNING of one of his most important articles written as the result of bibliographical researches carried out in Cambridge, the American scholar Paul Needham wrote: 'The most valuable printed book given to Cambridge University Library in its long history of generous benefactions is its Gutenberg Bible.'[1] The 42-line Bible (so called because each page has two columns of text with 42 lines to a column) was printed anonymously at Mainz by the inventor of printing in Western Europe, Johann Gutenberg, about 1455, and is a book of which a good complete copy is today worth well in excess of £1 million. The Library had to wait until comparatively modern times – 1933 to be precise – to acquire a copy of this monumental work, which came as part of a gift of 150 Bibles, made by Arthur William Young, a graduate of Trinity College. Dr Needham discovered that it had an additional importance in that it was used as printer's copy for a later edition of the Bible produced by Heinrich Eggestein at Strassburg in about 1469, of which the Library also has a copy (Oates 110[2]) [**113**].

2. J. C. T. Oates, *A catalogue of the fifteenth-century printed books in the University Library, Cambridge* (Cambridge, 1954).

For the past five centuries and more, Cambridge University Library has been most fortunate in its gifts. Its copy of Cicero *De officiis*, printed at Mainz by Fust and Schoeffer on 4 February 1466, was bought in Bruges on 17 April 1467 by Caxton's patron, John Russell, Chancellor of England, who later also owned the Virgil printed by Antonio Miscomini in Venice in 1476. This Cicero is the earliest surviving printed book to have reached England. Both books came to the Library as part of the collection of John Moore, Bishop of Ely (1646–1714), whose library was presented to the University in 1715 by King George I and has since been known as the Royal Library [**179**].

A volume containing five separate treatises, which belonged to a doctor of Augsburg named Ulrich von Ellenbog, was bound for him in his native city in 1476 and afterwards belonged to the Benedictine Abbey at Ottobeuren. It has been in Cambridge University Library since 1870. As this volume contains copious notes in the hand of Ellenbog himself, it came to the notice of Robert Proctor (1868–1903), the great incunabulist of Oxford

69. Inscription inside the front board of 'Ellenbog's Book'.

and of the British Museum, who, in the year of his tragic death in the Alps, published one of his celebrated articles which, while being as always technical and typographical, is one of his more humanely readable essays. His careful analysis of the tracts themselves, and of Ellenbog's notes, enabled him to fill out the picture of the activities of one of the earliest printing presses in Augsburg, situated in the monastery of Saints Ulrich and Afra.[3] The pieces are now Oates 128, 901, 903, 915 and 919 [69].

Victor Scholderer drew attention to the existence in the University Library of a copy of Jacobus de Clusa, *Quodlibetum statuum humanorum*, containing the manuscript date 1476 (now Oates 1144).[4] It is important for our knowledge of the career of a printer whose works are rarely seen, Johannes Hug of Göppingen, who evidently worked for Conrad Fyner, the only documented printer at Esslingen in the fifteenth century. Scholderer also reported on another incunable in Cambridge University Library: the *Speculum iudiciale* of Gulielmus Durandus, signed by Georg Husner and Johann Bekenhub on 22 November 1473 at Strassburg (Oates 143). The differences which the Cambridge copy reveals when compared to the British Library and Bodleian copies of this book are of importance for our appreciation of some of the technical problems facing the early printers of such a huge volume.

3. Robert Proctor, 'Ulrich von Ellenbog and the press of S. Ulrich at Augsburg', *The Library*, n.s. 14 (1903) 163–79, reprinted in his *Bibliographical essays* (1905), pp. 73–88.

4. V. Scholderer, 'Notes on the incunabula of Esslingen', *Gutenberg Jahrbuch* (1950) 167–71.

70. Geoffrey Chaucer, *Queen Anelida and the false Arcyte* (Westminster, William Caxton, *c.* 1477). One of the Library's unique Caxton quartos.

The unique and perfect copy of the *Doctrinale* of Alexander de Villa Dei (Oates 3300) once attributed to a semi-mythical printer named Laurens Coster, and now assigned to the anonymous 'Speculum Printer' who in all probability worked at Utrecht about 1472, forms part of a generous bequest to the Library by George Dunn, who died in 1912, many of whose incunabula are also in the British Library and some at Oxford. Of England's first printer, William Caxton, the Library owns forty-seven separate editions, or fragments of editions [70]. Among them are eight verse pieces, formerly in a tract-volume, now separated; four are unique. One is the *Disticha* of Cato in English, two consist of minor poems by Chaucer, three are by John Lidgate, the rest anonymous (Oates 4061, 4062, 4063, 4065, 4066, 4067, 4068 and 4070). Then in 1960, too late to be included in Oates's catalogue, the Library acquired from Ripon Cathedral one of four surviving copies of a vocabulary in French and English, printed by Caxton about 1480. A facsimile with linguistic introduction by Professor L. C. Harmer and bibliographical notes by J. C. T. Oates was published by Cambridge University Press in 1964.

How the Library's collections of early books grew from the fifteenth century onwards has been told in lucid and well-documented prose by J. C. T. Oates in the long introduction to his catalogue of the Library's incunabula, published in 1954. The Library was indeed fortunate to have the life-long services of such an excellent scholar as Oates (1912–90), whose many publications have chronicled its history as no other writer could have done, for his style was all his own.[5]

Henry Bradshaw, Fellow of King's (1831–86), University Librarian from 1867 until his early death, had a particular interest in incunabula from the Low Countries, visiting Holland and Belgium several times for sales, and keeping in regular correspondence with the Dutch incunabulists J. W. Holtrop (1806–70), Librarian of the Royal Library at The Hague, and his successor, M. F. A. G. Campbell (1819–90).[6] Bradshaw's enthusiasms and preferred fields of study were largely passed on to his pupil and, ultimately, successor, Francis Jenkinson (1853–1923, Librarian from 1889), under whom the Library's collection of incunabula more than doubled. The greatest benefactor of this period was Samuel Sandars (1837–94), educated at Harrow and Trinity College, who gave money, manuscripts and printed books to the University Library, and on his death bequeathed about 1,500 books as well as £500 to be spent on 'rare English books'. Oates's index shows that Sandars gave 91 incunabula and bequeathed 112 more [71, **180**]. Apart from these gifts, the Sandars Lectures in Bibliography instituted in 1895 are his most perpetual monument in Cambridge.

The result of Bradshaw's and Jenkinson's combined policies is that Cambridge University Library has been pre-eminent since the nineteenth century in its holdings of Netherlandish incunabula, but much weaker

5. J. C. T. Oates, *A catalogue*; 'Checklist of the published writings of J. C. T. Oates', in J. C. T. Oates, *Studies in English printing and libraries* (London, 1991) pp. 397–409.

6. *Henry Bradshaw's correspondence on incunabula with J. W. Holtrop and M. F. A. G. Campbell*, ed. W. and L. Hellinga (Amsterdam, 1966–78).

71. Nicolaus Pergamenus, *Dialogus creaturarum* (Gouda, Gerardus Leeu, 3 June 1480). An adaptation of the old bestiaries and the first illustrated book issued by a Dutch printer. (Sandars Bequest)

than the British Museum in its holdings of early French, Italian and Spanish books. In 1957 a second exchange of duplicates was arranged with the British Museum: there had already been one in 1948. The present writer had the pleasure of taking ten incunabula (five Italian, two French and three German) from the British Museum to give to Cambridge, while John Oates brought the same number, mostly Low Countries books, to London. When he published his catalogue in 1954, Oates was able to record 4,249 incunabula made up of 3,714 editions and 535 duplicates, including a number of variants which he was the first to identify. This made Cambridge University Library into the third-largest collection in the British Isles, the British Museum having about 10,000 and the Bodleian about 6,000. Between 1954 and 1996 Cambridge University Library has added another 174 incunabula to its collections.

Not that the Library lacked treasures amongst the choicest of Italian incunabula. It has two copies of the 1499 *Hypnerotomachia Poliphili* printed at Venice by Aldus Manutius, a very common book, but the most beautiful of all illustrated books to appear in Italy before 1500 [72]. The attribution of its authorship to Francesco Colonna is now disputed by some scholars, who consider it to be the work of a certain Fra Eliseo da Treviso. The first of the Library's four copies of the *editio princeps* of Homer, printed at Florence in 1488/9, was presented by Cuthbert Tunstall (1474–1559), Bishop of London

72. Francesco Colonna, *Hypnerotomachia Poliphili* (Venice, Aldus Manutius, December 1499). The identity of the designer of the woodcuts is uncertain, but the interdependence of word and picture in this dream allegory is unprecedented in a printed text.

– translated to Durham in 1530 shortly after making his gift, which brought the first Greek books into the University's possession. There are fifty-nine editions of the sermons of Girolamo Savonarola, the hot-headed Dominican friar from Ferrara who was burnt at the stake in Florence for heresy in May 1498. Of the three editions of Dante's *Divine Comedy* printed in 1472, the Library has those printed at Mantua and Foligno, lacking only the one whose place of printing had been disputed between Iesi and Venice until it was firmly established by Scholderer in 1932 as being Venice. A huge and splendidly rare law book is Oates 1704: the *Lectura Super I–III Codicis* of Baldus de Ubaldis, printed at Venice on 23 September 1474 by Johannes de Colonia and Johannes Manthen. It was given to the University about 1484 by Thomas Rotherham, Archbishop of York, who presented many more printed books and manuscripts, some thirty-five of his printed books being still *in situ*, among them several law books of the kind which are usually not available in the British Library, since the British Museum was only founded in 1753, when such law books were no longer in circulation. Those who want them in Britain must search not only in the university libraries of Oxford and Cambridge, but also in such colleges as All Souls, New College and Trinity Hall, which specialized in law studies.

In 1977 the Broxbourne gift brought thirteen superb and in some cases very rare incunabula into the Library's possession. They had belonged to the late Albert Ehrman, who for a time lived at Broxbourne, Hertfordshire, and who had always aimed to collect at least one specimen from every town in Europe in which printing took place in the fifteenth century. Thus were added to the Cambridge holdings examples of books printed at Toscolano, Como, Cagli, Fivizzano, Lüneburg, Torrebelvicino, Schoonhoven (two), Pojano and Udine: all imprints which the Library would probably never otherwise have had an opportunity to acquire [73].

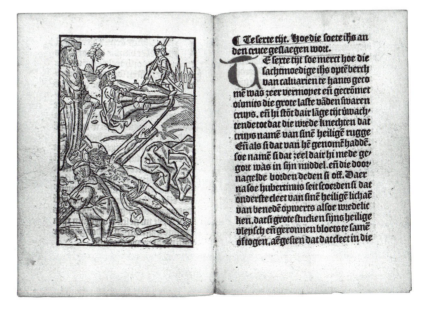

73. *Oefeninghe vander Passien en vanden bitteren liden ons heren Jesu Christi* (Schoonhoven, Canons of St Michael in den Hem, 10 November 1497). One of the Library's seven incunables from this monastic press, notable for their remarkable woodcuts.

Some of the Library's French incunabula are extremely rare, such as Oates 3075, the Book of Hours for the use of Poitiers, printed in Paris by Philippe Pigouchet on 8 August 1498; Oates 3203, the *Life of Christ* in French by Pierre Desrey, printed at Lyons by Guillaume Balsarin on 18 March 1498; and the only recorded copy of Alexander de Villa Dei, *Doctrinale*, printed by Martin Morin at Rouen after 1490 (Oates 3281), of which the *Gesamtkatalog der Wiegendrucke* in Berlin was only able to give an inaccurate and incomplete description (*GW* 1039).

The University Library is not strong in its holdings of Spanish incunabula. Nevertheless Oates recorded twenty-one editions, to which eight more have now been added. One of these eight, however, may be of the early sixteenth century: *Gratiarum actio directa ad Ferdinandum et Helisabeth pro victoria eis collata de Granatensi civitate ac regno, composita . . . Anno domini 1492 mense Januarij*. The book is attributed to Meinardus Ungut and Stanislaus Polonus at Seville, and is obviously later than January 1492, but *GW* 11291 believes it to be later than 1500. Norton does not mention this work, of which the Cambridge copy, acquired in 1955, is the only one recorded in the British Isles.[7]

Oates's first two Spanish incunabula deserve a note each. Gulielmus de Podio, *Ars musicorum*, printed by Peter Hagembach and Leonhard Hutz at Valencia on 11 April 1495 (Haebler 551,[8] Oates 4038), is the only copy in the British Isles. It leads us to the discovery that the University Library is surprisingly well-off for the handful of incunabula of musical theory which exist, as opposed to liturgical music printing. Oates 214 is Hugo Spechtshart, *Flores musicae*, Strassburg, Johann Prüss, about 1490. Then there are four editions by the celebrated author from Lodi, near Milan, Franchinus Gafurius (1451–1522): these are Oates 2322 (Milan 1496), 2626 (Brescia 1497), 2319 and 2320 (Milan 1492) and 2521 (Naples 1480). All these are also in the British Library and in many other libraries; but Cambridge University Library rounds off the list with an author who is not in the British Library: Johannes Spadarus. His *Defensio musices*, printed at Bologna on 16 May 1491 by Plato de Benedictis, receives a full description from Oates (no. 2492) because of its rarity: other copies are at the Bibliothèque Nationale, Paris, and at the Music Library of the University of Rochester, New York State. There is no known copy in Italy [74].

7. F. J. Norton, *A descriptive catalogue of printing in Spain and Portugal, 1501–1520* (Cambridge, 1978).

8. K. Haebler, *Bibliografía ibérica del siglo XV* (La Haya and Leipzig, 1903–17).

74. Use of the octave rather than the hexachord as the theoretic basis of scales is advocated by the Bolognese composer Johannes Spadarus in his *Defensio musices* (Bologna, Plato de Benedictis, 1491).

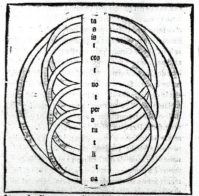

In questa figura potrai cognoscere la excellentia di queste octo uoce :non ti pare chel sia uero quel che dice il mio maestro:cioe che in esse include quello che nelle sei uoce de Guido:et insuper piu doe specie di diapente et lo tritono. Le uero che lo diapente ha piu perfectione in processo:e in sono che lo diathes saron:del sono non e dubio alcuno:ma del processo piglia la auctorita di Q do nel suo inchiridiõe: doue

75. Isaac ben Solomon Ibn Sahula, *Meshal ha-qadmoni* (*Proverb of the Ancients*; Brescia, Gershom ben Moses Soncino, *c.* 1491). In this allegorical tale the king rewards his diligent servant but punishes the lazy one.

Oates's second Spanish incunable is Aristotle, *Ethica ad Nicomachum*, in two volumes, attributed to the 'Printer of Bernardus de Parentinis', who was apparently Heinrich Botel at Saragossa (*GW* 2371, about 1478). Although this book was in the opinion of the Spanish bibliographer Francisco Vindel not printed in Spain, its Spanish origin is now firmly attested. No other copy is recorded in the British Isles (Oates 4039).

Finally, a few words on Hebrew incunabula, of which the University Library has forty-two editions in forty-nine copies, with an additional twenty in the colleges. David Qimhi (Kimchi), *Book of Roots*, now attributed to Obadiah, Menasheh and Benjamin of Rome, about 1469–70 (Oates 2731), seems to be the first Hebrew book ever printed. Thirteen copies are known. Isaac ben Solomon Ibn Sahula, *Proverb of the Ancients* (Brescia, Gershom ben Moses Soncino, about 1491, Oates 2723 and 2724) is the first illustrated Hebrew book. Cambridge University Library has two of the eight copies recorded [75]. Biblia Hebraica, Proverbs, commentary by David ben Solomon Ibn Yahya (Lisbon, Eliezer Toledano, *c.* 1492, Oates 4226) is the only copy in the British Isles of a book of which ten copies are known.

Sixteenth-century books

The University Library has probably been as fortunate in its gifts of 'post-incunabula' (a term used mainly to indicate books printed in the period 1501–20) as in those of incunabula. In 1934 Sir Stephen Gaselee, Librarian of the Foreign Office and a Fellow of Magdalene, gave the University Library 300 incunables and 77 post-incunables. Frederick John Norton (1904–86), Under-Librarian in the University Library from 1930 to 1972, was in his own right a distinguished Hispanist, and author with Professor Harmer of a highly successful Spanish grammar first published in 1935. His life-long passion, however, was for all books printed between 1501 and 1520. Not only did he publish in 1978 his great catalogue of Spanish and Portuguese books of this period, but he also collected French, German, Italian and other books of the same period. His collection, unrivalled in the world, passed into the University Library after his death, and has enriched the Library's holdings by some 660 editions.[9] Many of these are unique copies. It is hoped that a separate catalogue of the Norton books will be published [76].

9. Norton, *A descriptive catalogue*; J. J. Hall, 'The F. J. Norton collection of post-incunabula', *Bulletin of the Friends of Cambridge University Library*, 7 (1986) 10–12.

76. *Carta dela grã victoria y presa de Oran* (Barcelona, Carles Amorós, c. 1509). A scarce four-page pamphlet in prose and verse on the siege of Oran and its capture from the Moors in 1509. (Norton Collection)

77. A Psalter printed in Vilna, around 1525, by Francisk Skorina, who was the first translator and printer of the Bible in Russian, using the White Russian (Belarusian) recension of Church Slavonic.

78. Jean Pèlerin, *De artificiali perspectiva* (Toul, Petrus Iacobi, 23 June 1505). The earliest printed book on perspective, consisting mainly of full-page woodcuts in simple outline. This shows a travelling carriage and its component parts, the author calling himself 'Viator' on his title-page.

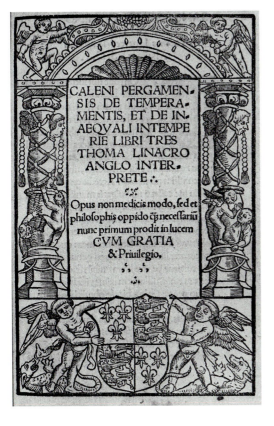

79. Galen, *De temperamentis* (Cambridge, John Siberch, 1521). Siberch used this elaborate title-page border, incorporating the royal arms, in two other productions.

In 1967 H. M. Adams, who had for many years been Librarian of Trinity
College, published his life's work, in which it is obvious that he records
many sixteenth-century rarities all over the University, not only in the
University Library.[10] The University Library has a copy of the Psalms in
White Russian, printed by Francisk Skorina at Vilna about 1525 [77]. It has
two editions of sermons by Gulielmus Peraldus, Bishop of Lyons, printed
by Johannes de Channey at Avignon in 1519. It has two editions of Jean
Pèlerin, *De artificiali perspectiva*, printed by Petrus Iacobi on 23 June 1505 and
7 September 1521, respectively. These have the imprint 'Tullis', which
Adams has translated in his index as 'Tulle', a town east of Périgueux, but
which really indicates Toul, near Nancy [78]. Another rare book, again
wrongly indexed by Adams, is the Statutes of Jutland, printed by Matthaeus
Brandis at Ripen in Denmark in May 1504, followed by another edition
printed at Copenhagen by Gotfridus de Ghemen in September 1508 (Adams
J 747,748).

The great Complutensian Bible printed by Arnao Guillén de Brocar at
Alcalá de Henares near Madrid (after 'Complutum', the Roman name for
Alcalá) is one of the most complicated books ever produced, having to use
the Greek, Hebrew, Latin and Chaldaic alphabets. Its various parts are
dated between 10 January 1514 and 10 July 1517, but the papal privilege was
not granted for its publication until March 1520, and is printed (as Norton
mentions) on a convenient blank page, possibly reserved for the purpose,
after receipt. Variant states of the book exist, and are distinguished in
Norton's lengthy description (Norton 27A – 27E). Cambridge University
Library has three copies, the first of which was presented by the Bishop
Tunstall whom we have already met. Another book given to the Library by
Bishop Tunstall was his own composition, *De arte supputandi libri quattuor*,
printed by Pynson in London in 1522 (*STC* 24319). It is, in Oates's words, 'the
first English book of practical arithmetic' [80].[11]

Mention should be made of the first printer in Cambridge, John Siberch,
from Siegburg near Cologne, who printed ten books in the University in
1521 and 1522. The University Library had apparently only two of Siberch's
productions when Henry Bradshaw prepared a bibliography of them (published posthumously by Jenkinson in 1886): two copies of the Baldwin, *De
altaris sacramento sermo*, 1521 (*STC* 1242), and one copy of the Galen, *De temperamentis*, translated by Thomas Linacre (*STC* 11536) [79]. It now also has a copy
of St John Fisher, *Contio* (*STC* 10898), and the strange little book by 'Papyrius
Geminus Eleates', of 8 December 1522, entitled *Hermathena* (*STC* 11719).

10. H. M. Adams, *Catalogue of books printed on the continent of Europe, 1501–1600, in Cambridge libraries* (Cambridge, 1967).

11. J. C. T. Oates, 'The Cambridge University Library 1400–1600', *Library Quarterly*, 32 (1962) 270–86.

12. Constance W. Bouck, 'On the identity of Papyrius Geminus Eleates', *Transactions of the Cambridge Bibliographical Society*, 2 (1958) 352–8.

Much argument has raged over the identity of the author, but the problem seems to have been satisfactorily settled by Constance W. Bouck in 1958: he was almost certainly Sir Thomas Elyot.[12] Cambridge University Library acquired its copy in Bradshaw's time. The Library has also two unique though incomplete settings of a list of indulgences issued by an unidentified Hospital of St Sepulchre (*STC* 14077c.151 and 152), printed by Siberch around 1522 and taken from a Siberch binding in the library of King Edward VI School, Bury St Edmunds. A copy of a woodcut of the Adoration of the Shepherds on a cancelled leaf from the first issue of Galen, *De temperamentis*, was presented by a former librarian, H. R. Creswick, in 1971, when Cambridge was celebrating the 450th anniversary of the arrival of printing in the city.[13]

13. *Siberch celebrations 1521–1971*, ed. Brooke Crutchley (Cambridge, 1971); E. P. Goldschmidt, *The first Cambridge press in its European setting*, Sandars Lectures in Bibliography 1953 (Cambridge, 1955).

80. Cuthbert Tunstall, *De arte supputandi libri quattuor* (London, 1522). This presentation copy on vellum bears Tunstall's gift inscription. The title-page border is based on a design by Holbein.

Chapter 6

The Royal Library
John Moore and his books

JAYNE RINGROSE

THE ENTRANCE HALL of the University Library today is dominated by portraits from the eighteenth century. Among these, Isaac Whood's two portraits of John Moore, Bishop of Ely, and Charles, second Viscount Townshend, survey incomers with a searching benevolence. George I's portrait implies royal patronage, and the two fine statues of George I and George II, by J. M. Rysbrack and Joseph Wilton respectively, moved in September 1994 from the Cockerell Building of the old University Library, may claim admiration [82, 83]. But the reader of manuscripts or early printed books is often unaware of the reasons for their presence, or of the provenance of the fine cases in the galleries, clearly dating from the eighteenth century, although now holding more modern books [181, 228].

81. John Pine's engraved bookplate for the Royal Library, 1737: 28,200 copies were printed in four sizes.

The elaborate book plate in the modestly bound manuscript, with Apollo and Minerva supporting the arms of the University, graced by a pyramid and books, which tumble from a pedestal bearing a medallion of King George I, and the significantly dated motto 'Munificentia Regia, 1715' may convey nothing to those seeking to establish the provenance of a book [81].

For our predecessors in the University it was not so. The year 1715 was known in Cambridge as the date of the greatest benefaction in the Library's history, when the king repaid the loyalty of the University to the House of Hanover in the year of the Jacobite rising, by presenting, at the suggestion of Charles, second Viscount Townshend, the library of the late Bishop of Ely, John Moore, who had died on 31 July 1714, one day before Queen Anne. The University's address of thanks, presented to the king on 29 September 1715, stated

> The noble Collection of Books & Manuscripts gatherd [*sic*] in many Years by the Great Industry & Accurate Judgement of the late Bp of Ely, tho' in itself exceeding valuable, is upon no account so Welcome to Yr University, as it is a Testimony of Yr Royal Favour; the Memory of wch will be constantly preserv'd by this Ample Benefaction, worthy to bear the Title of the Donor, & to be for ever styled the Royal Library.[1]

1. Transcribed from the copy in Cambridge University Archives, Grace Book Θ, p. 642.

82. John Moore, Bishop of Ely:
a copy by Isaac Whood, *c.* 1736, of
the 1705 portrait by Sir Godfrey
Kneller at Clare College,
Cambridge.

Moore himself was the grandson of a radical rector of Knaptoft in
Leicestershire. His father, an ironmonger, sent him to the University but
never intended him for episcopalian orders; his son had to repay him the
fees for his undergraduate years at Clare Hall, where he was eventually
elected Fellow in 1667. By 1670, Moore was attached to the household of
Heneage Finch, later Earl of Nottingham, who became Lord Keeper in 1673
and Lord Chancellor in 1675; henceforth, his rise in the hierarchy of the

Church of England was steady. Like his patrons, he supported the settle-
ment of the crown upon William and Mary in 1688. In 1691 Moore, who by
this time was minister of St Andrew's Holborn and a royal chaplain, was
made Bishop of Norwich, a see he was to occupy until 1707, when he moved
to the much richer bishopric of Ely [185]. Equally steady was his enthusiasm
for book collecting, which dated back to his undergraduate years.

One of the great problems in surveying the remarkable collection he was
to leave behind on his death in 1714, is the lack of documentation on how
and when he acquired his books. Accounts and journals, where these
survive at all, are largely uninformative. The prime source of information
about the provenance of the works in Moore's library remains the books
themselves; and all students will be indebted to David McKitterick, on
whose largely pioneering researches much of this account depends.[2]

The range and scope of Moore's collection was vast; it was well fitted,
perhaps more than almost any other private library being amassed at the
time, to form the basis of a national or university collection. Certain themes
can be discerned, however, some of them less expected for a divine. The
substantial number of books on medicine, for example, is very noticeable,
and reflects Moore's own practical interest in the subject, which began in
undergraduate days [182]. It was to give him a reputation as a bishop for
benevolence in prescribing for the poor. Thus we find him as early as 1663 in
Cambridge buying William Harvey's *Exercitationes de generatione animalium*
(Amsterdam, 1651), writing his name on the flyleaf, with the price: 3s 8d
[84]. He acquired works of ancients such as Galen, and the latest works of
practical interest, such as accounts of the waters of Tunbridge Wells, or
Bath. He was to acquire whole collections of medical interest, notably a
number of works, printed and manuscript, from the library of Sir Théodore
de Mayerne, Physician to King James I, which include manuscript notebooks and his copy of Vesalius *De humani corporis fabrica* (Basel, 1543) [85].

Another profession which Moore's interests seem to have touched on to
a remarkable degree was that of law, especially English law. John Baker's
cataloguing of the legal manuscripts in the University Library has shown,
in a way hitherto only suspected, the vast extent to which the large collection of legal manuscripts there is actually Moore's collection.[3] Again,
tracing the immediate provenance of many of the manuscripts is difficult,
but the collection includes a number which belonged to the Welsh judge
and antiquary Francis Tate (1560–1616), whose manuscripts record links
with many of the Elizabethan antiquaries and other collectors such as Sir

83. Statue of George I by J. M.
Rysbrack, *c.* 1739. A gift to the
University by the second and third
Viscounts Townshend, it stood in
the Senate House until 1884.

84. The flyleaf of Moore's copy of
William Harvey, *Exercitationes de
generatione animalium* (Amsterdam,
1651), inscribed with date and price
of purchase, 3s 8d.

2. David McKitterick, *Cambridge University Library: a history. The eighteenth and nineteenth centuries* (Cambridge, 1986).

3. J. H. Baker, *A catalogue of English legal manuscripts in Cambridge University Library* (Woodbridge, 1996). Professor Baker gives a full discussion of Moore's legal collections in his introduction.

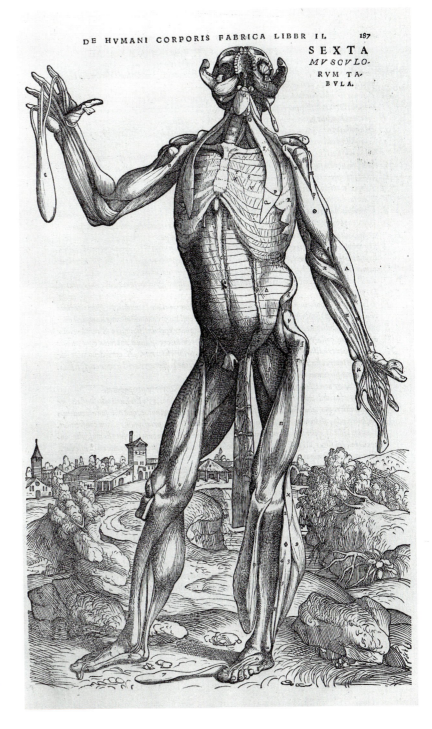

85. A plate from the first edition of Andreas Vesalius, *De humani corporis fabrica* (Basel, 1543), which set new standards of anatomical illustration.

Robert Cotton. MS Ee.1.1 may stand as a particularly notable example. Known as Liber Luffield, from Luffield Priory on the borders of Northamptonshire and Buckinghamshire, for whose use it was made in the 1280s, the book contains over seventy items, including statutes, legal treatises, a work on estate management and every kind of document relating to the Priory, including a collection of precedents by John of Oxford, a monk of Luffield, whose hand may be one of those which wrote the book, and who may indeed have been responsible for compiling it. It afterwards belonged to Sir Robert Cotton, who signed it on the first leaf, and gave it to Francis Tate in 1609.[4] Again, we do not know the full history of the way in which many of the legal volumes in the collection came into the bishop's hands. It would be interesting to know, for example, exactly how Moore acquired Ii.5.21, an autograph notebook of Sir Edward Coke, probably one of the manuscripts of Robert Nicholas (1595–1667), Serjeant at Law under the Commonwealth, which form one of the largest single identifiable legal portions in the Royal Library.

Moore was adding greatly to his library during his Norwich years when he kept the collection partly in Norwich and partly in London. It was not till he became Bishop of Ely that he was able to store all his books in one place, in rooms round the old cloister at Ely House. His best-known chaplain during his Norwich years was Thomas Tanner, afterwards Bishop of St Asaph, himself a collector of manuscripts, who served Moore thus from 1698 until 1701 when he became Chancellor of Norwich. Tanner had done a great deal of work in preparation for the account of Moore's library which was published in E. Bernard's *Catalogi librorum manuscriptorum Angliae et Hiberniae* (Oxford, 1697). This described the bishop's collection in unusual detail, printing (exceptionally) an account of his celebrated incunabula, and making it clear, from what was hastily listed in the appendices added as the book was about to be printed, that Moore was still at the height of his collecting, and was yet to add some of his (and our) greatest treasures to his collection. While the Book of Cerne (MS Ll.1.10) was listed as no. 113 in the collection, the Book of Deer (MS Ii.6.32) is listed as no. 664 in the main text and DCLXIV in the Appendix, and may have been acquired during the summer of 1697.

One group of printed books and manuscripts which was certainly acquired by Moore before the 1697 catalogue was printed came from the library of Sir Thomas Knyvett of Ashwellthorpe in Norfolk, and was plainly acquired by Moore while he was bishop.[5] The Royal Library now includes

4. D. Oschinsky, *Walter of Henley and other treatises on estate management and accounting* (Oxford, 1971), pp. 29–32. This edition makes use of at least seven manuscripts which belonged to Moore. In 1995 Dr Oschinsky bequeathed her entire estate, worth almost half a million pounds, to the University for the benefit of the Library, and in particular for the advancement of research in medieval history: a pleasing instance both of the usefulness of the Royal Library for current research, and of how a generous benefaction in one age can inspire further generosity in another.

5. D. J. McKitterick, *The library of Sir Thomas Knyvett of Ashwellthorpe c. 1539–1618* (Cambridge, 1978).

some 363 printed books and 57 manuscripts from this collection, built up in the latter part of the sixteenth century. Too late for the first pickings from the monastic libraries dispersed at the Reformation, Knyvett was nonetheless able to acquire some monastic items, such as MS Mm.1.25, a sixteenth-century book of lessons for saints' days in a mixture of English and Latin from 'amonge the bookes of Fakenham late Abbott of West-monster', as he noted in the book in 1560; or MS Mm.3.16 dating from the late thirteenth or early fourteeenth century, a manuscript of Avicenna from Norwich Cathedral Priory, which had belonged to John Hoo, Prior of Yarmouth. Remarkable for the beauty of its script is a fine Pseudo-Dionysius of the thirteenth century from Norwich (MS Ee.1.4), while a celebrated liturgical manuscript is MS Mm.2.9, a Sarum Antiphonary which may have been made for Barnwell Priory, on the edge of Cambridge. And it is ulti-mately from Knyvett that the University Library received MS Ff.1.6, the anthology of fifteenth- and sixteenth-century literature associated with the Findern family in south Derbyshire.[6] Knyvett's interest in the Abbey of St Albans, of which the neighbouring priory of Wymondham was a depen-dency, is exemplified in his possession of the St Alban's Formulary, MS Ee.4.20, the gift of Knyvett's half-brother, Robert Bowyer of the Middle Temple. Rather surprisingly, to the great benefit of subsequent scholars, he also acquired what was apparently the dedication copy of John Leland, *Antiphilarchia*, addressed to Henry VIII (MS Ee.5.14).

Knyvett's printed books show him to have been a keen collector of Italian works, and his interest in travel and foreign languages, in antiqui-ties and medals is plain. Thus the catalogue of his Roman coins in MS Ff.2.5 is apparently in his own hand, and we have, bound together by him, Marquard Freher's *De re monetaria* (Lyons, 1605) and his *Constantini Imp. Byzantini numismatis argentei expositio* (Lyons, 1604), as well as Kaspar Waser, *De antiquis nummis Hebraeorum Chaldaeorum et Syrorum* (Zurich, 1605). As might be expected, Moore acquired a number of medical books from the collection, including *La dissection du corps humain* by Charles Estienne, with the remarkable illustrations by Estienne de la Rivière (Paris, 1546). History and topography are well represented. Bartolomeo Platina, *De vitis Ponti-ficum Romanorum* (Cologne, 1568) was acquired by Knyvett in 1583; Torellus Sarayna, *De origine et amplitudine civitatis Veronae* (Verona, 1540) is another witness to his love of things Italian [86]. Such interests were complemented by his books of architecture; he had Leon Battista Alberti's *Architettura*, translated by Cosimo Bartoli (Florence, 1550), and the first edition of

6. *The Findern Manuscript: Cambridge University Library MS. Ff.1.6*, introduction by Richard Beadle and A. E. B. Owen (London, 1977).

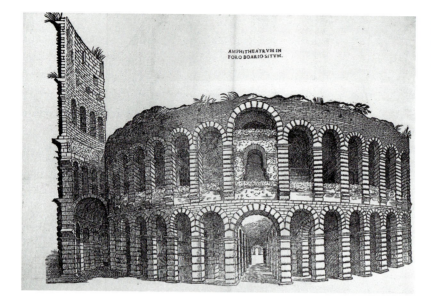

86. The amphitheatre at Verona in a woodcut by Giovanni Caroto from Torellus Sarayna, *De origine et amplitudine civitatis Veronae* (Verona, 1540).

Palladio's *I quattro libri dell'architettura* (Venice, 1570). These few examples may help to show how Knyvett's fine and wide-ranging collection of sixteenth-century books printed on the continent as well as in England continue to put the twentieth-century Library in his debt.

For, up to this time, the University Library had never formed a working library for scholars in a way that would be required in the future. Its coverage of existing publications was scanty; a few examples of the comparatively recent publications which were received for the first time with Moore's library may give cause for surprise. They included Newton's *Principia* (London, 1687), his *Opticks* (London, 1704), Halley's *Miscellanea curiosa* (London, 1705–7), Boyle's *Sceptical chymist* (2nd edn, Oxford, 1680), Hooke's *Micrographica* (London, 1655), John Wallis's *Opera,* in quarto (Oxford, 1657) and folio (Oxford, 1693–9), and Ray's *Synopsis methodica animalium* (London, 1693). William Harvey's *Anatomical exercises* (London, 1653) was among books newly appearing in the University Library in 1715, as well as Petty's *Political arithmetic* (London, 1683) and works by Locke. It may appear extraordinary that, but for Moore's copies, the Library would still have been waiting in 1715 for his ally Richard Bentley's great edition of Horace, published by the Cambridge University Press in 1711. Before Moore, the University Library lacked early editions of Milton, such as the first edition of *Paradise regained,* and had no collected edition of the works of Shakespeare, until Moore's fourth folio of 1685.

Moore's library was celebrated in his own day, not only for its noted incunables, such as the '1460' Mainz Catholicon and the finely decorated Pliny printed by Jenson in Venice in 1476 [183], but for the remarkable examples of early English printing. These included over forty Caxtons, among other printers, with Wynkyn de Worde and Richard Pynson well represented: Sel 5.51–63, for example, are a collection of pamphlets printed by de Worde in the early sixteenth century, and probably obtained for Moore in the 1690s by John Bagford, who occasionally acted as Moore's agent [87]. It is for this part of his library that Moore acquired his reputation as 'the Father of Black-letter collectors in this country'.[7] Well known among his Caxtons is the Bruges *Game and play of chess*, the *Dicts or sayings of the philosophers* (Westminster, 1477), and the Bruges *Recuyell of the histories of Troy*, of which the Library once owned two copies formerly belonging to him, one having been exchanged in 1960 for the Caxton vocabulary (see page 68). Of a piece with his interest in early English printing are his acquisitions in the field of medieval English and French vernacular literature. It is to John Moore that the Library owes Dd.1.1, the Northern Homily Cycle and other texts in a long format, perhaps designed to be carried in a saddlebag; Dd.1.17, the huge and bulky fifteenth-century collection of texts in Latin and English known, from the Glastonbury provenance of at least part of it,

7. T. F. Dibdin, *Bibliomania* (London, 1811), p. 421.

87. The Library's unique copy of *The boke of kervynge* printed in London by Wynkyn de Worde in 1508, a manual for serving a prince or nobleman at table.

as the *Liber Glastoniensis*; and the spectacularly fat volume, Gg.1.1, containing French and English texts, including an illustrated French Apocalypse [184].

The size of Moore's collection can only be estimated, but there may have been as many as 30,000 volumes, including 1,800 manuscripts. W. Nicolson, in 1714, wrote

> As yet, the present Bishop of *Ely's* Library is universally and most justly reputed the best furnish'd of any (within the Queen's Dominions) that this Age has seen in the Hands of any private Clergyman; the Reverend and Learned Proprietor, having from his Youth, been particularly diligent in collecting the fairest Editions of the *Greek* and *Latin* Classicks, Fathers, Councils, Ecclesiastical and Civil Historians, Law-writers, Confessions of Faith and Formularies of Worship, in all Languages, Ancient and Modern, Books of Physick, Surgery, Mathematicks & c. in one Word, the choicest *Supellex Libraria* that could be met with (by Himself, or his Friends) in public Auctions, or the Shops of private Stationers, at home or abroad.[8]

8. W. Nicolson, *The English historical library*, 2nd edn (London, 1714), p. xii.

Richard Gough was of the opinion that he had obtained many of his books by plundering the libraries of the clergy in his diocese, paying for some with sermons or other books, 'others only with *quid illiterati cum libris?*'[9] Plainly, many of his books, like the Knyvett volumes, came from the Diocese of Norwich. It is hard to suppose that very much came from the Diocese of Ely, which would already have been well picked over by earlier collectors.

9. R. Gough, *British topography* (London, 1780), vol I, p. 224.

Moore continued to collect after Bernard's *Catalogi* was published, and a list of yet further manuscripts, beginning with no. 831, was made by Thomas Tanner, and survives in MS Oo.7.50[(2)]. While on the whole the contents are less visually spectacular than those which he was apparently collecting while the *Catalogi* was going to press in 1697, they included some books of immense value, such as a group of archival manuscripts relating to Bury St Edmunds which came in August 1698. We owe to Moore MSS Ee.3.60 (The Pinchbeck Register), Mm.4.19 (The Black Vestry Register), Ff.2.29 with Ff.4.35 (The Red Vestry Register), Ff.2.33 (The Sacrist's Register) and Gg.4.4 (The Cellarer's Register, part I).[10]

10. For these and other manuscripts from Bury St Edmunds held in the Library, see *The archives of the Abbey of Bury St Edmunds*, ed. R. M. Thomson (Woodbridge, 1980).

Tanner's list also includes two of the most notable early manuscripts acquired by Moore, the two to which his name is still attached, the Moore Palladius (MS Kk.5.13) and, even better known, the Moore Bede (MS Kk.5.16). The Palladius manuscript, which contains the earliest complete text of the first thirteen books of the 'Opus agriculturae', was written in caroline minuscule at the abbey of St Denis in the second quarter of the ninth century, and was still there in the fourteenth century, as is attested by a fine *ex libris* inscription, and an anathema at the beginning.[11] The Moore Bede [88] is even earlier; it is generally considered to be of the eighth century, although probably not as early as 737 as was once thought. Additions on the last leaf indicate that the manuscript travelled to the continent and was known at the court of Charlemagne. It was afterwards at Le Mans, where it remained until the seventeenth century.[12] Both the Bede and the Palladius are part of a group of manuscripts – the last to be entered by Tanner in his manuscript continuation of the list of Moore's manuscripts (Oo.7.50[(2)] nos. 972–1025) – which appear to have been acquired mostly on the continent. The group includes twenty-eight Greek manuscripts, many of them signed by Jean-Baptist Hautin (1580–1640), the numismatist. Moore paid 'Mr Cunningham' seventy guineas for books on 21 August 1701, and this may well be the transaction by which the Moore Bede was acquired. Alexander Cunningham, a Scotsman and classicist, apparently bought the cache at auction, presumably in France. The Bede was seen by William Nicolson on 19 January 1702 when he dined with Moore in London, and has attracted constant interest ever since.

After Moore's death, the fate of the library was eagerly awaited, and Robert Harley, Earl of Oxford, sent his librarian Humfrey Wanley to inspect it with a view to buying it. Wanley reported that the collection was in disorder, with books not properly numbered, or else lent out, or mislaid, and with many books not worth acquiring. Harley considered the price of £8,000 asked by Moore's executor, Samuel Clarke, too high and withdrew. John Hudson, Bodley's Librarian, would have been willing to buy it, had Radcliffe's benefaction allowed. In the event, Dr Radcliffe left money to Oxford for the building of what is now the Radcliffe Camera, and only £100 a year for buying books.

11. R. H. Rodgers, 'The Moore Palladius', *Transactions of the Cambridge Bibliographical Society*, 5 (1969–71) 203–16.
12. *The Moore Bede: Cambridge University Library MS. Kk.5.16*, preface by Peter Hunter Blair (Copenhagen, 1959).

Dr Samuel Clark — Order is taken this 29th day of Octr 1715 By Virtue of his Mats Genl Lettrs of Privy Seale bearing date the 29th Septr 1714. And in pursuance of a Warrant under his Matts Royall Signe Manuall dated the 17th instant. That You Deliver and pay of Such his Matts Treasure as remaines in your Charge unto Samuel Clark Dr of Divinity Sole Executor of the Last Will and Testament of the late Right Reverend Father in God John Lord Bpp of Ely or to his Assignes the Sum of Six Thousand four hundred and fifty pounds for the Library of printed Books and Manuscripts of the said Bishop, which were left at Ely House in Holbourn at the time of his Decease or were Lent out by him before his Death. And These together with his or his Assignes Acquittance Shall be your Discharge herein ————

ar. 0
2715¢

Walpole
D. Finch
Newport

My Lord Denbigh I pray pay this Order out of Additionall Tonnage for the Civill List Since the 1st of August 1714

29th October 1715

Exd Record. 29° Oct 1714 as 1715 Denbigh

Examd p. Halifax

Eventually, by May 1715, it became known that the king would buy the Library and give it to Cambridge. The price agreed was £6,450. In the ensuing correspondence between Townshend and the University, the Secretary of State referred to 'His Majesty's generous Inclination to encourage his faithfull University of Cambridge . . . nor was it possible that much sollicitation should be necessary to induce him to furnish You with those Materials of Learning which he was secure would become so many weapons in Your hands to guard and maintain the faith of the Church, the Rights of the Crown and the Liberties of the British Constitution'.[13] This could almost have been a reference not only to the wealth of legal manuscripts which the collection contains, but to the collection of biblical, liturgical, theological and devotional works in English and Latin which supplemented those already in the Library, and which continue to interest scholars worldwide [89].

13. Transcribed from the copy in Cambridge University Archives, Grace Book Θ, p. 644.

For the time being, however, the weapons to guard the faith of the Church and the Liberties of the Constitution were to remain largely unused. When the books reached Cambridge, they were apparently stored at first on the ground floor of the western range of the Schools. By 1720, the Dome Room had been created on the first floor, linking the west and south ranges, and Moore's manuscripts were at first placed in it. Ultimately, George I's gift of the Royal Library was to change the appearance of the University, as the new east front of the Schools by Stephen Wright, and the creation of the East Room behind it, still show. The opening ceremony was not performed until 3 July 1758, and it was King George II ultimately who assisted the project handsomely with a gift of £3,000.

Moore's collections were not known by his own name, but received their title in Cambridge from the monarch whose reign he did not live to see, but who would certainly have commanded his loyalty. When, in 1756, all the Library's manuscripts were gathered into one sequence and placed in the Dome Room, Moore's own collection lost its separate identity as codices from all sources were mingled. This has not only disguised the provenance of many of the Library's manuscripts and early printed books for those who study them; it has served to conceal from specialist scholar and general user alike the identity of a man whose collections, more than anything else, first formed the University Library as a working library for study and research.

89. The Treasury Order whereby the king paid Moore's executor, Samuel Clarke, £6,450 for the bishop's library. (MS Add. 4357)

The *Voyages pittoresques et romantiques dans l'ancienne France*

MICHAEL TWYMAN

BARON TAYLOR'S *Voyages pittoresques et romantiques dans l'ancienne France* (Paris, 1820–78) was planned as a record of the glories of France and, in particular, of those monuments that had survived the ravages of the Revolution a generation earlier.[1] It could be described as a heritage publication ahead of its time. In its turn, it has become something of a monument in its own right, both to the Romantic attitude that inspired it and to the process of lithography by which it was realized. Neither the particular strand of Romanticism that lay behind it nor topographical lithography remained in vogue long enough to sustain it through to completion and, after a sixty-year history, it ground to a halt [90].

The publication was the brain-child of Baron Isidore Taylor (1789–1879), who directed it throughout. Taylor was born in Brussels of English parents, but became a naturalized Frenchman and received an artistic training in Paris. He contributed illustrations to several of the early volumes of the *Voyages pittoresques*, but his work as an artist represents just one strand of his activities; he is chiefly remembered for his sponsorship of artists of the Romantic movement and for his career as an administrator of the arts, which culminated in the post of Inspector-general of the Fine Arts and Museums of France.

Taylor explained that he conceived the idea of the *Voyages pittoresques* in June 1810 and sought the financial support of the Minister of the Interior. He claimed that the cost of reproducing numerous drawings by traditional engraving methods would have been enormous, and that it was only the discovery of lithography that made publication possible.[2]

The method of printing now known as lithography was discovered in Munich by Alois Senefelder at the close of the eighteenth century and relied on the mutual repulsion of grease and water rather than physical differences in relief. It took many different forms but, in essence, involved making marks with a greasy substance (crayon or ink) on slabs of compact limestone. Such marks were partially absorbed by the stone and given a

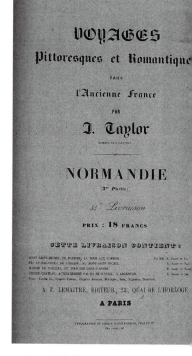

90. Baron Taylor's *Voyages pittoresques et romantiques dans l'ancienne France*: one of the original wrappers for the 39 *livraisons* of *Ancienne Normandie* vol. II (Paris, 1878).

1. C. Nodier, J. Taylor, A. de Cailleux, *Voyages pittoresques et romantiques dans l'ancienne France*, 20 vols. (Paris, 1820–78): Cambridge University Library, LA 6.1–20. For further information, see J. Adhémar, 'Les lithographies de paysage en France à l'époque romantique', *Archives de l'art français*, n.s. 19 (1938) 189–364; and M. Twyman, *Lithography 1800–1850: the techniques of drawing on stone in England and France and their application in works of topography* (London, 1970).
2. All quotations are from the *Voyages pittoresques*.

91. 'Carnac', *Bretagne* (1845): original drawing by Baron Taylor, lithographic drawing by Adrien Dauzats, printed by Thierry frères.

degree of permanence by means of various chemical treatments. Prints were taken from the stone by damping its surface and then charging the image on it with a greasy printing ink: the blank parts of the stone absorbed the water, leaving the image to attract the ink. Though it sounds extremely crude when described in this way, the process was capable of considerable and almost unbelievable refinement.

Lithography was taken up with enthusiasm for different purposes from the late eighteenth century in Germany, particularly for music printing, the reproduction of administrative documents, and the multiplication of artists' drawings. Elsewhere in Europe progress was slower, though in both Britain and France lithographic presses were established in the early years of the nineteenth century. But for a variety of reasons artists had to be persuaded that lithography, for all its undoubted benefits, could compete with the established processes of copper engraving, etching, aquatint and mezzotint. In particular, crayon lithography, which was the branch of the process that held most attractions for artists, had yet to be mastered by printers; though artists may have been able to make effective crayon drawings on stone, printers could not be relied on to do their work justice.

One turning point in this respect was the setting up of presses in France by Lasteyrie in Paris (1815) and Engelmann in Mulhouse and Paris (*c.* 1814, 1816). Another came with the substantial improvements made to the techniques of crayon lithography by artists and printers in the early 1820s, which are embodied in Engelmann's *Manuel du dessinateur lithographe* (Paris, 1822) and Hullmandel's *The art of drawing on stone* (London, 1824) [92]. That Taylor should have put such faith in this fledgling process for his ambitious publishing venture reveals foresight bordering on the foolhardy. His enthusiasm for it was aroused when he was shown some lithographs by the painter Charles Bourgeois: 'I foresaw', he wrote much later, 'that lithography was to be for the art of drawing almost what letterpress printing had been for literature.'

The turning point for Taylor came in 1818 when Engelmann demonstrated that lithography could be used for the reproduction of finished works and not just for preliminary sketches. At this point scarcely a publication of note had been produced with lithographic plates in either Britain or France, and certainly nothing approaching the scale of the *Voyages pittoresques*. As it transpired, Taylor's choice of lithography probably did as much as anything to promote the process at a time when it was not taken very seriously by many artists and publishers.

Charles Nodier, the prolific author who was commissioned by Taylor to write the text of the *Voyages pittoresques,* admitted the risk involved in

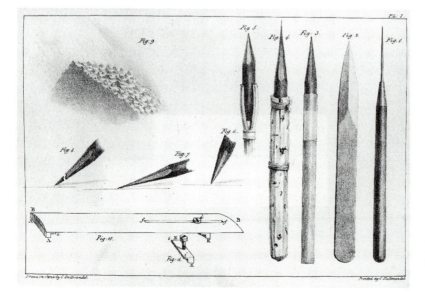

92. The lithographic draughtsman's equipment, from Charles Hullmandel, *The art of drawing on stone* (London, Hullmandel & Ackermann, 1824).

Taylor's choice of process when he wrote in 1820, with telling understatement, that 'The new process known as lithography has not obtained the unanimous approval of people of taste.' Yet he too appreciated that lithography had considerable advantages over other processes, claiming that the lithographic crayon 'seems to have been invented to fix the free, original and rapid ideas of the traveller wanting to capture his sensations'.

Though driven by its pictures, and remembered almost exclusively for them today, the *Voyages pittoresques* has a substantial text. Charles Nodier was the obvious choice for its principal author as he had already proved his commitment to the Romantic movement. He was assisted by the architect Alphonse de Cailleux, who continued with the work on his own after Nodier's death in 1844. The intention of the publication was to appeal not so much to the scholar as to the traveller interested in the ruins of France with all their noble associations. It is steeped in nostalgia, particularly for the Middle Ages. Taylor describes his aim as being to represent the monuments of Antiquity, the Renaissance, and the Middle Ages, but there can be little doubt where his real enthusiasm lay: in one of the last volumes he revealed that he had spent fifty years defending his belief that 'the arts of the *Bas-Empire* and the Middle Ages were not a decline but an advance'.

In its scale, as in its subject matter, the *Voyages pittoresques* was a product of Romanticism; even the fact that it was never completed has certain Romantic connotations. The idea was to cover the whole of France by its traditional provinces, but only nine were even started, which represents just over a third of the country by area. The whole publication as it exists today consists of around twenty folio volumes. The set in Cambridge University Library is bound as follows: *Normandie* (1820), *Ancienne Normandie* (1825), *Franche-Comté* (1825), *Auvergne* (1829, 1833), *Languedoc* (1834, 1834, 1835, 1837), *Picardie* (1835, 1840, 1845), *Bretagne* (1845, 1846, 1846), *Dauphiné* (1854), *Champagne* (1857, 1857), *Bourgogne* (1863), *Ancienne Normandie* (1878). Other sets of the publication are bound differently. Only the lithographs of the first half of the publication (those up to and including *Languedoc*) bear plate numbers, but the total number of plates probably lies between 2,700 and 3,000. The plates with their accompanying text were published in parts of unequal extent, and subscribers included a strong representation of European royalty, besides many French libraries and artists. The first subscription list includes almost 600 names, but subscribers dwindled to less than half this number for the volume on *Franche-Comté* (1825), and were fewer still for later volumes.[3]

3. See Adhémar, 'Lithographies', nos. 16, 111, 224, 340, 369, 635, 732, 745.

Drawn from Nature & on Stone. by J.D.Harding

Printed by C.Hullmandel

ST ETHELBERT'S TOWER.

Canterbury.

London Pub. by Rodwell and Martin. New Bond St. Jan.1, 1823.

4. See J. and E. R. Pennell, *Lithography and lithographers* (London, 1898), p. 56.

The publication was delayed by Taylor's frequent trips abroad on official business and by 1847 was causing something of a public scandal since it was still being subsidized by the French Government.[4] By this time, however, completion was hardly possible along the original lines, and later volumes can be seen as a desperate attempt to continue against a tide of changing circumstances. One consequence of this was that the plates became more architectural and less picturesque. It seems that Taylor's publication, and perhaps Taylor too, had begun to run out of steam. Nevertheless, his tenacity can be measured by a similar lithographic enterprise to record Britain county by county: *Britannia delineata, comprising views of the antiquities, remarkable buildings, and picturesque scenery of Great Britain. Kent* (London, 1822–3). Only the first part of the first volume on Kent was ever published; it consists of just twenty-five plates drawn by the leading lithographers of the day, several of whom were later to contribute to the *Voyages pittoresques* [93].

The folio volumes of the *Voyages pittoresques* stand as a fine monument to French lithography and book production. The letterpress text of the entire publication was entrusted to the notable French firm of Didot. Pierre Didot set the style, employing the austere modern-face typography he had used so successfully in his famous edition of Racine's works (Paris, 1801–5). This tradition was maintained by his successors through to the end. The typographic style of the *Voyages pittoresques* stems from the age of neo-classicism, and its use in a publication so self-consciously medieval in spirit emphasizes both the strength of what has come to be regarded as the French tradition in typography and the inherent conservatism of the printing trade. The contrast between the neo-classicism of the letterpress printing and the publication as a whole is most marked in the *Languedoc* and *Picardie* volumes, where extravagant lithographed borders surround the text pages. These borders consist of a medley of architectural detail, figures, animals and plants; some even include whole views set within cartouches. They were the work of many artists, the most prolific being Viollet-le-Duc who, perhaps more than anyone else in France, was responsible for the revival of interest in medieval architecture. The designs of these borders become increasingly complex and assertive; on some pages the text occupies scarcely a quarter of the printed area and gives the impression of a small rectangle obscuring the middle of a picture [94]. Though often derided, these lithographed borders of Viollet-le-Duc, Célestin Nanteuil, Tony Johannot and many others should at least be respected for their invention and craftsmanship.

93. 'St Ethelbert's Tower, Canterbury': 'Drawn from Nature & on Stone by J. D. Harding' from *Britannia delineata* (London, printed at C. Hullmandel's lithographic establishment for Rodwell and Martin, 1822–3).

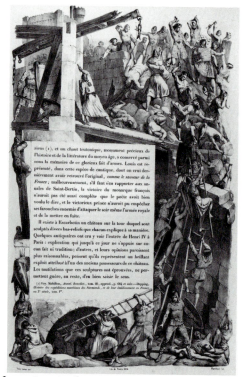

In this one publication it is possible to trace the progress of lithography, as Nodier had predicted in his introduction, and also possible – though Nodier could hardly have foreseen this – to trace its decline. The publication's lithographs fall into two main categories: the largest and most significant group comprises landscape and architectural plates, which vary considerably in size of image and have no obvious physical relation to the text (many of them are landscape in format and need to be looked at with the book turned sideways); the lithographs in the other group appear on letterpress pages and take the form of border decorations or vignettes at the ends of sections of text.

All the lithographic printing was initially entrusted to Godefroy Engelmann, whose improvements to the process had been responsible for Taylor's decision to use it. The plates of the first two volumes were all printed by him and he continued to undertake most such work until 1834. Though not responsible for the majority of plates in the publication, he should be regarded as its leading printer: he set a standard for other printers and must have inspired confidence in the new process among artists. By the time he died in 1839, all the finest lithographs of the *Voyages pittoresques* had been published.

Rather oddly, one might think, the first printers to contribute to the publication alongside Engelmann were Charles Hullmandel and William Day (later Day & Haghe), both of whom worked in London. They printed 176 plates for it, beginning with *Franche-Comté*. Numerically this may not have been a particularly significant contribution, but it was made during the finest period of the publication and of topographical lithography in general. If we are to believe the letters of recommendation from Taylor which Hullmandel printed in one of his pamphlets,[5] the quality of his printing was much admired in France. The lithographs printed by Hullmandel and Day were nearly all drawn by British artists, and it is possible that Taylor hoped to secure the services of such artists by involving British printers.

Apart from occasional plates printed by Bichebois in Paris, and Day (Day & Haghe) in London, Hullmandel was the only printer to share with Engelmann the production of plates for *Franche-Comté* (1825) and *Auvergne*

94. An elaborate border by Viollet-le Duc, from *Picardie* (1835).

5. C. Hullmandel, *On some important improvements in lithographic printing* (London, 1827), pp. 6–7.

(1829, 1833). The first volume on *Languedoc* (1834) saw the introduction of Thierry frères, who took over the role of leading printer through to *Champagne* (1857) and emerged as the most prolific printer of the publication as a whole. The remaining firm that made a significant contribution to the *Voyages pittoresques* was Lemercier, Bénard et Cie (later simply Lemercier). It made its début with the first *Languedoc* volume (1834) and continued through to the very end in 1878. The printers Taylor chose to use were at the time, or later became, the best-known lithographic firms of their day, particularly for pictorial work.

Those who turn to the *Voyages pittoresques* today do so primarily for its pictures: it is a 'museum without walls', redolent of its period, which displays the work of over 150 draughtsmen and lithographers. In this respect it has something in common with thousands of other books in the University Library, which are at least as important for their pictures as for their text. In recent years the Library has added two major collections to its already rich holdings of such material: the John Harley-Mason Collection of hand-coloured aquatint books of the late eighteenth and early nineteenth centuries, and the Norman Waddleton Collection of colour-printed books[186–93]. The *Voyages pittoresques* differs from most of the books in these two collections in that its pictures are monochrome (or simply have a printed background tint): as far as I am aware, none of the sets of the publication that survive has its lithographs coloured by hand.

Though some of the artists of the *Voyages pittoresques* can now scarcely be identified, others were among the leading figures associated with lithography at the time. It is usually possible to distinguish between those artists who produced original drawings and those who translated such drawings into lithographs. Sometimes the same person was responsible for both activities; but a division of labour was common and occasionally, as when the draughtsman was a specialist topographer, a third hand was brought in to draw figures. The distinction between artist and lithographic draughtsman was not always precise: Eugène Ciceri, for example, would sometimes supply a drawing for someone else to put on stone; on other occasions he would take on the role of reproductive lithographer; mostly, however, he would combine the activities of artist and lithographic draughtsman [95].

Though most of the artists of the *Voyages pittoresques* are now neglected, a few have survived the test of time, including Bonington, Brascassat, Charlet, Devéria, Géricault, Huet, Ingres, J.-B. Isabey, Carle Vernet and Horace Vernet. However, the bulk of the work was undertaken by a dozen

Rue de l'Eglise à Quimper.
Bretagne.

95. 'Rue de l'Eglise à Quimper', *Bretagne*, vol. II (1846). Original and lithographic drawing by Eugène Ciceri, printed by Thierry frères.

or so artists, some of whom remained faithful to Taylor throughout much of the publication's history. The most productive in the earlier volumes was Alexandre Fragonard (1780–1850) who, with his son Théophile (1806–76), contributed over a period of twenty-five years. Louis Villeneuve (1796– 1842) was another important early figure; after making a few plates to the first volume, he appeared in every subsequent one until his death. Louis Bichebois (1801–50), Nicolas Chapuy (1790–1858), and Léon Sabatier (d. 1887)

96. 'Abbaye de Conques',
Languedoc, vol. II (1834). Original
and lithographic drawing by
Nicolas Chapuy, printed by
Lemercier, Bénard et Cie.

were all professional lithographic draughtsmen who worked regularly for
the *Voyages pittoresques* during its middle period; they illustrated many
other publications too and exhibited regularly at the Salons [96]. Emile
Sagot's name appears frequently from 1840, either as draughtsman and
lithographer or as a draughtsman only; in the final four volumes he
emerged as the leading lithographer.

97. 'Grande porche de l'église Ste Cécile d'Alby', *Languedoc*, vol. I (1834). Original and lithographic drawing by Adrien Dauzats, printed by Engelmann.

By far the most regular and prolific contributors were Eugène Ciceri (1813–90) and Adrien Dauzats (1804–68). Lithographs by Ciceri are found in every volume from *Picardie* (1845) onwards; Dauzats, who made his first appearance in *Franche-Comté* (1825), continued as one of the most regular lithographers in every volume until the last. Ciceri was the only significant lithographer to emerge during the second half of the publication, and was often at his best when working from other people's drawings. He was first and foremost a craftsman and, technically, there was no-one working in these later volumes who could match the soft, silvery greys of his lithographs. Dauzats made more lithographs for the publication than anyone else; his plates are mainly architectural and have a precision and severity very different from those of Ciceri [97].

98. 'Eglise de Saint-Nectaire', *Auvergne* (1829). Original and lithographic drawing by Eugène Isabey, printed by Engelmann.

Eglise de Saint-Nectaire.
Auvergne

Tour du gros Horloge, batie sous la domination des Anglais en 141...

99. 'Tour du Gros-Horloge,
Evreux', *Ancienne Normandie* (1825).
Original and lithographic drawing
by Richard Parkes Bonington,
printed by Engelmann.

The plates of the *Voyages pittoresques* are perhaps more remarkable (considering the range of artists represented) for their uniformity than for their variety. The common subject matter of rugged landscape, threatening skies, bustling market places, overhanging eaves, gothic decoration and crumbling masonry provides a strong unifying factor. The conventions of lithography also have the effect of reducing the impact of individual style. Of the French artists represented, the painter Eugène Isabey provides a refreshing change. His seventeen lithographs in the publication are all in the two *Auvergne* volumes (1829, 1833). He abandoned the mechanically laid tints of the professional lithographer and built up his tones in a more spontaneous way with vigorous and irregular crayon hatching; in addition, he made good use of the scraper to produce highlights, almost in imitation of the transient effects of impasto paint. Limited as he was in the *Voyages pittoresques* to the land-locked province of Auvergne, he was unable to indulge in his speciality of seascapes. Instead, he made the most of skies to create an overall mood. Such prints provide a powerful antidote to those of the architectural draughtsmen whose lithographs dominate the publication [98].

It may seem surprising that as many as fifteen British artists and lithographers should have contributed to a publication so strongly associated with France's heritage, but it has to be remembered that British landscape painting had begun to be appreciated in France and that several important British painters worked there and even exhibited at the Paris Salons. British-born artists, or artists who worked in Britain, made over 200 plates for the *Voyages pittoresques*, well over half of which were by Louis Haghe (1806–85) and James Duffield Harding (1797–1863). Haghe was one of those artists who found inspiration in European views and medieval subjects. He was ideally suited to the *Voyages pittoresques* and his contributions to it spanned his whole career as a lithographer. Some of his finest lithographs are found in its early volumes; most of them were made from his own drawings, though he also worked as a reproductive lithographer after several French artists. Harding's work for the publication spans much the same period as Haghe's, and some of his early prints for *Franche-Comté* (1825) show carefully built-up tones and a respect for visual impressions rarely seen in his later work. All but one of Harding's lithographs for the publication were printed in London by his long-term associate Hullmandel, whereas many of Haghe's plates for the *Languedoc* volumes (1834, 1835) were printed, and presumably drawn, in Paris. Among the other British artists who made more than the occasional lithograph for the *Voyages pittoresques* were George Barnard, Bonington, Thomas Shotter Boys, and R. L. Gale.

The outstanding British contributor was Richard Parkes Bonington (1801–28) [99]. Though born in Britain, he emigrated with his parents to France in 1817, where he received his training as an artist. Apart from visits to England in 1825 and 1827, he worked in France throughout his very short life, exhibiting at the Salons and also in London. All his lithographs were originally published in France, including the fifteen in *Ancienne Normandie* (1825) and *Franche-Comté* (1825). As a lithographic draughtsman he inherited the traditions of British topography, but little else; his method of drawing on stone with its airy tonality and lightness of touch belongs, if the distinction needs to be made, to France rather than Britain. His finest lithographs were made for the *Voyages pittoresques*, and two prints for it, 'Rue du Gros-Horloge, Rouen' and 'Tour du Gros-Horloge Evreux', have become canons by which we, consciously or otherwise, judge topographical lithography. They are outstanding prints even in Bonington's œuvre, though they make their impact as much through their striking compositions as by anything specifically lithographic. Nevertheless, his lithographic technique grew to meet the demands put on it and in these two prints he handled a range of tone from silvery greys to rich blacks with great confidence. Unlike Eugène Isabey, Bonington worked within the accepted conventions of the genre. An Englishman working in France, he managed to combine his native tradition of topographical recording with a technical sensitivity and freedom from stylization found only in the finest French lithography.

For those interested in the methods used by artists when drawing on stone, the *Voyages pittoresques* provides as complete a record as one could hope to find within the pages of a single publication. The first volume on *Normandie* (1820) reflects the experimental nature of the process at the time; it includes a few pen and ink drawings and some crayon lithographs that are no more than sketches on stone. The first two volumes also contain a few tinted lithographs. This was a technique used in the very early days of lithography that involved a second working, usually buff in colour, to compensate for the colour of the stone on which the drawing was made. Tinted lithography was used again in response to a renewed enthusiasm for the idiom from *Picardie* (1835) onwards, but it was not until *Dauphiné* (1854) that it became the predominant style. The most commonly used method throughout the whole publication was monochrome crayon lithography

100. 'Tombeau de Philippe Pot, à Dijon', *Bourgogne* (1863). Photolithographic plate by Lemercier.

which, by the mid 1820s, involved a high degree of skill on the part of both draughtsman and printer. The method went far beyond the simple notion of drawing with greasy crayon as one might on paper, and involved a complex syntax of crayon hatching to produce tones. Most of the ancillary methods that had been developed to make it easier for draughtsmen to produce tonal images on stone were used somewhere in the *Voyages pittoresques*, including Hullmandel's patent 'lithotint', which allowed artists to work with washes of ink diluted to different strengths.

In the years immediately following Bonington's finest lithographs, Nièpce made his first hesitant steps towards fixing photographic images. In 1837 J.-L.-M. Daguerre, who had already contributed drawings to the *Voyages pittoresques* and also subscribed to it, went a stage further. Two years later he announced his particular form of photography to the French nation. Almost immediately it achieved such success that unskilled amateurs could record their own 'voyages pittoresques'. A lithograph of 'Notre-Dame de Paris', which claimed to have been the first made after a Daguerreotype, was published in the trade journal *Le Lithographe* in the very year of Daguerre's announcement.[6] Taylor and Nodier even contributed text for one of the most important early collections of printed photographs: *Excursions daguerriennes: vues et monuments les plus remarquables du globe* (Paris, 1841–3). The temptation to use photography, however, at least openly, seems to have been resisted until the later volumes of the *Voyages pittoresques*.

6. *Le Lithographe*, 2 (1839).

The threat to the lithographic draughtsman came when photographic images could be put on stone and printed lithographically. Experiments of this kind were being undertaken in Paris by the lithographer Lemercier, in association with Lerebours, Barreswil and Davanne, around the middle of the century. Subsequently, Poitevin developed a process of photolithography (patented in August 1855) which the lithographic printer Lemercier used under licence for, among other publications, the *Voyages pittoresques*. In the *Bourgogne* volume (1863), twelve plates were printed by Lemercier using a photolithographic process [100].

The rise and fall of the topographical lithograph in France can therefore be charted in this one publication. Even if Taylor had not died a year after the publication of *Ancienne Normandie* in 1878, it is doubtful whether his ambitious project, which was still far from complete, could have continued much longer. By this time, both the means of recording the world through drawing and one of the most popular methods of printing images had changed almost beyond recognition.

Chapter 8

Agriculture, food and famine in Japan

PETER KORNICKI

ALTHOUGH JAPANESE has only been taught at Cambridge since 1947, the Japanese collection in the University Library dates back to 1715, when Bishop Moore's library was presented to the University by George I. It contained a copy of *Azuma kagami* (Mirror of the east), a historical work that was published *c.* 1620 and bears an inscription written at Oxford in 1626; it was undoubtedly one of the first Japanese books to reach England. A few chance donations of Japanese books came the way of the University Library towards the end of the nineteenth century, but it was in the early years of the twentieth century that the collection assumed respectable proportions, and it is now the second largest in Europe, after the Staatsbibliothek in Berlin. The oldest items are four Buddhist invocations printed in Japan in the 760s, which, by a margin of several hundred years, are the oldest printed items anywhere in the Library [194]. The superb collection of modern books was largely built up from scratch by Eric Ceadel, a Cambridge graduate in Classics who learnt Japanese early in the Second World War and spent the rest of it either teaching Japanese to intelligence officers or translating captured documents; he was appointed to a lectureship in Japanese in 1947, and in 1967 became the University Librarian. To this modern collection has recently been added a vast archive of microfilms of nineteenth-century books, through the generosity of Mitsui Marine and Fire Insurance, and the collection is continuing to grow, in spite of the high yen, and is in ever-growing demand. By the end of 1998 it will, together with the Chinese and Korean books, be housed in the Aoi Pavilion, an extension to the Library made possible by the generosity of Mr Tadao Aoi.

The most valuable part of the Japanese collection is the Aston Collection of more than 2,000 early Japanese books, which was put together in the 1860s and 1870s by two young consular officials, W. G. Aston and Ernest Satow, and which was acquired by the Library in 1911, well before there was any prospect of teaching Japanese. Aston and Satow made themselves experts on the history of books and printing in Japan and put together an outstanding collection, which contains much that is either unique or of very great rarity; most items were printed with wood-blocks, but there are also a number of manuscripts, some early books printed with metallic movable-type and even some printed with wooden movable-type. Many visitors from Japan come to consult the collection, most recently to work on the early maps or to look for evidence of the identity of Sharaku, the mysterious but brilliant print-artist of the 1790s. Amongst the collection's treasures are a Buddhist doctrinal work printed on Mt Kōya in 1288 [**196**], and some seventeenth-century illustrated manuscripts [**197**]. At present, only a small part of the collection has been closely studied, and it offers a superb resource for the future study of Japanese mapmaking, travel literature, sinology, drama and prose literature. Following the publication of a complete catalogue of the Aston Collection in 1991, the University Library became the base of a much larger project which aims to describe all premodern Japanese books in European libraries, and data gathered from collections all around Europe, from Moscow to Lisbon and from Stockholm to Naples, is added to the database maintained in the Library.[1]

One of the most neglected areas of book-production in pre-modern Japan is that connected with agriculture and food, and this is well represented both in the Aston Collection and in a number of other European collections. Early Chinese botanical works and herbals are known to have been imported into Japan at least by the Heian period (794–1185), but it was the importation in 1604 of the Ming herbal *Bencao gangmu* (Herbal epitome, 1596) that had the most profound impact on the development of botanical and pharmaceutical knowledge in Japan. *Bencao gangmu* brought to botany a more sophisticated classification scheme, and more lucid explanations based on a wealth of empirical knowledge, than any previous work, and its influence was overwhelming in both China and Japan; its author, Li Shizhen (1518–93), was in Joseph Needham's judgement 'probably the greatest naturalist in Chinese history, and worthy of comparison with the best of the scientific men contemporary with him in Renaissance Europe'.[2] A copy was found in Nagasaki by Hayashi Razan, adviser to the *shōgun*, and given by him to Tokugawa Ieyasu, the founder of the Tokugawa shogunate. Hayashi himself published some extracts from it in 1612, and there were subsequently innumerable Japanese editions and adaptations of it as well as legions of derivative works. The obvious gap between the Chinese plants described and illustrated in *Bencao gangmu* and the plants that could be observed and named in Japan created a tension that only began to be resolved at the end of the seventeenth century with the publication of works such as *Yamato honzō* (Japanese herbal, 1709) by Kaibara Ekken, who

1. For the history of the Cambridge collections and a complete catalogue of the Aston Collection, see N. Hayashi and P. F. Kornicki, *Early Japanese books in Cambridge University Library* (Cambridge, 1991).

2. J. Needham, *Science and civilization in China*. Vol. vi: *Biology and biological technology, Part I: Botany* (Cambridge, 1986), p. 308.

101. *Honchō shokkan* (Mirror of food in our country). A study of food eaten in Japan written by Hitomi Hitsudai and published in 1697. The text is in Chinese, still then the normal language of scholarship, albeit with reading marks to assist Japanese readers, and there are no illustrations: a high degree of literacy is called for! Shown here is the opening page of volume II, which deals with *miso* (bean paste). After discoursing on the name, the author remarks that *miso* is used every day in Japan in soups and describes how the beans are boiled, crushed and fermented to make the paste.

illustrated and described a large number of plants found in Japan and having no literary history whatsoever.

The botanical interest aroused by *Bencao gangmu* stimulated further enquiries in a number of practical directions, related to food production, pharmacology and dietetics. Herbals devoted to foodstuffs first appeared in the seventeenth century, inspired both by *Bencao gangmu* and by imported Chinese works on the subject, and mostly written by medical men, often in easy language to popularize knowledge about the medicinal value of different foods. The last work in this tradition was *Honchō shokkan* (Mirror of food in our country [=Japan], 1697), by Hitomi Hitsudai, whose father was a paediatrician and who enjoyed personal connections with the family of the *shōgun* [101]. Unlike his predecessors, he was able to break away from the strait-jacket imposed on many minds by *Bencao gangmu*; his approach was critical and embodied his own empirical investigations into the foods eaten in his day by ordinary people in Japan, and their nutritional value. As a result he was not preoccupied with plants or pharmacology, and gave most space to animal foods, especially fish, shellfish and the various dried, salted and processed foods derived from them. He was little concerned with cookery and the preparation of food, but he did take an ethnological interest in the ritual and ceremonial functions of food, for example of the rice cakes, known as *mochi*, at the New Year.

Cookery books already had a long history in Japan. The two oldest known were prepared in the late fifteenth century and circulated in manuscript. Of these, one focusses on the use of knives in the preparation of food, and the other consists mostly of illustrations. Although enticing illustrations have become an essential element of the cookery book today, few cooks would be comfortable relying on

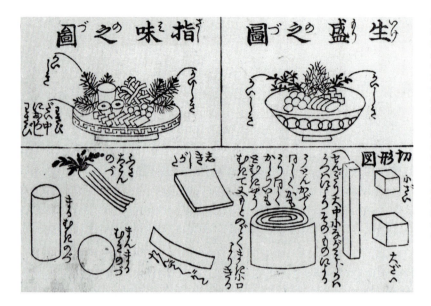

102. *Shōjin kondateshū* (Recipes for vegetarians). A book of recipes for vegetarians, published in 1819. Vegetarianism in Japan was principally associated with Buddhism, which forbade the taking of life and so the consumption of meat, poultry and fish. Although at first it consisted of little more than vegetables and seaweed, in the Kamakura period (1195–1333) *tōfu* was introduced from China and the range of vegetarian foods grew under the influence of Zen Buddhism. The upper half of the page illustrated here shows ways of arranging food formally, and the lower half shows the shapes into which food can be cut for decorative purposes.

pictures alone, and it is only with the appearance in 1643 of the first printed cookery book, *Ryōri monogatari* (Tales of cookery), that we find anything similar to a modern book of recipes. It clearly filled a need, for it was reprinted at least five times in the course of the seventeenth century. The first half of *Ryōri monogatari* was a study of the ingredients most commonly used in Japan, and so showed its connections to herbal literature, but the second half was unashamedly practical, being taken up with recipes. Modern devotees of *tōfu* and *sushi* would, however, be surprised to find that, in spite of the reputation of Japanese cuisine today, many of the recipes were for meat dishes, including venison, wild boar, rabbit and even bear. Over the following two centuries, cookery books became a well-established part of the book trade, and a variety of niche markets developed as increasingly specialized works were printed. There were vegetarian cook-books, represented in Cambridge by one published in 1819 [102]; books on cake-making, of which the first appeared in 1718, and which explicitly made public, for the first time, secret treasured recipes; books devoted to Chinese food, which became popular in the middle of the eighteenth century – the first of these, published in 1761, was physically shaped to resemble a Chinese rather than a Japanese book and included illustrations of the cooking implements and dining furniture needed for the authentic Chinese experience; and whale-meat cookery books, of which the best known was printed only for private sale in 1842. After Japan resumed contact with the

West in 1854, western food, wine and beer began to make their appearance in shops and restaurants, and in 1872 *Seiyō ryōri shinan* (Instruction in western cookery) was published with a preface urging the Japanese to eat western foods like beef, lamb, chicken and pork in order to become healthier. These days, of course, the emphasis is reversed, but in the 1870s anything 'western' had an automatic cachet and quickly became a fad.

Agriculture was also a beneficiary of the botanical interest aroused by Chinese herbals. Some of the earliest Chinese farming manuals had reached Japan by the tenth century, but it is only in the seventeenth century that the gap between learning and agriculture was bridged and the first Japanese farming manuals were compiled. The earliest efforts were based on the geographically limited experiences of their authors, so while they were evidently useful in the localities in which they were produced they had no universal applicability and consequently circulated locally in manuscript until pried from obscurity by modern scholarship.

Why did farmers now need book-learning all of a sudden? By the end of the seventeenth century, the government of the *shōgun* and the many domains scattered throughout Japan were in serious financial difficulties; among samurai, indebtedness to merchants was endemic. Since the samurai class as a whole, the shogunal government and the domains all relied for their income on rice production, there was intense pressure to increase supply. There was a very delicate balance here: as exactions on the farming peasantry increased to raise samurai incomes, so the danger grew of uprisings staged by desperate cultivators – which grew ever more frequent – or of malnutrition or even famine: most samurai, however, realized that pressing the farmers to the point of starvation was not the best way to increase production. Caught in the middle of this stand-off between the samurai and the cultivators were samurai-turned-farmers and wealthy independent farmers, who were often the first victims of any riots and who, accordingly, were the people most likely to write farming manuals to assist the cultivators in their efforts to increase production. For, once the possibilities for extending the area under cultivation and for reclamation had been exhausted, there remained only the possibility of increasing the yield, and for that some knowledge of basic agricultural science and of good practice in farm management was essential.

The classic farming manual was Miyazaki Yasusada's *Nōgyō zensho* (Complete book of agriculture), which was first published in 1697 and remained in print until the late nineteenth century [103, 104]. What is particularly significant about this hugely influential work is the author's commitment to an independently worked-out scientific method. He was a *déclassé* samurai from Kyūshū who spent some thirty years preparing it: he consulted previous literature on the subject, necessarily Chinese, though his aim was to provide solely for the needs of Japanese farmers dealing with domestic crops and conditions; to make his work of universal rather than purely local significance he travelled widely throughout Japan, interviewing experienced agriculturalists on the methods and techniques they used and their experiences of different soils and crop varieties; and he practised agriculture himself, with a view to experimenting and to testing the information he had gathered.

As a result of the circulation of *Nōgyō zensho* and other works, in the course of the eighteenth and nineteenth centuries Japanese agriculture underwent a startling transformation. The number of rice varieties jumped from a few hundred to several thousand, as the breeding of new varieties produced strains that were suited to particular conditions, offered higher

103. *Nōgyō zensho* (Complete book of agriculture). Miyazaki Yasusada's encyclopaedic study of agriculture for the use of farmers was first published in 1697, but there were several later editions and shown here is a harvesting scene from the edition of 1787 in an impression of 1815. In the lower right-hand section, men are harvesting the rice, while the upper half shows several methods used for transporting the harvested rice along the narrow paths between the paddies; in the lower left-hand section, women are threshing the rice while, above, the rice straw is hanging up to dry before being piled up in a rick.

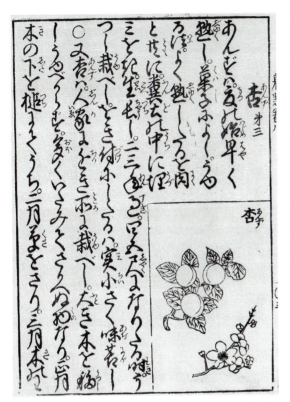

104. *Nōgyō zensho* (Complete book of agriculture). Another illustration from Miyazaki Yasusada's *Nōgyō zensho* (1697). Shown here is the beginning of the section on the cultivation of apricots, written in easy Japanese with Chinese characters glossed in Japanese. The text starts: 'Apricots ripen early in summer and are good for snacks. To grow them, bury a ripened apricot, with the flesh still attached, in soil that has been fertilized; after it has grown up, when two or three years have passed and it is four or five feet high, it must be transplanted. If left where it is, the fruit will be small and bitter.'

3. Needham, *Science and civilization*, p. 330.

yields, or matured more quickly thus permitting double cropping. By the nineteenth century, yields per hectare were much higher than they had been in the seventeenth, and the range of crops grown was far more diverse as farmers took advantage of local conditions to plant cash-crops, such as indigo or tallow-trees.

In spite of all these successes, abnormal weather conditions, volcanic eruptions and other natural disasters caused a succession of crop failures and famines throughout the Tokugawa period (1600–1868), which brought not only untold economic losses and hardship but also in many cases thousands of deaths by starvation. The three worst famines occurred in 1732–3, 1782–7 and 1833–9, but while there had also been a number of severe famines in the seventeenth century it was not until the end of the eighteenth century that famine herbals began to circulate widely.

In China the recurrence of famines had already given rise to what has been called an 'esculentist' movement in the fourteenth century, in Needham's view 'one of the great Chinese humanitarian contributions', as botanists sought to identify natural plants that could safely be eaten in times of food scarcity.[3] The major text was *Jiuhuang bencao* (Famine-relief herbal), which was written by an Imperial prince and first published in 1406; a Japanese edition was published in 1716, and much of its content was included in two other Chinese compilations, which were also reprinted in Japan.

These had, of course, limited practical value in Japan, given the differences between the flora of Japan and China. The first literary effort at famine relief in Japan was *Kyūga taii* (Elements of starvation relief), a manuscript prepared in 1713 and concerned mostly with the provision of soup kitchens, and so clearly intended for the attention of the government. The first intended for the sufferers was Takebe Seian's *Minkan bikōroku* (Provisions for the people in case of famine), which circulated in manuscript before being published in 1760 and subsequently reprinted in 1771, 1833 and 1835. Takebe wrote this work in a few months in 1755, in the midst of a famine in northern Japan, where his family had served for generations as doctors to

105. *Kyūkō shokumotsu benran* (Guide to foodstuffs in time of famine) This sheet was produced to help people find alternative foods in time of famine by Itō Keisuke (1803–1901). This work, which he dictated to two scribes, identifies plants by name and states which parts are edible; at the end are suggestions for their use as food. In the preface he emphasized that his work was not based on Chinese or western works, but on what was available in Japan. There are no illustrations and it was therefore necessary to know the plants in question by name.

the lords of the domain. As an intellectual, he was powerless to alleviate the suffering he saw around him in any meaningful way, other than by providing life-saving knowledge of edible plants in the wild. He had extensive familiarity with the literature of agriculture and botany and was, of course, familiar with *Jiuhuang bencao* but he had of necessity to address himself to circumstances in Japan. His references to earlier works such as *Yamato honzō* and *Nōgyō zensho* (see above) show the intellectual origins of his enterprise and the perceived importance of concentrating on the flora of Japan, however stimulating Chinese scholarship might be. Consequently, much of *Minkan bikōroku* was original, such as the six alternative ways Takebe devised of making *miso* (bean paste), which were quoted in many subsequent famine herbals. He also wrote in a deliberately easy style, eschewing the difficult Sino-Japanese language of most scholarship: the point was to be accessible. From this time onwards there were many books published on famine relief, all aimed at those living on the land. One of the simplest was a sheet printed in 1837, in the middle of the so-called Tenpō famine, containing a simple guide to emergency foodstuffs [105].

What is incalculable is the effect these famine herbals had on the population. Hayami has written of the Tenpō famine that 'Between 1834 and 1840, only eight of Tokugawa Japan's sixty-eight provinces registered a population increase, while twenty-seven showed a decrease of five per cent or more.'[4] Travellers recorded seeing the corpses of those who had starved to death lying unburied by the roadside, and reported the growth of infanticide. At best it is a matter of speculation how many might have escaped this fate by resorting to the alternative foodstuffs recommended in these books.

In the course of the Tokugawa period, the availability of books on all subjects grew to an extraordinary extent as commercial publishers came into their own. The result was a book market of a size and sophistication that was without equal anywhere outside western Europe and that could support the publication and distribution of a huge variety of minority publications, from guides to the cultivation of 'morning glories' to studies of European coinage. Books on agriculture and botany were an important part of that market, and what still needs to be investigated is the relationship between the book-learning represented by the books discussed in this chapter and actual agricultural practice. In the mid nineteenth century most of this learning was displaced by the introduction of Linnaean classification and scientific agriculture, which was encouraged by government ministries in the 1870s in the belief that anything Western must be better. Nevertheless, the products of this earlier learning remain in the University Library to show that the study of these subjects had independently reached a high level in Japan before the age of close contact with the West, and that it was already accepted in Japan that study and learning could be of benefit even to the most practical of pursuits. Literacy and books were functional for farmers, and that made the later diffusion of new agricultural technologies so much easier.[5]

4. Hayami Akira, 'Population changes', in *Japan in transition: from Tokugawa to Meiji*, ed. M. B. Jansen and G. Rozman (Princeton, 1986), p. 295.

5. Further reading on agriculture and botany in Japan in English: T. C. Smith, *The agrarian origins of modern Japan* (Stanford, 1959); H. H. Bartlett and Hide Shohara, *Japanese botany during the period of wood-block printing* (Los Angeles, 1961). The Chinese background is expertly covered in Needham, *Science and civilization*, vol. VI, parts 1 and 2 (Cambridge, 1984–6).

106. *Nōka gyōji* (The tasks of the farmer). The first part of this work deals with the cultivation of rice and of cotton, which was the principal cash crop. The second part was written by the prolific Ōkura Nagatsune, and deals with other cash crops and prevention of water damage. Shown here is a device to be installed in a waterfall to catch stones and prevent them from damaging dikes and irrigation systems, which were vital for controlling the supply of water to the paddies.

そでみ貝の
もろく波に
いヘ末て
菜の
水くえて
まふとて
うしてのこと
ことう
水と竹
よふとて
田
稲菜と
こりてのて
こと
なくぐ

107. *Jokōroku* (Keeping pests at bay).
This is a detailed study of pests
affecting rice cultivation and of
ways of eliminating them. The
principal method in use in the
Tokugawa period (1600–1868) was
the use of oil poured on the water
in the paddies, which was effective.
The author, Ōkura Nagatsune,
states that he wrote it for farmers
in northern Japan, who knew little
about this method of pest control,
but it circulated widely throughout Japan. The first part was
published in 1826, and recommended the use of whale oil for
the purpose; there was a conflict
of interests here, for Ōkura is
reported to have received funds
from whale-oil merchants. The
second part, published in 1844,
considered substitutes for whale
oil in regions where it was
unavailable. The upper part of the
picture shown here depicts a man
ladling oil out of a wooden bucket
while another man spreads it
around with a straw brush.

108. *Menho yōmu* (The task of
growing cotton). Another work
by Ōkura Nagatsune, published
in 1833 and dealing with all aspects
of the cultivation of cotton.
The illustration shows women
ginning cotton to prepare the
seeds for subsequent planting;
after being dried in the sun, they
were to be stored in bails made of
rice straw until the sowing season.
In the farmhouse can be seen a low
screen with poem cards pasted on
it; by this time something more
than functional literacy was not
as uncommon in farming villages
as is often thought.

Chapter 9

The Darwin Papers

Frederick Burkhardt

THE UNIVERSITY Library's collection of the papers of Charles Darwin has made it the world centre for Darwin studies and a major centre for research in the history of science in the nineteenth century. The vast number of manuscripts in the collection, the range of their subject matters, and the detailed nature of the information that they contain, provide a resource for a depth of understanding of the life and work of a scientific genius that is rare, if not unequalled. The Darwin Archive, with its hundreds of manuscripts and thousands of letters, is the documentary record of Darwin's entire working life, and, as such, it is recognized as one of the great treasures of our cultural heritage [109].

The history of the Archive

The majority of manuscripts in the Archive were originally in the possession of Francis Darwin, Charles's third son, who had worked closely with his father and who undertook the editing of his father's letters. After the death of Francis Darwin in 1925, his son Bernard assumed custody of the Darwin manuscripts and moved them to Gorringes, his own home in Downe, Kent, only a short walk from Down House, where his famous grandfather had lived and worked for forty years. In 1926, Down House, which had been leased by a school for some years, stood empty. In the following year the Darwin family decided to put the still untenanted house up for sale. In an effort to save the historic site, Arthur Keith, president-elect of the British Association for the Advancement of Science, made an appeal for funds in his inaugural address to the Association. George Buckston Browne, a wealthy retired surgeon, on reading the appeal in *The Times* the next morning, bought the property and turned it over to the British Association to be preserved in perpetuity as a memorial to Charles Darwin. By 1929, Down House had been repaired, and officially opened as a Memorial Museum.

Meanwhile, the Darwin manuscripts remained at Gorringes. In 1932, Bernard had a catalogue prepared using a system that had been devised by Francis Darwin. The catalogue was made up as a record of the manuscripts packed in five metal deed boxes labelled 'A' to 'E'.[1]

On 4 September 1942, Sir Alan Barlow, a co-executor with Bernard Darwin of the Francis Darwin estate, announced a proposed gift of Darwin manuscripts in a letter to A. F. Scholfield, the then Cambridge University Librarian. The gift was to be divided between the Down House Memorial and the University Library. 'The principle of division', he wrote, 'is to let Down have a popular exhibit, & items specially relating to Down, but to keep together in the University Library the rest of the material in order that it may be available to any future student of Darwin & his work.'[2]

It was not until 1948 that the Library received its part of the donation. The initial delay was due to wartime conditions in the London area. Gorringes was just a mile from the RAF fighter station at Biggin Hill, and in 1942 circumstances were not conducive to systematic record-keeping or storage. When the deed boxes were collected and checked at the University Library against the Gorringes catalogue, it was found that Box 'B' had not been received at all, that some items had to be exchanged with Down House, and that a significant number of items were missing from the boxes in which they had originally been packed. Some of the missing items were later found by Bernard Darwin and his wife; others that had been borrowed were retrieved, but Box 'B' was not discovered until 1954, when it emerged during the clearing of Gorringes prior to Bernard's move to a flat in London. Inexplicably, Box 'B' was not then sent on to the Library, but was put into storage with other belongings of the Bernard Darwin household. In 1962, some months after Bernard's death, its discovery was reported to his son and executor, Robin Darwin.

On 22 March 1962, Robin Darwin invited Dr Sydney Smith and Lady Barlow, Charles Darwin's granddaughter and Sir Alan Barlow's wife, to inspect the 'Black Box', as Box 'B' was thereafter called. It was immediately clear that the contents did not coincide with the items listed under Box 'B' in the Gorringes catalogue, but it did contain documents missing from the other boxes. In a letter to Lady Barlow dated 5 April 1971, Robin Darwin

1. See the introduction to the *Calendar of the correspondence of Charles Darwin 1821–1882*, with supplement, ed. F. Burkhardt and S. Smith, 2nd edn (Cambridge, 1974), p. 2.

2. *Calendar*, p. 2.

109. Charles Darwin, 1840. Pencil sketch by George Richmond.

110. Darwin's Journal, in which he recorded the periods he was away from home, the progress of his work, and important events in his family life. Found in the Black Box.

refers to the Black Box as the box 'into which we stuffed anything which came to light on my father's death'. Packed into the box were a substantial number of Darwin's working notes; also recovered was Darwin's personal pocket diary, which he started in 1838 and kept for the rest of his life. The box also contained a large collection of letters to Darwin, mainly from his family, covering the years from 1821 to 1840, and drafts of letters in Darwin's hand, dating from 1876 to 1882. These had not been listed in the Gorringes catalogue. Robin Darwin agreed to deposit Box 'B' in the Cambridge University Library, with a condition that prohibited any rearrangement or numbering of the documents. Scholars were to be allowed access, and the

'Black Box' was thereafter frequently mentioned by scholars as the source of manuscript material [110].

On 28 October 1963, Robin Darwin reported to Lady Barlow the discovery of fifteen more parcels of Charles Darwin papers that he recognized 'as part of the lot which I rescued from a bonfire some 8–9 years ago'.[3] The parcels contained over 4,000 letters to Darwin in alphabetical order of correspondents, dating from the years immediately following the publication of the *Origin of species* to the year of Darwin's death in 1882. The letters had been stored in corrugated board cartons under damp conditions, and some letters at the bottom of the cartons had been reduced to compressed cardboard pulp.

After Robin Darwin's death in 1973, the Library began negotiations with the executors of his estate to obtain legal possession of the contents of the Black Box and the letters to Darwin that had been saved from the bonfire. Agreement on terms of purchase by the University was reached in November 1975, and the documents were legally as well as physically integrated with the rest of the Darwin Archive.

At the time of the shipment of October 1948, the Gorringes catalogue was the only list of the Darwin documents in the estate of Francis Darwin. In 1955, a more detailed listing was made for the use of scholars working on the papers, and, five years later, a *Handlist* was published. In the Preface, H. R. Creswick described how the materials were received and the basis on which the *Handlist* was made:

> They [the papers] were in parcels each containing small packets of manuscript wrapped in tissue paper on which the subjects had been noted in Darwin's hand. They were presumably just as Darwin had left them, and accordingly this arrangement was preserved when they were bound, the volumes now representing as closely as possible Charles Darwin's papers in the order in which he left them.[4]

The *Handlist* also contains some material that was not listed in the Gorringes catalogue, notably a collection of copies of Darwin's letters made when Francis Darwin was preparing his *Life and letters of Charles Darwin*. Francis had sent out an appeal to his father's correspondents, asking to borrow letters they had received from him. Of the considerable number he received, he had copies made and then returned the originals to their owners. Also recorded in the *Handlist* were original letters donated by some of Darwin's correspondents. By far the most important such gift was from

3. *Calendar*, p. 2.

4. *Handlist of Darwin Papers at the University Library Cambridge* (Cambridge, 1960).

DARWIN & his HOBBY.

Go it Charlie !

111. Albert Way's sketch of Darwin
beetling while a Cambridge undergraduate. Found in the Black Box.

Darwin's closest friend, Joseph Dalton Hooker, who gave his life-long
collection of letters from Darwin, dating from 1843 through to 1881.

The 157 bound volumes and boxes covered by the 1960 *Handlist* represent
only the papers in the collection as of 1955. Accessions since then have
brought the number of volumes and boxes of manuscripts to 265 [111].

Darwin is a figure of such transcendent cultural importance, and the
object of such great scholarly and public interest, that any document in his
hand is a treasure to its owner. The Darwin Archive is a collection of many
hundreds of such documents and millions of Darwin's words. No brief
description can do justice to it. The best one can hope to do is to provide
some examples that illustrate the richness and importance of its holdings.

The Beagle *manuscripts*

The five-year voyage of HMS *Beagle*, which determined Darwin's whole
career, produced almost daily records of observations made whenever he
was not sea-sick or in bad health. The University Library received the extensive scientific notes of Darwin's observations on the zoology and geology of
the voyage, his lists of specimens collected, diagrams of geological sections, and drawings made of specimens during the voyage. When the Black
Box arrived, it was found to contain a large collection of letters written to
Darwin by family members and friends during the expedition. Despite the
hazards of seafaring mail deliveries of the time, only one letter from the

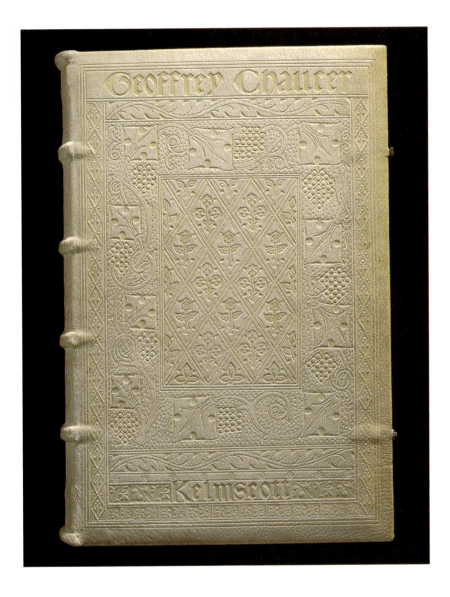

112. *The works of Geoffrey Chaucer,*
printed by William Morris at the
Kelmscott Press, 1896. One of
thirteen copies printed on vellum.
Bound in white pigskin at the
Doves Bindery after a design by
Morris, 1898. (Presented by John
Charrington, 1918)

113. *Biblia latina* (Mainz, Johann Gutenberg and Peter Schoeffer, *c.* 1455). The first substantial work printed from movable metal type, the so-called Gutenberg, or 42–line, Bible.

114. An early binding by Roger Payne (gold-tooled red morocco, with green onlays), produced at Eton in 1764: Virgil, *Bucolica, Georgica, et Æneis* (Birmingham, 1757). (From the library of Sir Geoffrey Keynes)

115. A page from the manuscript of *Vigils*, poems by Siegfried Sassoon (1886–1967), carefully written out, and with watercolour illustrations, by the author. A limited edition was printed in 1934, from copper plates engraved by Charles Sigrist to resemble the author's handwriting, but without the illustrations. (From the library of Sir Geoffrey Keynes)

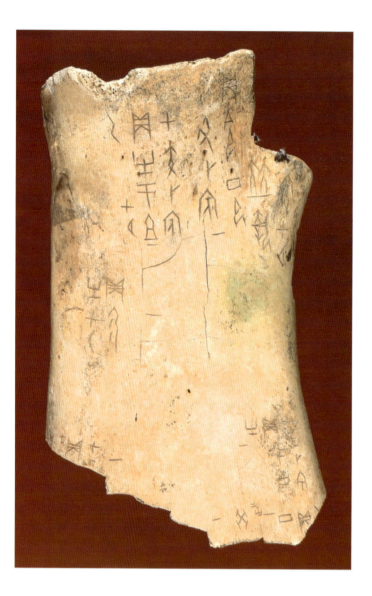

116. A Chinese oracle bone
(fragment of a bovine scapula),
c 1200 BC. The oracle bones were
used for divination and contain
the earliest known texts in
Chinese. Heat applied to hollows
chiselled out on the reverse of
specially prepared scapulae
and turtle shells produced
characteristic cracks, which
were interpreted as answers to
the questions posed of the oracle.
The inscriptions provide much
information about matters of
contemporary concern, including warfare, hunting, agriculture,
medicine, meteorology, astronomy
and genealogy. The University
Library possesses over 800 oracle
bones, the bequest of Lionel
Charles Hopkins (1854–1952).
They are the oldest documents
in the Library.

117. An 1837 edition of the
'Authorized' or King James'
Version of the Bible, printed by
Cambridge University Press.
This copy was bound in specially
designed carved wooden covers
for display at the Great Exhibition
of London in 1851 as an example
of the standards that the
University Press could achieve.
(Bible Society collections)

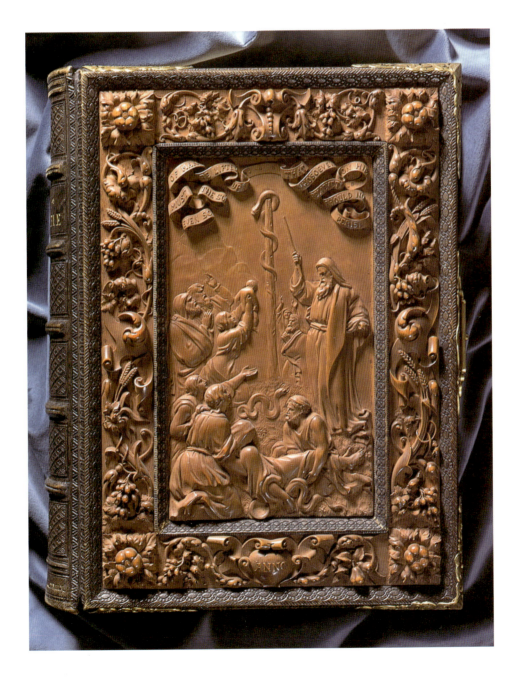

118. An example of legal-deposit intake: Vladimir Nabokov, *Camera obscura*, translated by Winifred Roy (London, 1936). Nabokov disliked the translation and would not sanction a reprint, producing his own version as *Laughter in the dark*. Since most copies were apparently destroyed in a warehouse fire, this is a scarce book: Nabokov's bibliographer traced only two copies with dust jacket.

119. Legal-deposit intake of the 1920s; these shelves contain mainly novels, stored in the tower in their original dust jackets.

120. This medieval map of the world, with the encircling ocean framing Asia, and Europe and Africa below, was drawn in 1367 and illustrates the religious concept that the holy direction of east (Oriens) must be at the top and Jerusalem (Irlm) in the centre. (Rustat Fund)

122. Codex Bezae, folio 348*v; one of the ninth-century leaves, showing the blue ink used for the colophon of Mark's Gospel.

121. Codex Bezae, folio 104r; showing the red ink used by the scribe for colophons and for the first three lines of each book.

123. Initital letter to Psalm 47 in MS Ee.4.24.

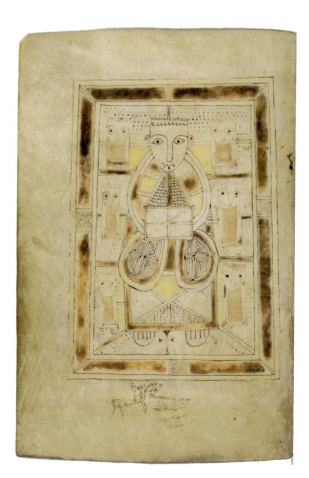

124. Book of Deer: frontispiece
of the Gospel of St John.

HIE MAR CVS
IN HV MA
NITA TE

HIC MA R CVS MA
I EI

NEM
TENET
B

125. Book of Cerne: frontispiece to St Mark's account of the Passion, with his symbol, the lion.

Armipotentis alexandri h p̄scr̄ta tenent
Arrḡe casus n̄ non ꝓ prelia seua
Ꝑ mare ꝑtias que quonda̅ gesserat ipe
Ipe manu ualida que nulli potere nouit
Omnia quin poet igni ferroꝙ̄ penut
Ac fere ꝑ totum bellor̄ incendia mundu̅

Miscuit atꝙ̄ o̅r̄s excelsas b̄ruit urbes
Qui mare q̄ t̄as qꝙ̄ aera t̄ruit ipsum
Classiliꝫ ꞇ popul̄ iacul̄ paritꝙ̄ sagittis
Uis queꝙ̄ quem ferri hominu̅ ue potuica niq̄
Uince pualuit uino paritꝙ̄ ueneno
Uictuſ ꞇ extinctuſ herebi penet̄lia scandit

126. MS Kk.4.25: drawing
of Alexander the Great.

127. Life of St Edward the
Confessor: Edward's death,
and his presentation to Christ
by the Apostles Peter and John.

a troit arpent dune les loigna
e flestri e de murra:
par es teuts trois rois dura:
la bastardie. puis returna:
sun truuc e cep certein
u teus henri le pmerein
apres lui roi aedward:
furent troi sinant: bastard
araud ne willame: dieit
urent. ki ueirs dire doit
e willame le secund
par reat de ceinte: dunt
esloigne sun par arpent trois.
dut henri ki fu quarte d rois
pres aedward: ben reuerdi
u premer cep ki re uerti:
fut par sa uolunte de memo
ahaud espusa. ki pleine:
e ducit e de su bunte
e franchise e de brute
ille la nece roi aedward
la racine out dune regard
a sa nece racine a ert
luri. fruit fist en aport
ne lemperice mahaud nasqu
e fruit: quant li reis henri:

emit iohan si duir de meime
e uaire la maiste le meine
e ki en terre unt memoire
deu lui dune mut gnt gloire
un regne li gnte e dinie
meudre bailaut unt. enrime
a replem de sa saunt
est-il. e regnes enturt
luir e gnt charte dune:
artut. cum solail e lune
re sunt roi ore sunt baru
regne. dun sanc onuin.
engleterre e normendie
en uant mielt la cumpanie
i mielt seit la phie
espundre: e ment la die
ki uns mest ke cest sufist
esclarcir loseur escrit
roi aedward a sa fin it
est mils ki dolur gnt ne ert
la char li est ia deiu morte
sa gent reapele e re cunforte
e cest esforce de parler
lui ad dit. lanc amui cher
olie est ma mort de plende
it deu le uout ne puet re
meis

us les regarde. e les ont loue
eit la reine. s ki greue
i se pleint. plure. e sulpure
es cheueus eit. se dun de gire
e plurez dist li rois amie
e ma mort ne dolez mie
apres mei e cest mort:
iuerai a seun port
uuerai of mun seignur
uz urs a ioie e a baudin
r uus pa cuz ki este eit
a seu gent e mi ami:
a reine kest ma muiller
i beus ne pu par cincer:
i ma este suer e amie:
ortez li leau cumpanie
alle mad este e espuse
e de mie mut penise
onurer la. cum a si bone:
peut. e haute matrone
uaire eit plenement
e lui maneez e sa gent
oient engleis soient normant
onurez les eit lui iuuant:
n la iglise seint pere: a bi:
n la iiur. seie en seueli

elt bi uiure abone enrente:
li de ses mauſ rele m̄ ſente
uns uoiſ uer̄ de normendie
de pouere emeſſáſe uie
ki del aumoſne lurei ſu:
ānt cum neſqū ſultemi
tit de membre e nerfz
i pe li ſint au doſ a crſ
et menuſ li ſint emeſſe per
tre ſtreler ſeſt a puier
ur prer̄ ſeſt de un egin
quel ſen ua par le chemin
n auget v ſeſt aſiſ
ſe ẽt memeſ li cheualt
li chemin n agge ſant flot
Del grantz uert̄z ſeit aedwardt
a geñt uite recunter
tant ſe eſt ẽt a weſtmuſter
lauent a quike peine
o fu memes la ſimaine
e li roiſ aedward tranſi
uimund. ſe plet e clement
i roiſ aedward debonere
e ne me clenne ne p̄ faire
ume ſur peſtre e ueſtir
une poiete miue echeuir

De puet la fame eſtre ceue
a ſaer̄ reſtore adla ueue
p ar la puere e la uertu
s eut aedward. a ſun ſacru
t eſt nuls ki de maus̄ euaille
a weſtmuſt p̄ ſaute naille
s il auogles igariſter
O ſ lur diutr̄ biun oil auor̄
m aiſ ore muet ſant parmrir
i de mīr̄ en grant deſir
e tute partz de beuz ai pre
alade ſu. con pouerte
v menguttet de ceſte uie
eie o meſ mauſ: aie
y ort pluſtoſt̄ fin ſeſ diz
li cuntraiſ neſtort garu
al gambeſ eaſ peez ſe dreſce
eí ſeiñt choſe ki le bleſce
a ceuſ ki iſint tiñ enſemble
er ueilliſ de la itu ſemble
a rne eſt eremmelee:
u roi la fame e remmee
e buſoigniuſ fiſt teu cuſtor̄
e nant e auteſ ſauiont
uiſe gracet e uertuz
auont lurei aedw̄. fiſt tut

h aiſ de uue reſtorer
h auont uuke coñ ſuñ per
e umoiſ ke li roiſ fu mort
a uitit cū uuſ ben record
Eſ auogleſ de uñ ki noirt
f orſ uñ ſiul oil dunt il uer̄ pout̄
o enez ſunt par le paiſ:
e ñ poureſ me ſeiſet mendiſ
s en piuſ dire inuelle. e noiſ
s aet auogleſ uireñt uñ oil
d weſtmuſter ſiuñt ciſt uenú
e la uireñt au ſeint ſacru
a treiſ dient de bonaure
a ike la ſoleit ſaire
q uant eſtoier euimund obſcur
a nogleſ dinãt luur̄
o reſt clerſ cſt eſt la lune
y ſolail: clarte nuſ dune
d e noſtre clarte grant aedward
a miſchütiſt kar dunr̄ part
p i ore luur auez duble
p e uimund n auoieſ oiſ truble
q ſuit ke ciſt ki la uite:
v eme: ke ne uert gute:
v n autre oil ad reten
e tut leſ autreſ ad uen

129. Hours of Alice of Reymes
showing the owner kneeling
before an archbishop.

130. Hours of Alice of Reymes: nativity scene.

128. Life of St Edward the Confessor
showing the shrine of St Edward
in Westminster Abbey.

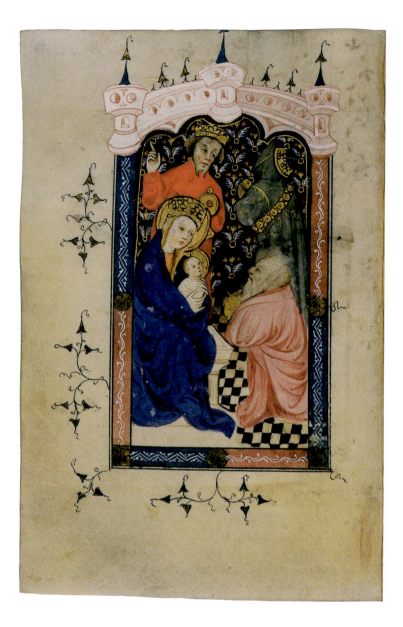

131. The Adoration of the Magi
from a Book of Hours produced
at Bruges around 1400. (MS Ii. 6.2)

132. Crucifixion from the
Benedictional of Robert
de Clercq, abbot of Dunes.
(MS Nn.4.1)

133. A child's Hebrew alphabetical exercise from about the tenth century. (T-S K5.13)

134. An Arabic tale of a lioness and a lion cub, with accompanying illumination, from about the fourteenth century. (T-S Ar.51.60)

entire family correspondence during the voyage was lost.

Also included in the Archive is material related to the *Beagle* voyage; in preparing to publish his observations, Darwin augmented his own notes by extensive reading about other voyages and works by contemporary naturalists. The manuscripts of the *Beagle* and material related to the voyage make up more than twenty substantial bound volumes.

Darwin himself made use of both his zoological and his geological notes when preparing the results of the voyage for publication. The *Zoology of the voyage of HMS Beagle*, which was published in nineteen numbers of five parts, describing Fossil Mammalia, Mammalia, Birds, Fish, and Reptiles, was superintended by Darwin, who wrote the background notes and descriptions of the habitats and ranges of the species described by the taxonomical experts. The geological diaries produced three volumes on the geology of South America. The first of these, *The structure and distribution of coral reefs*, published in 1842, proposed a brilliant new theory of these formations. It has been rightly said that even if Darwin had produced no other work, *Coral reefs* would have gained him a distinguished place in the history of science [135].

135. 'Slinging the monkey. Port Desire. December 25, 1833'. From a sketchbook compiled by Conrad Martens during the voyage of HMS *Beagle*.

Darwin's notebooks of 1836–44

Of the many notebooks that Darwin filled with his observations, records of experiments, and jottings of ideas that occurred to him, this early series has a special importance, for it was in them that he first set down his doubts about the fixity of species, and his search for the data that would establish the case for their mutability. The idea, as he put it, 'that one species does change into another' occurred to him early in 1837 when the ornithologist John Gould reported that the mockingbirds and finches Darwin had collected in the Galápagos were not varieties but true species. Working on the hypothesis of transmutation, Darwin collected facts on variation, on the geographical distribution of species, and on any other phenomena that might have relevance to the mutability of species. The first of these notes were made in the second half of a notebook (called the 'Red Notebook') that he had started during the last months of the voyage, and which was eventually included with the *Beagle* material sent to Down House. It, together with four others, designated 'B', 'C', 'D', and 'E', covering the years 1837–9 and usually referred to as the 'Transmutation Notebooks', were deposited in the University Library in 1948 [136]. They provide a fascinating, sometimes cryptic, set of clues that Darwin thought might lead him to the solution of the 'mystery of mysteries' of how species came about. Then, in September 1838, a reading of Malthus's *Essay on the principles of population* furnished him with the great clue of natural selection and a new theoretical basis for his inquiries. These were years of extraordinary intellectual activity in which many books were filled with notes.

A week after the birth of his first son, William Erasmus Darwin, on 27 December 1839, Darwin began a notebook of observations on the psychological development of the infant. The notebook was kept until 1854, with observations on all of his children as they grew up. This, along with the 'metaphysical notebooks', began the research that, in 1872, led to his book, *The expression of the emotions in man and animals*.

The essays of 1842 and 1844 and the publication of Origin of species

By the summer of 1842 Darwin's researches on the species problem had reached a point at which he felt ready to write a brief outline of his theory. This he set down in a manuscript which has come to be known as the 'Pencil

136. A page from notebook 'B', showing the development of Darwin's concept of branching evolution.

with slightly different constitutions would succeed
under different climates. There is reason to
believe that constitution & colour are correlated
in a good measure & also the susceptibility to the
attacks of flies is correlated with colour; as
is liability to the poison of certain plants.
But we are far too ignorant to speculate on the
relation in nature of the various differences; I have alluded to these subject.
these that if we are unable to account for the
characters which distinguish our
domestic breeds in different countries, & which
nevertheless we generally admit have arisen during the
course of ordinary generations, we ought not to
lay much stress on our ignorance of the
precise cause of analogous differences between true
species. I will here say nothing on the
origin of the races of Man, which are so strongly marked;
I think I can see some little light, chiefly through sexual selection of a
without entering on details, by reasoning under
appear quite gratuitous. —

The foregoing remarks led me to say a few words
on the protest lately made by some naturalists
against the doctrine that any part or
detail of structure has been created for the
good of its possessor; They believe that a

sketch' of 35 pages. In the summer of 1844, the sketch was enlarged into an essay of 230 pages. Both manuscripts are preserved in the Darwin Archive; both present to a surprising degree the general outline of the theory as it was set out in the *Origin of species* in 1859. Darwin did not consider the theory ready to be published, but in view of his precarious health he wrote a sealed letter to his wife to be opened in the event of his death. In the letter, he asked her to arrange for the publication of the essay, and set aside money to defray the expenses. He also suggested names of naturalists who might prepare the manuscript of 1842 for publication. Eventually, in 1909, Francis Darwin edited and published both the sketch and the essay under the title *Foundations of the Origin of species*.

When Darwin submitted the manuscript of the *Origin of species* to his publisher, John Murray, he gave it the title 'An Abstract of an Essay on the Origin of Species and Varieties through Natural Selection'. The 'Essay' itself was the manuscript that contained 'the references and facts in full' in support of his evolutionary theory. The *Origin*, he took pains to make clear, was simply an abstract of the larger work. The story of how the *Origin* came to be published as a separate work is a dramatic one.

After writing the 1844 essay, Darwin continued to collect data, guided by his hypothesis of natural selection, but devoted much of his attention to writing papers and books examining the geological and zoological results of the *Beagle* voyage. These were followed by eight arduous years devoted to his taxonomical monographs on the Cirripedia. Only when that work was completed in September 1854, did Darwin turn his attention exclusively to work on the species hypothesis. A year later, Alfred Russel Wallace published a paper entitled 'The law which has regulated the introduction of new species'. It clearly indicated that Wallace was thinking along the same evolutionary lines as Darwin. Darwin's friend, Charles Lyell, warned him that he might be forestalled, and urged him to publish at least a preliminary sketch of his views. On 14 May 1856, Darwin wrote in his diary: 'Began by Lyell's advice writing Species Sketch'. As he worked, Darwin became convinced that a persuasive case could not be made without incorporating the mass of supporting data he had accumulated in almost twenty years of work on the subject. Abandoning the plan of publishing a sketch, he worked steadily on a longer manuscript, to which he gave the title 'Natural Selection'. By 1858, Darwin was referring to it as his 'Big Book' and it had grown to over 200,000 words.

On 18 June 1858, a letter arrived from Wallace in which was enclosed an essay that stated briefly but clearly a case for the evolutionary origin of

137. A leaf from the manuscript of the *Origin of species*.

species that was strikingly similar to Darwin's theory. To save Darwin's claim to the theory, Lyell and Joseph Dalton Hooker, who had read the 1844 essay, arranged with Darwin to produce evidence of the years he had been at work on the theory. Darwin provided an extract from the essay of 1844 and a copy of a letter to Asa Gray, dated 5 September 1857, which contained a brief summary of his theory. The two friends then submitted this material to the Linnean Society of London to be read jointly with Wallace's essay. The paper, 'On the tendency of species to form varieties: and on the perpetuation of varieties and species by natural means of selection, by Charles Darwin and Alfred Wallace', was read at the Linnean Society meeting of 1 July 1858.

Soon after the publication of the joint paper, Darwin set to work on abstracting the manuscript of 'Natural Selection'. The entry for 1 October 1859 in his diary reads: 'Finished proofs. 13 months and 10 days on Abstract on Origin of species. 1250 copies printed.'[5]

5. *The correspondence of Charles Darwin*, ed. F. Burkhardt and S. Smith (Cambridge, 1991), vol. VII, p. 504.

Of the original manuscript of the *Origin* as published in November 1859, only a few leaves have survived [137]. In *Life and letters*, Francis Darwin noted that Darwin used the backs of his manuscripts for writing and thus destroyed most of the manuscripts of his books.[6] Some leaves were occasionally given to friends of the family as mementos. Nineteen of these rare holographs are preserved in the Darwin Archive. Of the 'Big Book', the Archive holds twelve chapters of the text before it was abstracted for publication as the *Origin of species*.

6. *The life and letters of Charles Darwin, including an autobiographical chapter*, ed. Francis Darwin (London, 1887–8), vol. I, p. 121.

The portfolios of working notes

In his 'Autobiography', Darwin described his 'manner of writing':

> As in several of my books facts observed by others have been very extensively used, and as I have always had several quite distinct subjects in hand at the same time, I may mention that I keep from thirty to forty large portfolios, in cabinets with labelled shelves, into which I can put a detached reference or memorandum. I have bought many books and at their ends I make an index of all the facts that concern my work; or, if the book is not my own, write out a separate abstract, and of such abstracts I have a large drawer full. Before beginning on any subject I look to all the short indexes and make a general and classified index, and by taking the

138. Some of Darwin's working notes from portfolio '12' on embryology.

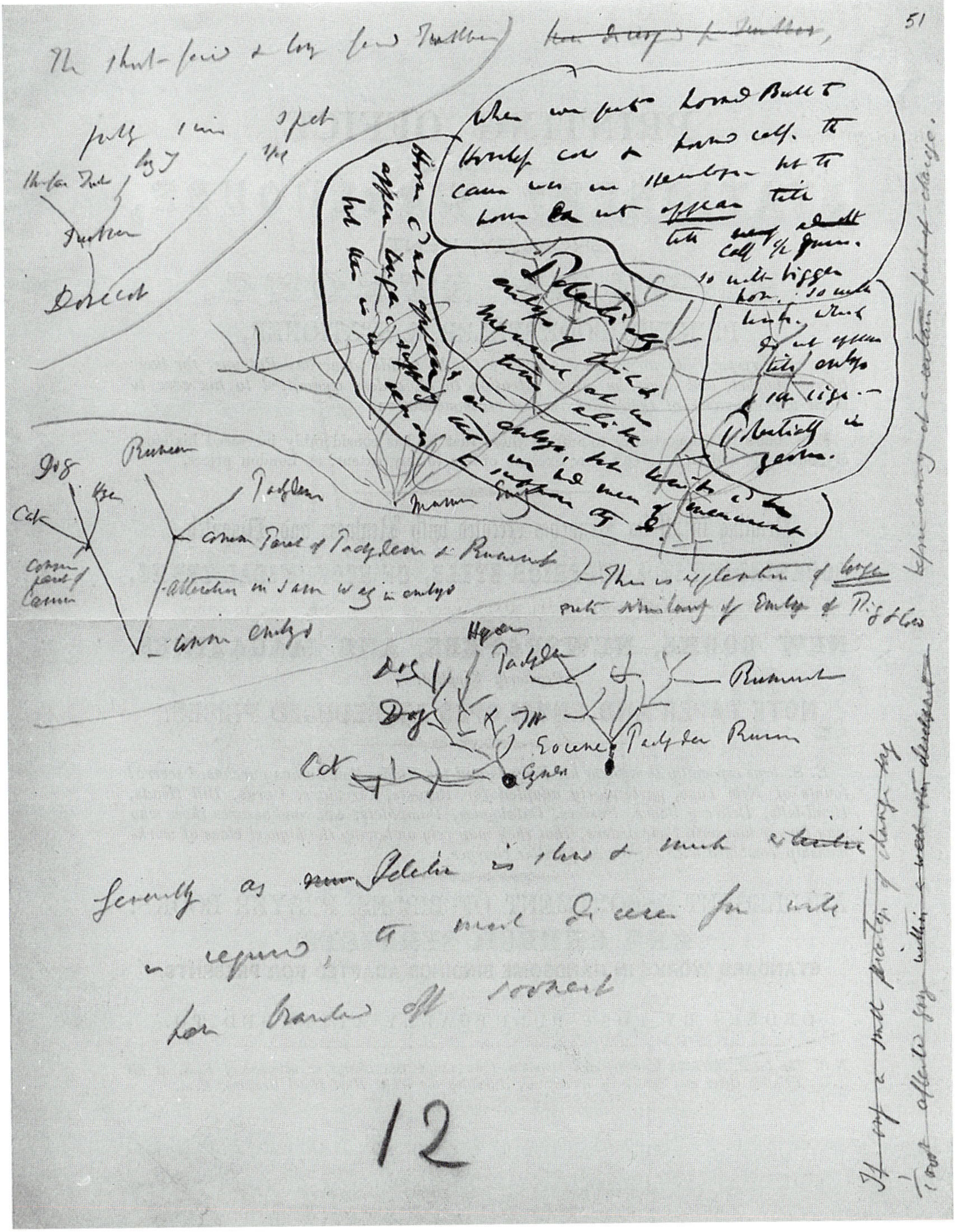

one or more proper portfolios I have all the information collected
during my life ready for use.[7]

7. *The autobiography of Charles Darwin
1809–1882, with original omissions
restored*, ed. Nora Barlow (London,
1958).

Four of the portfolios used in writing chapters of 'Natural Selection' and
the *Origin* are preserved intact in the Archives. These include notes and
letters for the chapters on 'Struggle for Existence' and 'Laws of Variation'
[138]. Other portfolio collections were clearly intended for use in the successive revisions of the *Origin*. The portfolio system of organizing his material
was adopted after the 'Transmutation Notebooks' of 1837–9 had been filled
and numerous pages were excised for inclusion in the portfolios for the
later works. Almost all of these loose pages have now been retrieved and
restored to their original locations in the notebooks. Additional collections
of notes and letters for later works exist, including extensive material for
both the first and second editions of *Descent of man* (1874, 1875), *Insectivorous
plants* (1875) and *The formation of vegetable mould through the action of worms*
(1881). Three large collections of notes on his reading and experiments were
used for Darwin's botanical papers of the 1860s and 1870s.

The 'Autobiography'

In 1876, at the age of 67, Darwin spent an hour a day writing a manuscript to
which he gave the title 'Recollections of the Development of My Mind and
Character'. He added to it during the next six years of his life, and it eventually amounted to 188 pages. It was not intended for publication but merely
for the interest it might hold for his children. In 1887, his son Francis published it as chapter 2 of his *The life and letters of Charles Darwin*, calling it
Darwin's 'Autobiography'. A number of passages, mainly concerning religion, were suppressed at the request of Darwin's widow and some other
members of the family. The full text was transcribed and published by his
granddaughter, Nora Barlow, in 1958.

Darwin's library

In 1905, Francis Darwin gave custody of the remaining books from his
father's library to the chair of botany at Cambridge. The books remained in
the Botany School until 1935, when A. C. Seward, then Professor of Botany,

139. Some of Darwin's marginal
notes on his copy of Louis Agassiz's
Essay on classification (1857).

transferred them to Down House. There the books remained until 1960, when Harry Godwin acceded to the chair. He arranged for the transfer of the books of special historical importance, and those books that Darwin had annotated and marked for reference, to the University Library. At the same time, Godwin moved, from the Botany School to the University Library, a collection of pamphlets consisting mainly of reprints of papers sent to Darwin by their authors, and articles collected by him in the course of his work, including reviews of *Origin* and subsequent Darwin publications.

Darwin was an omnivorous reader and, as his marginalia make clear, he read thoroughly and critically [139]. Often his comments ran to pages, which he then pinned in the back of a volume. The opportunity these annotations afford, in effect, to read the books and pamphlets along with Darwin, is an experience to be treasured. Detailed abstracts Darwin made on borrowed books and journals are preserved in five bound volumes in the Archive.

8. *Life and letters*, vol. I, p. v.

The Darwin correspondence

Until the early 1860s, Darwin destroyed most of his correspondence. In his *Life and letters*, Francis Darwin wrote that it was his father's custom:

to file all letters received, and when his slender stock of files ('spits' as he called them) was exhausted, he would burn the letters of several years, in order that he might make use of the liberated 'spits'. This process, carried on for years, destroyed nearly all the letters received before 1862. After that date he was persuaded to keep the more interesting letters, and these are preserved in an accessible form.[8]

There were exceptions to this early practice. Many letters from members of the family were saved, some from the early days when he was a student at Edinburgh and then at Cambridge, and as noted earlier, both sides of the correspondence of the *Beagle* voyage were preserved. So too were letters from his Cambridge mentor and friend, John Stevens Henslow, and correspondence from his fiancée Emma Wedgwood, whom he married in 1839. After the

Beagle voyage, whenever he received a letter in answer to some request for information, Darwin would cut out the part he wanted and file it in one of his portfolios with the other notes on the subject he was investigating at the time. These fragments are also preserved in various portfolios in the Archive.

Darwin's work was to an unusual extent dependent upon correspondence. This was only in part due to his ill health and the consequent reclusive life he led at Down for long periods. To a larger degree, it was owing to the nature of his work, which required communication with scientists in every part of the world. In the pursuit of his hypotheses, he collected data from every field of natural history and from any corner of the world that might provide information relevant to his theory. Some correspondents were not only consulted as experts in fields that Darwin knew little about but played an important part in the development of his thought. Among these were the zoologists Edward Blyth and George Robert Waterhouse, and the botanists William Henry Harvey, William Herbert, Hewett Cottrell Watson and John Scott. Other citations in Darwin's works show the important influence of the geologist Edward Forbes, the palaeontologist Hugh Falconer (an acute but friendly critic of the evolutionary hypothesis) and the entomologist Benjamin Dann Walsh.

Like Galileo, Robert Boyle, Robert Hooke and other great theorists, Darwin actively sought information from craftsmen and practitioners. From his earliest efforts to shed light on the emergence of new species through variation, Darwin had given a large place in his observations to the variation of animals and plants under domestication. As early as 1839 he distributed a printed questionnaire, *Questions about the breeding of animals*, of which the Archive possesses one of the two known copies. Information from animal and plant breeders was later used extensively in his publication, *The variation of animals and plants under domestication* in 1868. Among the animal breeders, William Bernhard Tegetmeier had an exceptional place as Darwin's guide and collaborator on pigeons, fowls and bees. Darwin's second cousin, William Darwin Fox, who introduced Darwin to entomological collecting when both were undergraduates, and kept what Darwin called a 'Noah's Ark' at his Cheshire parsonage, was also a frequent correspondent and source of breeding information. A plentiful correspondence exists with a number of gardeners and nurserymen like Thomas Rivers. James Torbitt, with whom Darwin exchanged letters about potato rot, was a Belfast wine merchant and grocer. Much of the information from such sources that Darwin cited in his works came from direct acquaintances like

John Horwood, a neighbour's gardener who helped Darwin build a hot-house, or from discussions he listened to at meetings of London pigeon-breeders' clubs in what Darwin described as 'gin palaces'.

Most impressive and illuminating of all is Darwin's correspondence with scientists who were his intimate friends, with whom he not only exchanged ideas, but shared his problems and anxieties. Hundreds of letters to and from Charles Lyell, Thomas Henry Huxley, Asa Gray and, later, George John Romanes constitute an extensive running dialogue about their common interests and work. Of all these friends, Joseph Dalton Hooker was the closest. For forty years he supplied Darwin with specimens from botanic gardens, gave him taxonomical help, and criticized his manu-scripts. At first unimpressed by Darwin's evolutionary theory, he slowly became a convert. So close were they that Darwin once wrote to Hooker that he was sometimes not sure whether an idea was his own or Hooker's. The Darwin Archive has almost 1,400 letters of their correspondence, constitut-ing one of the great sustained personal and scientific epistolary records in the history of science [140].

Since the Black Box materials were added to the Archive, the Library has acquired a large number of family letters by gifts of descendants, including the papers of Darwin's second son, George Howard Darwin; Darwin's letters to his wife and to his son George; Emma Darwin's reminiscences of Darwin's last two years; and the famous 1838 pencilled memorandum, 'This is the Question/ *Marry*/*Not Marry*' [141]. A recent acquisition includes the earliest material extant in Darwin's hand: a diary in the form of letters to a friend, written in 1822; this was the only item still missing from the shipment sent to the University Library in 1948. The entire collection listed in the Gorringes catalogue of 1932 is now accounted for.

Since 1974, the University Library has been the headquarters of the *Correspondence of Charles Darwin*, the editors of which are engaged in the preparation of a definitive edition of all the letters to and from Darwin that have been located to date. In addition to the 2,600 letters written by Darwin held in the University Library, there are also about 6,600 original letters written to him. The remaining letters are in the hands of private owners and over 200 libraries in 20 countries; photocopies of these additional letters make a total of almost 15,000 in all. The Darwin Correspondence Project is thus making available 60 years of personal and scientific corre-spondence, most of it as yet unpublished.

not give yourself any trouble about them, for I know how fully & worthily you are employed.

Besides a general interest about the Southern lands, I have been now ever since my return engaged in a very presumptuous work & which I know no one individual who w.ᵈ not say a very foolish one. — I was so struck with distribution of Galapagos organisms &c &c & with the character of the American fossil mammifers, &c &c that I determined to collect blindly every sort of fact, which c.ᵈ bear any way on what are species. — I have read heaps of agricultural & horticultural books, & have never ceased collecting facts — At last gleams of light have come, & I am almost convinced (quite contrary to opinion I started with) that species are not (it is like confessing a murder) immutable. Heaven forfend me from Lamarck nonsense of a "tendency to progression" "adaptations from the slow willing of animals" &c — but the conclusions I am led to are not widely different from his — though the means of change are wholly so — I think I have found out (here's presumption!) the simple way by which species become

140. Letter to Joseph Dalton Hooker, 11 January 1844, in which Darwin announces his belief in evolution.

141. Darwin's deliberations on the relative merits of the married and single state.

Chapter 10

The Acton Library

O W E N C H A D W I C K

L ORD ACTON was the Regius Professor of Modern History in the University of Cambridge from 1895 until he was near death in 1902 [142]. He had inherited and then collected a huge private library for his own historical purposes. When he died, these books, though still in Acton's various houses, were owned by the American millionaire Andrew Carnegie, who had stepped in to save Acton from having to sell them to make ends meet; of course Carnegie did not want them and gave them to the politician and writer John Morley; who did not want most of them and gave nearly all to the University of Cambridge, as Acton's university, on condition that they be kept together as a collection [198].

142. John Emerich Edward Dalberg, first Baron Acton (1834–1902), in his library at Aldenham, Shropshire.

There were some 70,000 books, so these were not easy to put on shelves in the then University Library in the Old Schools building, especially if they had to be housed together. It was agreed that each book should be given the classmark 'Acton'. When the new library was opened in 1934, the ground floor of the south-east wing was allotted to the collection.

The basis of Acton's personal library consisted of books which he inherited. He was the squire at Aldenham in Shropshire and some books were in the Aldenham library from long before he was born – for example Thomas Tanner's great study of all the abbeys of England and Wales, *Notitia monastica*, of 1744. His father's father was an English adventurer who became the Prime Minister of Bourbon Naples and, in southern Italy during the last age before they were overthrown by French revolutionaries, he naturally acquired books. Not all these books came to the family seat at Aldenham because Acton's father's brother became a cardinal and it is possible that some of his grandfather's books are now in the Vatican Library. It is possible, however, to trace in the Acton Library books which came from the Neapolitan period of the family. One, for example, is the *Decisiones Consilii Rotalis Romani sub auspiciis Ferdinandi IV* (Rome, 1802), the legal decisions of the Rota court when Rome, for a short time, was under the domination of the king who entitled himself King of Sicily and Jerusalem. The book has in it a draft Neapolitan passport, permitting entry to Austrian territory, for the young man who, later, was to become our Acton's father.

Acton's father married a German, a Dalberg. In the days before Napoleon, the Dalbergs had been one of the great families of German nobles with their seat at the castle of Herrnsheim near Worms in the Rhineland. One of Acton's great-grandfathers on his mother's side was the brother of one of the eminent men of Europe, Karl Theodor, the last Elector-Archbishop of Mainz, who was one of the Germans to back the incoming Napoleon and so was made Duke of Frankfurt. He was an intelligent and cultured man and collected a good library. He had a special interest in the histories of Spain and Portugal and of Sweden and Russia. Through his nephew and then his nephew's daughter, his castle and its books came to our Acton [143].

Hence, the basis of the library at Aldenham and afterwards at Cambridge consisted of two late eighteenth-century libraries, one collected by an Englishman in southern Italy, the other collected by a German in the Rhineland. Because these two naturally had different interests in what they collected, the range of the library was already unusual. Some of the Dalberg books stayed with our Acton's wife, who lived at Tegernsee near Munich and insisted on living in Bavaria although she was married to a

143. The Rhine at Mainz, from Matthaeus Merian and Martin Zeiller, *Topographia Archiepiscopatuum Moguntinensis, Treuirensis et Coloniensis* (Frankfurt, 1646).

Shropshire squire. Others of the Herrnsheim books moved to Aldenham and there Acton had to add a new library to his mansion to house the books which came from Naples, those which came from Herrnsheim and those which he collected.

There was a third substantial source of books which he did not assemble himself. Because he was a Roman Catholic he could not go to Oxford and although Cambridge could legally have accepted him, though not for a degree, colleges did not wish to do so. So he was sent to the University of Munich, then famous for its devout but humane Catholicism and for its new and higher standards in Catholic scholarship.

Munich University transformed him intellectually. He owed this to two professors in succession. He started on classics, with Ernst von Lasaulx as his professor, and he became Lasaulx's favourite pupil. Then, with his passion for historical study, he turned to history and became the favourite pupil of Ignaz von Döllinger, the Professor of Church History. The historical training which he received there was so exciting to him, and of such a standard, that later in life he affected the entire atmosphere of English historical study.

When Lasaulx died, after Acton had left the university, Acton bought his books. The collection thus acquired was very different in subject matter from those from Naples or Dalberg; these books were of the ancient world, of philosophy, especially ancient philosophy and the philosophy of history, and ethics whether ancient or modern. Acton's library had increased its range in a third direction. Twelve years after Lasaulx's death, and probably before, Acton employed a graduate librarian to care for and arrange the books at Aldenham.

Meanwhile he was buying steadily. The first thing to notice is extraordinary. Here is a historian who has acquired three different lots of books, each from a collector with different interests. Other books were given to him as presents as they are given to us all – Gladstone, for example, gave him a copy of the *Odes* of Pindar. There was another source of miscellany: to get what he wanted he sometimes bought, in bulk, whole private collections that were up for sale, and such purchases obviously included books in which he had no interest. Yet everyone who uses the Acton Library is conscious that this is a unity – a single mind dominates the shelves. It may have been awkward – it was certainly inconvenient to the then University Librarian – that John Morley should make it a condition that Acton's library must be kept together. The condition had grave disadvantages. Its carrying-out, however, enables the user to find this astounding unity which has been imposed, and which could only have been imposed, by a person of the deepest learning.

He was not a bibliophile; he did not buy books because they were very rare or because they looked beautiful. He bought them because they were tools towards knowledge. When the University Librarian, the sweet-natured Francis Jenkinson [62], saw the collection which the University had forced him to accept, he told a friend sadly that there was hardly a book in it which interested him; for what he loved were medieval manuscripts or books printed before 1500 or the books of the English sixteenth century – and Acton was not very interested in the Middle Ages (although he did study Peter Damian and Gregory VII and the letters of St Boniface) and his passion was for Europe since the Reformation. Acton liked splendid bindings and interesting old books but acquiring these was not his motive. He wanted books because they were doors with fascinating country beyond, when they were opened. If a book which he wanted was already in ruins, that did not stop him buying it. Already as an undergraduate he began to read booksellers' catalogues and to buy books in second-hand shops. Over the next twenty years or perhaps a little more, when he had plenty of money to spend, he bought largely and steadily and intelligently. Eventually the collection – Aldenham books, Herrnsheim books, Lasaulx books, his massive purchases – made one of the great private libraries of Europe and, since people referred to it publicly, it became well known, and when society talked of Acton they talked of his library.

He had two main aims which were the cause of, and guide to, his purchases. He was a dedicated Whig, or Liberal, and a believer in progress, and he wanted to study how humanity had gained liberty in its constitutions and its social life. Then he was a Roman Catholic by birth. In popular northern opinion in his two countries of Britain and Germany, the Roman Catholic Church had steadily resisted the coming of liberty, a resistance summed up in the word 'Inquisition'. Hence his second interest was the history of the Papacy, from the Counter-Reformation to the French Revolution. To students with such strong views as he held, these two themes contained ample temptation to mere propaganda. But Acton was a true historian – he was determined to know, resolute not to overlook information that told against the thesis which he wanted to prove, and hence the thoroughness with which he probed every corner of his two subjects by means of his book-purchases.[1]

1. Henry R. Tedder, 'Lord Acton as a book-collector', *Proceedings of the British Academy*, 1 (1903–4) 285ff.

AVE VIRGINEA IMPERIALIS ROSA

SS. Rosarium est Vinculum, ac singulare ad everte-
ndas hæreses Præsidium, Ecclesia in Oficio SS. R...

Christus bellum agit, cu Præd: Ordo contra Mundi
Potentes scu̶ni Fidei, opponit, Stufa Ordinem
in f. Perallu. c. 20 §. 60 Solicit.

Infidelitas

Hæresis

Apostasia

Blasphemia

It was a good time to buy. Many monasteries had excellent libraries and they were in a bad way. Houses that once had many monks and scholars among them now had a handful. Catholic states treated monks badly – the French Revolution abolished them in France and Belgium; one consequence of Napoleon's power in Germany was the loss of many monastic libraries; Portugal dissolved all its monasteries in 1834 and Spain all in the next year, Italy dissolved most of them from 1866 onwards, and Swiss cantons did the same by dribbles during the century; most of the Polish houses vanished under Russian rule. On occasion monks, now desperately poor because their endowments had been seized, had to sell precious books if they were to survive.

Not all these books came onto the second-hand market. States could appropriate them for the national library, as was done in Bavaria and in Rome. Monks were good at keeping their way of life, by moving to Protestant countries where they would be safer or moving from one Catholic state to another – out of Spain to France when the Spanish dissolved the monasteries, out of France to Spain when the French dissolved them; and some books went with them. Nevertheless, many libraries were for sale in the bookshops. The British Museum had a prosperous time.

In Acton's collection are superb books from the libraries of monasteries. We can track where several of them came from. A book of 1662 by a Dominican, about the Inquisition, came from the Capuchin house at Castelvetrano in Sicily [144]; another, of 1648, on the same subject, from the house of the Franciscans at Bergamo. The Discalced Carmelites at Castelvetrano provided him with the *Bulla Cruciatae explicata* of Francesco Bardi (Palermo, 1656). The Capuchins at Verona supplied Johannes Medina, *De poenitentia* (Ingolstadt, 1581). Cardinal Petra's *Commentaria ad constitutiones apostolicas*, published at Venice in 1729, came from the house of the Discalced Carmelites in Florence.

Naturally the Bavarian religious houses supplied some of the best. The *Magnum bullarium* (Lyons, 1692–7), then the indispensable collection of papal bulls and still, for some purposes, indispensable, was given to help found a Carmelite house at Schöngau in Bavaria, not far from Acton's wife's home at Tegernsee. There was a Jesuit house at Landsberg in Bavaria; why their books did not go to the Bavarian State Library, it is hard to say, but several of these Jesuit books ended up with Acton. These were not the only Bavarian books. Durandus's textbook on law (*Speculum juris*, Frankfurt, 1592) was in the university library at Ingolstadt, which since the Counter-

144. Frontispiece from Johannes Maria Bertinus, *Sacratissimae Inquisitionis rosa virginea* (Palermo, 1662).

Reformation had been dominated by Jesuits. When the Jesuits were abolished by the Pope in 1773, the university library gave the book to the Theatine monks of Ingolstadt. It was not the only one of Acton's books which the university gave to the Theatines during the Jesuit crisis; and then the Theatines in their turn lost their library in the revolutionary age and so the book came to Acton.

From the regular canons at Gars near Munich came Zunggo's history of the canons (*Historiae generalis et specialis de ordine canonicorum regularium S. Augustini prodromus*, Regensburg, 1742–9), but it did not come by the Bavarian route, because it passed through a French bookseller [145]. There were books from the very historic Irish house at Regensburg. The oddest of the Bavarian acquisitions is a lovely copy of Jean Mabillon's *Annales ordinis S. Benedicti occidentalium monachorum patriarchae* (Lucca and Paris, 1739–40), for it belonged to the ducal library in Munich [146]. How did the Duke of Bavaria, after Napoleon turned him into a king, manage to lose so splendid a book? We know that Professor Döllinger borrowed books from the Royal

145. Book-label of the library of the regular canons at Gars near Munich.

146. The monastery at Monte Cassino from Jean Mabillon, *Annales ordinis S. Benedicti occidentalium monachorum patriarchae*, vol. II (Lucca, 1739).

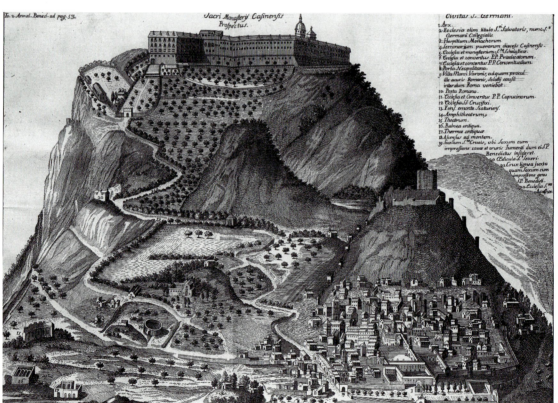

Library in Munich and that Döllinger freely lent books to Acton. One does not like to think that this was the route by which it came into the Acton Library.

At least two of the books which Acton acquired – Franciscus Patricius, *De regno* (Paris, 1567), and the Jesuit Juan de Mariana's famous *De rege* (Mainz, 1605) – state at the front that they are duplicates from the Royal Library at Munich, so we know that that library sometimes sold books.

The revolutionary Portuguese state had little interest in the past and freely allowed its monastic books into the auction rooms. Quite a number of Acton's books came from the Oratory at Lisbon – for example, Giovanni Domenico Mansi's supplement to Philippe Labbe's *Acta Conciliorum* (Lucca, 1748–52), a still useful book – and more from the Portuguese university town of Coimbra which had been packed with religious houses. The Discalced Augustinians of Coimbra supplied him, eventually, with a good number of books.

The monastic books are on various subjects, but the collection as Acton made it contains splendid materials for the history of the monastic orders before the French Revolution.

A few of the books have interesting comments in them, like: 'Reading this book is banned by decree of the Index'; or, in one case: 'This book belongs to the library of St Dominic at Bologna from which it cannot be removed, the penalty of removing it is excommunication, so Popes Urban VIII and Innocent XII.' There was a book from Paris which belonged to the Vincentians but did not come from them into the market because in 1728 the Mazarin College gave it to one of its adolescent pupils as a prize for her knowledge of the catechism.

Mostly of course he was not buying ex-monastic books. The university library at Halle found their copy of a 1567 commentary on the Decretals to be a duplicate and simply sold it on the market; and Acton picked it up. There was *Thuringia sacra* (Frankfurt, 1737) which was sold in 1851 by the university library at Leipzig, probably because it was a duplicate, and was bought by C. A. Schnabel and thence by Acton. The very good collection of the Protestant Reformation was put together by himself; for example he bought Enders's edition of Luther's German works when it first came out. What he did get out of ex-monastic libraries were the pamphlets or tracts against Luther, such as Catharinus, *Apologia pro veritate catholicae* (Florence, 1521), which had belonged to the Capuchins; Cochlaeus, *Consyderatio de futuro concordiae in religione tractatu* (Ingolstadt, 1545), which came from the

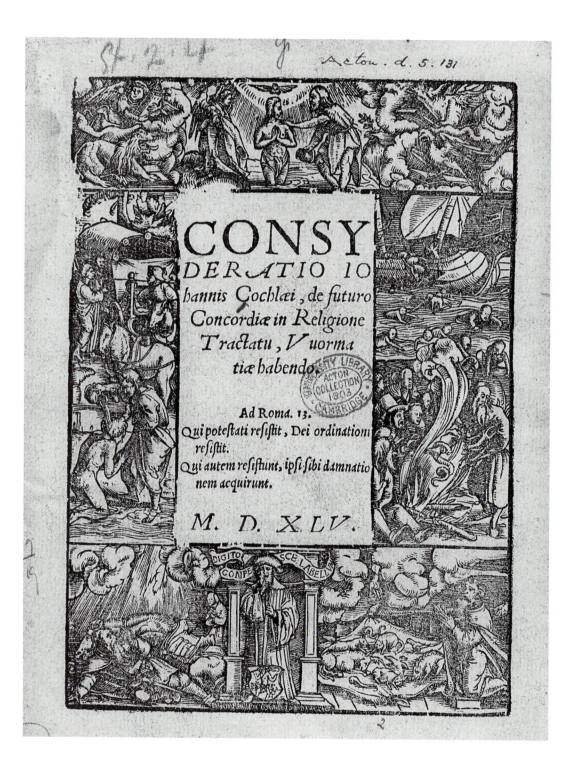

Franciscans at Ingolstadt [147]; and the canons and decrees of Trent (Dillingen, 1564) from the abbey of St George at Villingen in Württemberg.

During the course of their history some of these books must have had an odd time. The Palatine Library was collected in the age of the Reformation by an extravagant Elector Palatine at Heidelberg. When his successor, Frederick V, who was son-in-law of King James I of England, accepted the crown of Bohemia in 1619, a Catholic army occupied Heidelberg and sent the Palatine Library to the Vatican. A volume from the Palatine Library, the life of Pope Benedict XIII, appears in Acton's collection. Perhaps the Vatican disposed of a few duplicates – or perhaps it left the Vatican by some less reputable route.

There is a book on concordats, *Collezione di provvidenze pontificie dipendenti dai concordati sopra l'immunità della giurisdizione ecclesiastica* (Turin, 1770), which belonged to King Charles Emmanuel III, King of Sardinia and Savoy [**199**]. During all of Acton's life there was still a king of Sardinia, though for the later half he was also king of Italy. How did such a royal book come into Acton's possession? The kings of Savoy and the kings of Italy were not ardent readers of books and it is possible to guess that not a single one of them would have read a book on concordats. Yet it is not likely to have been sold from a royal library. The inference must be that, during the conquest of northern Italy by General Bonaparte, the devastation reached even to books.

As he developed his library, Acton's interest shifted with a change in his own historical enquiries. Before about 1870 or 1874, when he was in danger of excommunication by Rome, his interest was the Papacy and all Catholicism in Europe till the French Revolution. He was an enemy of the idea of infallibility and he wanted to show how it was wrong. Now his interest widened, to the society and ethics of Europe, including the beginnings of modern social sciences. For example, he bought Karl Marx's *Das Kapital*. The second area in which the library developed specially was in French books and pamphlets. He had inherited fine books from Germany and from southern Italy and he bought many books published in Spain. Now he turned to the French bookshops and built up what became an outstanding feature of his collection, a superb library of French history, especially of French local history [148]. He was the first English historian to have this rare interest in French local history, which brought such valuable results in the decades after his death.

Acton bought in London from C. J. Stewart, King William Street, off the Strand; from D. Nutt, 'Foreign and Classical Booksellers', 270 The Strand;

147. A tract by a fierce opponent of the Reformation: Johannes Cochlaeus, *Consyderatio de futuro concordiae in religione tractatu* (Ingolstadt, 1545).

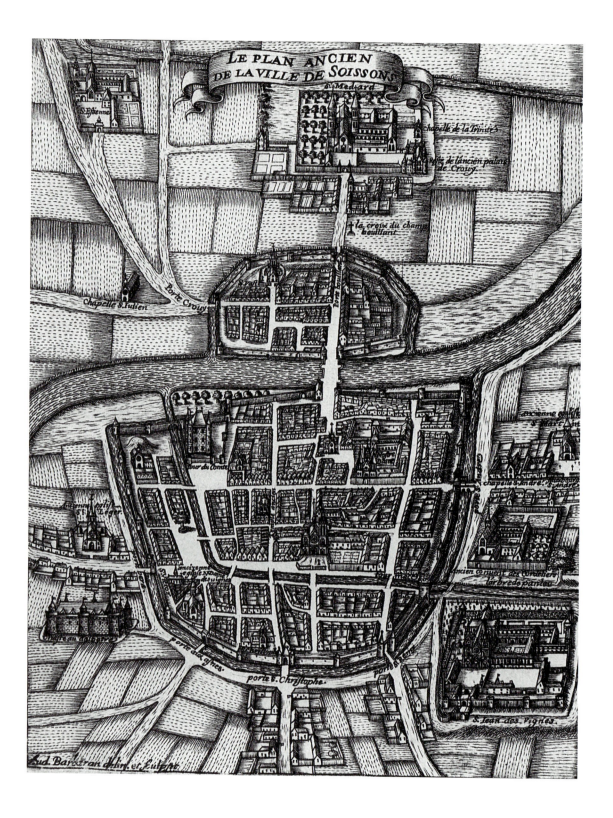

from Stanford, famous to us as mapmakers; from Bickers and Son; from Burns Oates; and from Williams and Norgate. In Cambridge he bought from Deighton Bell, and from Arthur Cox whose business was soon to become Galloway's; in The Hague from Martin Nijhoff's Librairie Ancienne et Moderne; in Paris from Ernest Thorin at the Librairie Ancienne et Moderne, 58 Boulevard Saint Michel, and from the Librairie Ecclésiastique de Toulouse et Taranne, which despite the name was at 33 Rue Cassette, Paris; and also from the French bookshops Librairie Nouvelle, Librairie Universelle and Librairie Spéciale pour l'Histoire de France; in Munich from Rieger who ran the university bookshop, and from the bookseller Theodor Ackermann, 10 Promenadeplatz. There is no sign as yet of any regular purchases from an Italian or Spanish bookseller.

It has been regarded as an established truth that Acton built the main part of his library during the twenty years after he was an undergraduate and that from about 1874 he bought far less, but this cannot be true. What is true is that, during the later 1880s, as he bought and as his children grew more expensive, he had to pause because he had not the money to continue; and he and his advisers came to the conclusion that, if he was to save himself from the creditors, he must sell his books. The London auctioneering house, Puttick and Simpson, printed in 1890 a first catalogue of Acton's books for sale and issued it to the public, to be sold on six days of sale beginning on 16 July 1890 'at ten minutes past one o'clock precisely'. Although it was only a first catalogue, it must have roused the interest of every serious student of history and society.

This was when Gladstone stepped in to save Acton from what he regarded as disgrace and persuaded Andrew Carnegie to buy the library on condition that Acton could keep it until his death. If Acton had refused this offer he would have lost the books, but, in accepting it, he must have been aware that if he had auctioned the library he would have received far more money than he was given by Carnegie. He preferred to keep the books and to be saved from creditors, to selling the books and being very comfortable.

From the moment he was assured of being able to do so, the buying began again; more modern books now, more German than French. There is a bill from Ackermann in Munich, dated 28 December 1896, with a list of books bought and the days when they were bought, and it shows that Acton was sometimes ordering three or four books twice a week – and expensive books: one set was 73 marks, another more than 88 marks [149]. More than one bookseller started to worry. When Ackermann presented his bill to

148. Frontispiece to Claude Dormay, *Histoire de la ville de Soissons* (Soissons, 1663).

149. Part of a bill presented by the Munich bookseller Theodor Ackermann, covering Acton's purchases from June to October 1896, and amounting to 1,350 marks.

Acton that December, it was for more than 1,350 marks. We find little notes from booksellers, not only foreign, pleading for settlement of a debt.

Then the burden fell on Jenkinson, the University Librarian, whose natural world this was not, and who by his generosity, indefatigable labours and wisdom turned the benefaction into one of Cambridge's great possessions.

He had a first difficulty: Aldenham Park was rented out, and it had its (so to speak) 'private' collection of books about the house, which must somehow be distinguished from the great library. Many books were in Tegernsee; the same series of volumes might be partly in Tegernsee and partly at Aldenham and partly in Acton's room at Trinity. The books from Aldenham, transported to Cambridge in February 1903 by five vans and in 443 packing cases, lay in heaps about the Arts School and the old Syndicate Room in the Old Schools.

The first sight of them made Jenkinson grateful but also alarmed. The gratitude was due to the realization that he had been given a collection which, in its themes, was not paralleled in any other library in Europe. The alarm came from a perception of the physical and intellectual problems which faced him. Many books were unbound. There were hundreds of rare pamphlets which would require long research if they were to be catalogued aright. Many series were found to be incomplete; Acton might buy the first two volumes and then fail to buy the third, or purchase in a sale the first and third volumes but have no second. He was also the most generous or imprudent man with books; he frequently took a rare book from his library and thrust it into the hands of an undergraduate – another way to find a series incomplete. The habit shows, as nothing else, how he was not a bibliophile but how the books were tools to knowledge and nothing more. And did he own all the books on his shelves? As late as 1906, a volume which belonged to the Royal Library at Munich was found at Tegernsee. Two years after that, the Royal Library pointed out that they had discovered Acton's signature on a borrower's ticket for four volumes of Döllinger and where were these four volumes? About that time, Lord Stanmore claimed back a privately printed volume of his father's correspondence which he had lent to Acton.

So the first tasks were:

1. to find shelves;
2. to make a preliminary catalogue and find out about rare books and pamphlets, which would require extra staff, in order
3. to bind what needed binding – 13,791 volumes were to be bound, partly by the Library staff and partly by Gray of Cambridge;
4. to try to find single volumes which could fill the gaps – Jenkinson sent out to the European book trade a list of volumes wanted, and eventually succeeded in buying 1,515 volumes of what he needed, at a cost of £417 12s 0d – it was beginning to be almost an Acton–Jenkinson library;
5. to decide what to do about two peculiarities: the duplicates of existing volumes in the University Library and the discovery that in many volumes Acton's working slips were still in place to mark passages of special importance to him. What was to be done with the slips?

He needed a team. With the aid of Adolphus Ward of Peterhouse he collected an excellent team to research into these books and to arrange and catalogue them. Ward had been Professor of History at Manchester and there knew Alice Cooke, a Manchester girl who had specialized in the history of monks and friars in the Middle Ages. When she won an assistant lectureship at the University of Manchester she was one of the first women in England to be appointed to a university post. There she had shown her ability as a cataloguer of the Spencer library at Althorp and the fledgeling John Rylands Library. She had a quiet friendliness which made her easy to work with. For nearly five years, from 1903 to 1907, she worked at the huge task which confronted Jenkinson. The witnesses agreed that she was the best of all the assistants in this task. She left in 1907 only because she won a full lectureship in medieval history at Leeds, in a competition in which the candidates included the great Maurice Powicke. Later she was to return to Cambridge as Director of Studies in History at Newnham College, but by that time the Acton work was done. She was one of those assistants who are indispensable to the work of a great library but who receive credit only from the very few of their employers who are in the know.

When she went, Ward's hand was still at work and she was succeeded, from 1908 to 1912, by T. A. Walker, Fellow of Peterhouse, Dean of Peterhouse, Bursar of Peterhouse, Librarian of Peterhouse and Vicar of Cherry Hinton; and despite this busy combination he did well with the Acton books and pamphlets. When he left, the job was almost done.

Jenkinson must have asked himself questions about the utility of what they were doing. Not many classical scholars would now want to use German theses on ancient literature which were printed between the 1820s and the 1840s and came from the working library of Lasaulx. In the way in which the collection had been made, on occasion by buying a bulky lot, it was inevitable that Acton bought two or even three copies of the same book. The librarian whom he employed at Aldenham in 1873, Henry Tedder, had as part of his duty the thinning-out of duplicates and certainly got rid of more than 1,000 books. When the Acton Library reached Cambridge in its vans and packages, it had hardly any duplicates. What it did have was the same book in different editions or languages. Acton did not think his collection complete if he had a sixteenth-century edition and there then came on the market a seventeenth-century edition of the same book. One of the oddest examples of this is Paolo Sarpi's celebrated history of the Council of Trent. Of Sarpi's book, he acquired the original Italian of 1619; the English, which was at once printed in London because of the danger of publishing in a Catholic country; a French translation; and a German translation of 1761. Acton commanded these four languages. The copy which he read was the German.

That was not Jenkinson's chief problem: it was that the University Library already possessed many books of which they were now given another copy. Sometimes the books which they possessed were well bound whereas Acton's copy was not; sometimes the series which they possessed was complete and Acton's was incomplete. Yet the University had accepted Acton's books as a totality to be kept together. He was, so to speak, under an obligation not to get rid of anything. Jenkinson called this the problem of 'surplusage'.

A ruthless Librarian, who had not enough space on his shelves, would in a mysterious way have got rid of duplicates, even though his bosses in the University had accepted the library as a unity to be kept together. Jenkinson, though he was the least ruthless of men, did precisely that. First, he asked John Morley, the donor, whether he would like any of the duplicates, apart from the *Biographie universelle* which he had demanded to keep; for no one could blame the librarian if the donor accepted back some books; and Morley was clearly willing, because eventually he received altogether 940 books which Cambridge saw no point in keeping.

Then he asked the second Lord Acton whether he would like some of his father's books, and persuaded Morley to give the new Lord Acton 6,000 books. Even that was not enough. From an early moment in the operation, intelligent scholars of other universities realized that there must be duplicates and asked whether their own inadequate libraries might not be passed the duplicates which Cambridge did not want. The librarian at Tübingen University was quick to express a hope that they might get Acton books. No less a scholar than Mary Bateson, for example, asked Ward, of Peterhouse, who had helped Acton edit the *Cambridge modern history* and was now working closely with Jenkinson, whether the unwanted duplicates might not be given to the National Library of Ireland.[2] Ward replied very cautiously: they might not have the power to give away any of the books which they had accepted; and before there could be any question of it a considerable time must elapse. It is impossible to tell whether, when Ward talked of a considerable time, he was thinking of the years that must elapse before the collection was fully catalogued and ordered – this took in the end some ten years – and so when they would know what were duplicates and what were not; or whether it also came into his mind that after years have elapsed donors do not grieve so much if gifts are given away by the recipients. It took Jenkinson six years before he felt that the time was ripe for a sale of duplicates; but this sale had to be very private, no one must see that the University of Cambridge was disposing of part of a benefaction. He offered duplicates to a bookseller in Tunbridge Wells on the strict condition that no one should know where the bookseller found what he had for sale.

2. Letter from Mary Bateson to Ward, 13 June 1903. My thanks to John Wells for his help with these papers, in University Archives ULIB 6/1.

This diminution of the duplicates, however, first to John Morley, and via John Morley to the second Lord Acton, and then to Tunbridge Wells, does not disclose the humanity of Jenkinson. Like every other worker on Acton's library, he was moved by the power of the single mind moving among all this material; that is, he did not want to give away or sell books, even if he had them already, when the disappearance of the book would imply that Acton's range was narrower than it truly was. He kept a lot of duplicates, even though they were duplicates, because their presence in the Acton Library illustrated the mind of Acton.

This was particularly important with the slips. Acton often put slips into his books, to mark a sentence or passage which struck him. The passage on that page might also be given a light pencil-line in the margin. The slips were systematic in that they were almost all the same size, some 5 cm by 1 cm, and most were cut from booksellers' catalogues of second-hand books, usually English booksellers but sometimes German. Because they had lived in the book for years, all were dusty, most were crumpled and some were dirty. Probably most librarians would have thrown all these slips away as worthless. Jenkinson kept them all, at the page where he found them [150]. They illustrated the omnivorous mind of this indirect benefactor of the University Library. Jenkinson's brother-in-law testified that Jenkinson, the bibliophile for whom Acton's books were not his real interest, was almost more interested in the slips than any other part of what Acton did.[3]

There were a few oddities left after such a unique operation. As we browse, revering, in the shelves, and wishing that we had read more than any of us have, we come across J. P. Whitney's *The Reformation* of 1907. It was the best textbook of its time, of a type which Acton dismissed as too outline to matter. Acton would not have bought it probably, and he did not buy it certainly, because by 1907 he was dead. There could not but be curious twists in the work of making useful such a big monument to a private thirst to know the past.

3. H. F. Stewart, *Francis Jenkinson* (Cambridge, 1926), p. 56.

150. Acton's 'slips' in his copy of Karl Gustav Geib, *Lehrbuch des deutschen Strafrechts* (Leipzig, 1861).

Chapter 11

The Stefan Heym Archive

PETER HUTCHINSON

STEFAN HEYM (born 1913) is not only a writer, but a journalist, a politician and a prime dissident. His versatility, his forthrightness and his long creative period mean that he has experienced and engaged with many of the important events of our century. His archive thus provides scholars with the resources for study not only of his own work within fascinating periods of German literature, but also of aspects of political and social history, publishing history, and even, in due course, espionage techniques. The bulk of the material is, though, devoted to literature, and the most exciting research can be done with reference to the genesis of Heym's fiction: from first ideas and sketches to detailed plans; from such plans to first draft; from first to second, third, and sometimes even fourth draft; and even the changes from galley to page proof. Here, in a possibly unparalleled form, we can see the writer in his workshop; we can see how characters, events and ideas are shaped, modified and finalized. Further, as a result of Heym's bilingualism in German and English, we can regularly see this process in two languages.

From an early age, Heym knew he wanted to be a writer. He was highly ambitious and confident of his own ability, and it is in fact due to such firm confidence that his archive is so remarkably full. He wanted to preserve for posterity every important stage of his life, not just as a writer, but also as a man. Thus we can find here originals or copies of virtually every line he has published, ranging from his first poem, an anti-war piece of 1930, to his opening address to the German Parliament in 1994. We also find much unpublished material: an extensive correspondence with publishers, agents, friends, fans and critics; speeches (on audio- and video-tape); a slide collection; various photographs; and clippings from newspapers throughout the world (initially reviews of his novels, but later extending to all events in which he participated). The state of preservation of almost every item is excellent, despite the fact some of the material was composed on the battlefields of the Second World War.

To appreciate the significance of the Archive, it is necessary to have some acquaintance with Heym's adventurous life. He was born as Helmut Flieg

UNABHÄNGIG
PROGRESSIV
AKTUELL

Deutsches Volksecho

DAS BLATT FÜR
DIE DEUTSCH-
AMERIKANISCHE
FAMILIE

VOL. I (XI)—No. 9 · Reentered as second class matter February 27, 1937, at the post office at New York, N.Y., under the Act of March 3, 1879." · New York, den 17. April 1937 · Published weekly by the Deutsches Volksecho Publishing Co., Inc, 5 Beekman Street, N.Y. Subscription rates: $1.20 for 6 months; $2.50 a year. · PREIS 5 Cents

Sonderinterview für das Volksecho:

THOMAS MANN AN DIE DEUTSCHEN IN U.S.A.

Thomas Mann, der grosse deutsche Dichter und Nobelpreisträger, der durch die Nazis ins Exil getrieben wurde und jetzt in Amerika weilt, gab dem Vertreter des VOLKSECHO ein Sonderinterview.

Thomas Mann ist für eine kurze Vortragsreise nach Amerika gekommen. Nur ein einziges Mal, am 21. April im Mecca Temple, wird Thomas Mann in einer Riesenversammlung zu den Massen der Deutschamerikaner sprechen.

Thomas Mann zur Einheitsfront

Auf die Frage, wie Thomas Mann sich zur Einheitsfront gegen Hitler in Deutschland stelle, antwortete er:

"Es ist aufs Lebhafteste zu wünschen, dass es zu einer solchen Einheitsfront kommt." Zwar gebe es grosse Gegensätze zwischen den Gegnern des Hitler-Regimes, fuhr Th. Mann fort, aber die Steigerung des Widerwillens gegen Hitler müsse einigend wirken. Die Gegner Hitlers haben gemeinsame Wünsche. "Das Verlangen nach religiöser, geistiger und wirtschaftlicher Freiheit, vor allem die Sehnsucht nach Freiheit muss sie zusammenführen."

(Fortsetzung auf Seite 3)

Thomas Mann und Frau an Bord der "Normandie" bei ihrer Ankunft in New York.

TODESANZEIGE

Wir haben die schmerzliche Aufgabe, die Familie, die deutschen und ausländischen Fliegerkameraden, die deutsche Wehrmacht und das deutsche Volk von dem plötzlichen Tod eines der besten Söhne Deutschlands und seines grössten Fliegerhelden

GERHARD FIESELER

zu benachrichtigen, nachdem die deutsche Regierung aus politischen Gründen diese Nachricht unterdrückt.

Gerhard Fieseler wurde am 15. April 1896 in Glösch bei Köln geboren. Nach harter Jugend ging er als Setzerlehrling im Weltkrieg, meldete sich bei den Fliegern und machte seine Feldpilotenprüfung. Fieseler wurde rasch zum Unteroffizier und dann zum Feldwebel befördert. Später ging er als Jagd- und Kampfflieger nach Mazedonien und errang dort 19 Luftsiege.

Nach dem Kriege betätigte sich Fieseler als Fluglehrer und Kunstflieger. Bald wurde er einer der grössten Kunstflieger der Welt, er erfand viele neue Figuren, die von der internationalen Kunstfliegerei übernommen wurden, wie z. B. das berühmte «Looping nach vorn».

Fieseler begann selbst Flugzeuge zu konstruieren. In seiner kleinen Flugzeugfabrik in Kassel, die er 1930 gründete, konstruierte und schuf er den vielbewunderten Sportapparat «Fieseler 5». Fieseler begann die Arbeit in dieser Fabrik mit 15 Arbeitern. Heute ist daraus ein grosses Werk geworden, das die bekannten Doppeldecker «Figa» baut.

Mit Gerhard Fieseler verliert die deutsche und internationale Fliegerei einen der grössten Kunstflieger, der folgende Rekorde errang: 1928/1933 deutscher Kunstmeister, 1933 Europameister für Kunstflug, 1934 Weltmeister im Kunstflug.

Gerhard Fieseler starb als einer der unzähligen deutschen Flieger und «Freiwilligen» die die Hitlerregierung ihrer verbrecherischen Politik im spanischen Abenteuer opfert. Wie Hunderte andere deutsche Flieger verkaufte sie Fieseler, ihren besten deutschen Flieger an die Francoregierung. Sie bestritt anfänglich mit frecher Stirn diese Tatsache, musste sie aber später wie auch die schwere Verwundung Fieselers zugeben. Wie der Tod von vielen anderen Opfern des spanischen Krieges verheimlichte die Hitlerregierung auch feige seinen Anfang Februar 1936 eingetretenen Tod.

Das Hitlersystem mordet nicht nur seine politischen Gegner, sondern tausende der besten Söhne Deutschlands, die in Spanien und in der Heimat fallen. Beängstigend steigt die Zahl der Selbstmorde in der Armee. Hunderte junger Deutsche können den barbarischen Drill in den Zuchthauskasernen nicht ertragen, verlieren den Glauben an die Partei, die sie früher vergötterten und jagen sich, wie die begabte, junge

Graf von Welczeck,

Sohn des gegenwärtigen deutschen Botschafters in Paris, eine Kugel in die Brust.

Wir senken unsere Fahnen, die Fahnen des alten und ewig jungen Deutschland an der Bahre dieser neuen Opfer der brutalen, menschenmordenden Hitlerregierung und schwören, nicht zu ruhen und nicht zu rasten, bis das undeutsche, fluchbeladene Hitlersystem gestürzt ist.

BERLIN, 10. Februar 1937.

DEUTSCHE FREIHEITSPARTEI.

Das erste nach Amerika gelangte Dokument der Deutschen Freiheitspartei. Die deutsche Freiheitspartei hat in den letzten Wochen viel von sich reden gemacht. In Berlin und anderen Städten Deutschlands wurden Flugblätter der neuen Anti-Hitler-Partei versandt; in der Freiheitspartei sind, nach den Angaben ihrer eigenen Flugblätter, alle oppositionellen Gruppen Deutschlands vertreten. *(Photokopie eines uns zugegangenen Originals.)*

in the German industrial city of Chemnitz. His early years were relatively uneventful, but his literary career actually began abruptly and frighteningly – on 7 September 1931. On that day the social-democratic newspaper of Chemnitz published seven short, satirical stanzas by him entitled 'Exportgeschäft' (The export business). The poem attacked the decision by the German General von Seeckt to send instructors to Chiang Kai Shek's army in China. It was a bold move to publish such a poem at this point of German history (the newspaper itself was banned two years later), and it was even bolder for the (Jewish) author to couch his criticism in such openly sarcastic terms – and to sign the poem with his own name. The consequences were immediate: Flieg was beaten up by fellow sixth-formers and had to spend several days away from school. Further, although the school did quietly admonish those who had attacked him, it suggested Flieg leave and not return. The teenager managed to finish his secondary education at a liberal school in Berlin, and he went on to the University in that city. Here he wrote poems and newspaper articles, most of which concentrated on the social conditions of the poor. However, he had not been a student long before Hitler came to power and the fraud of the Reichstag fire was perpetrated. A few days later a warrant was issued for Flieg's arrest. The authorities searched his parents' house in Chemnitz, believing him to be there, and this gave his brother the opportunity to rush to Berlin and warn him of the danger. Flieg escaped to Czechoslovakia several hours later, on 12 March 1933. He was only nineteen years old.

Flieg changed his name to 'Heym'. He made his way in Prague by writing articles and reports for German-language newspapers, and composing poems, all of which are preserved in the Archive. In 1935 he won a scholarship to the United States, obtained his MA at Chicago in 1937, and then obtained the post of chief editor of a German-language newspaper in New York, *Deutsches Volksecho*, one of whose goals was to attack elements of Nazism in the USA. The paper was also outstanding at obtaining interviews with German exiles [151]. The enterprise had to close in 1939, and Heym then made a living as a salesman, all the while composing short pieces for newspapers and trying to write for the stage. The turning point came when his agent encouraged him to think in terms of a novel. He did, and *Hostages*, a work about the underground in Czechoslovakia, became a bestseller and also a Paramount film (the Archive holds a video). Heym was financially secure for the first time in his adult life, and one of the main beneficiaries of his new-found wealth was his archive: every piece of paper

151. A *Volksecho* article based on Heym's interview with Thomas Mann, immediately after the latter's arrival for a lecture tour in 1937. Only two complete runs of *Deutsches Volksecho* have survived, one of them in the University Library.

relating to his novel was carefully preserved; every review of the work was cut out of its newspaper and pasted into a large volume designated for cuttings; every speech he now gave – and he was invited to give them throughout the United States – was preserved in successive drafts and final copy.

Shortly after his first success, Heym was conscripted into the US army. Given his linguistic and intellectual skills, he was soon allocated to a new and unusual section, one concerned with 'psychological warfare'; and after training in the United States and in England, he took part in the Normandy invasion. His task was to interrogate prisoners, assess the morale of the enemy, and produce leaflets and other material which could be shot, or dropped by plane, over enemy lines. He was also involved in broadcasting to the enemy over loudspeakers, urging them to surrender.

There are some fascinating documents in the Archive which relate to this period, and the conservation department of the Library has ensured

152. An example of the propaganda leaflets. Most used the German language alone, but this one was also produced in English. The plate shows the front of the German version, the reverse of the English.

My Name is Joe Jones

I am an American soldier. I come from Steubenville in the State of Ohio.

My comrades and I have made a long journey to get here. Our people have given us the best and the most fighting equipment of any army in the World.

We do not believe in miracles. We believe in airplanes, guns, grenades, tanks and machines.

In a few months we have overrun and destroyed the German army in the West. What we undertake we carry through.

We want peace, quiet and order. And not only for 25 years.

I am Joe Jones, an American soldier. I demand nothing personally from the Germans and am accustomed to respect the rights of my fellow men. I am fighting a soldiers' war.

I like to live and I respect the lives of others. But whoever attacks me will learn that Joe Jones can be otherwise.

Whoever wants to be my enemy will quickly learn that I too can be an enemy so hard and so ruthless that he will never forget me.

Which Joe Jones do you want to know?

JOE JONES
expects an answer

Mein Name ist Joe Jones

Ich bin ein amerikanischer Soldat. Ich komme aus Steubenville im Staate Ohio.

Meine Kameraden und ich haben eine weite Reise gemacht, um hierher zu kommen. Unser Volk hat uns das beste und das wirkungsvollste Kriegsmaterial aller Armeen der Welt zur Verfügung gestellt.

Wir glauben nicht an Wunder. Wir glauben an Flugzeuge, Kanonen, Granaten, Panzer und Maschinen.

In wenigen Monaten haben wir die deutschen Armeen des Westens überrannt und vernichtet. Was wir uns vornehmen, das führen wir durch.

Wir wollen Frieden, Ruhe und Ordnung. Und nicht nur für 25 Jahre.

Ich bin Joe Jones, ein amerikanischer Soldat. Ich verlange persönlich nichts von den Deutschen und bin daran gewöhnt, die Rechte meiner Mitmenschen zu achten. Ich führe Krieg als Soldat.

Ich lebe gern und achte auch das Leben anderer. Aber wer mich angreift, der muss wissen, dass Joe Jones auch anders kann.

Wer mein Feind sein will, der wird schnell erfahren, dass ich auch ein harter und unerbittlicher Feind sein kann. So hart und unerbittlich, dass meine Feinde mich nie vergessen.

Welchen Joe Jones willst Du kennenlernen?

JOE JONES
erwartet eine Antwort

BRÜCKEN-KOPF Remagen S.3.

Frontpost

„Der Starke braucht die Wahrheit nicht zu scheuen.“
Ernst Moritz Arndt

März Nr. 5   Nummer 53 — 12. HG

NACHRICHTEN FÜR DEUTSCHE SOLDATEN. HERAUSGEBER : DIE AMERIKANISCHEN TRUPPEN IN WESTEUROPA.

Durchbruch nach Bayern

PARIS. — Die Amerikaner haben Darmstadt genommen und sind in raschem Vorstoß nach Aschaffenburg und damit in Bayern eingedrungen. Alliierte Truppen haben den Rhein von Wesel bis Worms an vielen Stellen überschritten. Das westrheinische Gebiet von der Schweiz bis an die holländische Grenze ist von alliierten Truppen besetzt und jeglicher deutsche Widerstand hat aufgehört.

In breiter Front über den Rhein – Alliierte im Ruhrgebiet

Die amerikanische Dritte Armee überschritt den Rhein an sieben Stellen zwischen Koblenz und Boppard und nahm in raschem Vorstoß Darmstadt. Weiter nach Osten vorstoßend haben General Pattons Panzer den Main erreicht und sind über eine unbeschädigte Brücke in Aschaffenburg eingedrungen. Im Dreieck Mainz-Frankfurt - Aschaffenburg ist jeder organisierte deutsche Widerstand zusammengebrochen.

Bei Remagen

Nach letzten Meldungen sind die Amerikaner in die Vororte von Frankfurt eingedrungen.

Die Amerikaner haben aus ihrem Brückenkopf bei Remagen in östlicher Richtung die deutschen Stellungen durchbrochen, die Reichsautobahn Frankfurt—Köln überschritten und sind bis 30 km östlich des Rheins durchgestoßen. Am Südabschnitt des Brückenkopfes wurde Neuwied genommen. Am Nordabschnitt stiessen die Amerikaner über Hennef bis unweit Siegburg vor.

Nach längerer Vorbereitung stießen die britische Zweite und die amerikanische Neunte Armee über den künstlich eingenebelten Rhein nördlich der Ruhr vor und errichteten mehrere Brückenköpfe.

Gegen Duisburg

Gleichzeitig setzte die Erste Alliierte Luftlandearmee von 3000 Transportflugzeugen und Lastenseglern 40 000 Luftlandetruppen ab. Diese drei Armeen vereinigten sich und haben am rechten Rheinufer einen festen Brückenkopf von 46 km Breite und 17 km Tiefe errichtet.

Wesel und Rees wurden erobert, alliierte Einheiten stehen unweit Duisburg und Drosten. Die Nazi-Gauleiter im Ruhrgebiet haben die gesamte männliche Bevölkerung aufgefordert, ins Innere des Reiches zu fliehen. Westlich des Rheins gibt es von deutschen Soldaten nur noch solche, die kriegsgefangen sind. In der Pfalz allein haben mehr als 110 000 die Waffen gestreckt. Dies ist seit Stalingrad der größte deutsche Menschenverlust in einer einzigen Schlacht.

Moskau : Großoffensive begonnen

MOSKAU. — Der Moskauer Rundfunk meldet: Die russischen Armeen sind von Königsberg bis zur Donau zur Offensive übergegangen.

Im Raum zwischen der Donau und dem Plattensee stehen Einheiten der Heeresgruppe Tolbuchin 55 km vor der österreichischen Grenze. Die Städte Stuhlweissenburg, Gran a. d. Donau, Felsögalla und Papa wurden genommen.

Im ungarischen Raum folgt die russische Offensive den wochenlangen deutschen Versuchen, vom Plattensee aus zur Donau durchzubrechen. Diese vergeblichen Versuche kosteten die Deutschen 70 000 Mann an Toten, sowie 750 Panzer und Sturmgeschütze.

In Oberschlesien brachen die Russen aus dem Raum Oppeln aus, haben Neustadt und Neisse erobert, und sind dort in das Sudetengebirge und in die Tschechoslowakei eingedrungen. In diesem Abschnitt fielen mehr als 30 000 Deutsche.

An der Danziger Bucht sind die Russen zur See durchgebrochen, haben Zoppot erobert und den deutschen Kessel gespalten. Der Restkessel von Königsberg ist in Auflösung begriffen. Heiligenbeil, die letzte deutsche befestigte Stellung, ist gefallen.

that they will remain in a pristine state in perpetuity. One collection of exceptional items consists of the propaganda leaflets devised by Heym and his team [152]. A second comprises copies of *Frontpost*, a mini-newspaper dropped by the American air force over German lines [153]. The idea of such a paper came from Heym, and he was responsible for much of the content. These papers were produced in great haste, often on mobile printing presses, and by a unit which was constantly on the move. Heym jealously preserved copies of them all (there are over fifty); given the circumstances under which they were created, their present condition is outstanding. Also in the Archive are Heym's complete typescripts for broadcasts given on Radio Luxemburg: these were intended to inform the enemy of Allied progress and to weaken morale. For his bravery during this period, Heym was awarded the Bronze Star [154].

Heym's numerous war adventures, and also his doubts about American policy in Germany after the war, are brought out in his great novel *The crusaders,* a work of some 300,000 words. Heym worked on this for three years, made very long and detailed plans, undertook massive revisions. The

154. The certificate which accompanied Heym's award of the Bronze Star following the Battle of the Bulge.

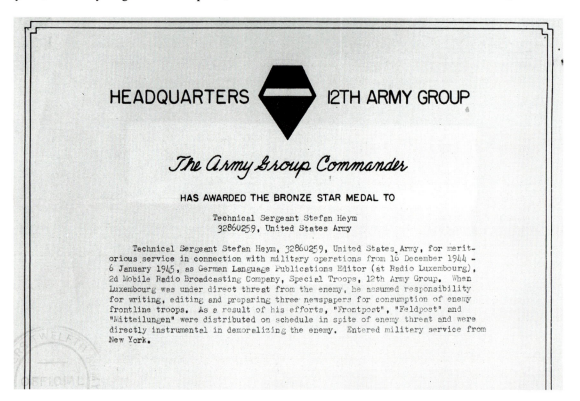

HEADQUARTERS   12TH ARMY GROUP

The Army Group Commander

HAS AWARDED THE BRONZE STAR MEDAL TO

Technical Sergeant Stefan Heym
32860259, United States Army

Technical Sergeant Stefan Heym, 32860259, United States Army, for meritorious service in connection with military operations from 16 December 1944 – 6 January 1945, as German Language Publications Editor (at Radio Luxembourg), 2d Mobile Radio Broadcasting Company, Special Troops, 12th Army Group. When Luxembourg was under direct threat from the enemy, he assumed responsibility for writing, editing and preparing three newspapers for consumption of enemy frontline troops. As a result of his efforts, "Frontpost", "Feldpost" and "Mitteilungen" were distributed on schedule in spite of enemy threat and were directly instrumental in demoralizing the enemy. Entered military service from New York.

success of the novel, however, justified the labour: four printings were made within three weeks of publication, and over two million copies, in English, and in some 18 other languages, have been produced to date. The Archive holds all these translations, as well as the translations of all other works by the author, in languages ranging from Armenian to Vietnamese.

Heym was a socialist. Despite an affluent family background, he seems to have been attracted to socialism from his teens, and practically all his early pieces are on social issues. A left-wing tendency is dominant in the final pages of *The crusaders* and throughout his next major novel, *The eyes of reason* (1951). In the late forties and early fifties, the US turned against socialism and Senator McCarthy began hounding left-wing intellectuals. In 1951, then, Heym and his wife left the United States and tried to find a country in Europe in which they might settle. They were eventually offered a home in the German Democratic Republic (GDR), and Heym has remained there ever since.

Eighteen months after he arrived in the GDR, the country provided Heym with material for one of his most famous works. In June 1953, there was an uprising in East Berlin and several other large cities. It was the first major revolt in the communist bloc, and it was swiftly crushed by Soviet tanks. The government of the GDR was bewildered. How could working men rise up against a state supposedly run *for* the workers? There was obviously only one way in which the uprising could be explained: it was a West-inspired plot, aimed at toppling the government and then taking over the country.

It was at this point that Heym swung firmly into journalism again, writing a lively column which supported the ideals of socialism but which regularly attacked the way in which they were being implemented. On the uprising, he censured the government for being out of touch with the workers. So shaken was that government by what had happened that it allowed his articles to be printed. He went on to attack bureaucracy, local party officials, party directives; he was severe in his exposure of whitewashing, of proving the Party was always right; he constantly spoke up for the workers. He was also a sharp critic of capitalism. Heym's column, the most popular in the GDR, stood out from mainline GDR journalism through its boldness, originality and vitality. Three years later, though, pressure was put on the author to give it up. Naturally, the Archive has all the papers relating to this activity, but it also has something else: thousands of letters from readers and carbon copies of Heym's replies. Some congratulate Heym on his courage; some urge him to espouse a cause in which they are involved; very few criticize him. These letters offer a touching insight into the way people thought in those bleak years of the mid-fifties, when people were fleeing the GDR in their thousands every week.

Heym's novel based on the June uprising was to become the most famous unpublished work in the Republic. Although its working title, *A day marked X*, suggested its general adherence to the Eastern government view of the uprising – that is, that the West played a major role in events – Heym also exposed many weaknesses in Eastern government. He was particularly critical of the Socialist Party.

In East Germany, publishing houses were state-owned, and so publishers' readers were censors by another name. They clearly would not allow a work like this to appear. Heym could have published the novel in the West, which quickly picked up news of what was going on, and for years his inability to have the title accepted for print was a key item in their attacks on the censorship system of the other German state. Yet Heym knew that publication in the West at this period in time would be dangerous. He waited; re-wrote sections of the novel several times; completely changed his view of events; and substantially modified the theme of a West-inspired conspiracy. The text was finally published in West Germany in 1977, with the East having promised to bring it out at the same time. In the end, though, it appeared in the West alone. Heym's frequent reworking of the manuscript, and its translation, can be recognized in Plate [155]. As with the majority of his other novels (and there are twelve in all), the author has had most of the working papers bound handsomely.

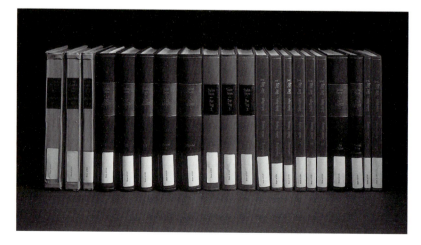

155. Twenty-one volumes of material covering events, character studies, outline, revision, translation, discarded material and final typescripts of *Der Tag X/A day marked X*.

The Berlin Wall was erected in 1961, and the East German government tightened its control over intellectuals and writers. In 1965 Heym, and several others, were viciously attacked by Erich Honecker at a major Party conference. Curbs on his literary activities became more severe; nothing by him was to be published in the country; his speeches and readings were cancelled; his trips abroad were curtailed; study of his works was banned in the universities.

Heym fought the ban vigorously, using the platform of socialist gatherings outside the Republic to deliver some of his most lively attacks. From now on, the Eastern leaders undoubtedly wanted Heym to leave, for he represented a constant, and popular, source of criticism. The secret police, the 'Stasi', which had previously watched him only moderately closely, devoted greater attention to him. His house was consistently bugged. Over the next decade every aspect of his life was scrutinized. It was not until the secret police files were opened that Heym was to learn what had actually been done.

156. Early in 1977 Heym found a notebook near his house, which contained jottings by a group of secret service agents who had been detailed to watch him.

Every object in his house was photographed. His private diary was put onto microfilm and translated into German. All his mail was read, and since there was much English correspondence, this too was all translated into German. His telephone calls were taped. Every visitor to his house was photographed. At various stages he was followed everywhere [156].

Heym's secret police file was one of the largest in the country, and it is a part of his life. He has photocopied most of it, and in due course he wishes the photocopies to come to Cambridge. They will have to be embargoed for twenty-five years after his death, but they will then reveal numerous aspects of GDR espionage and state control. A small foretaste is shown in Plate [157]. So important was Heym in the eyes of the GDR, that even his request for a visa to make a brief trip to the West had to be approved by the head of the government.

Heym was, to the surprise of many, never imprisoned for what he did; his arrest would have caused an uproar in both parts of the German nation. He knew that he had support from the ordinary people in the East, but many of his works were banned and he was never featured on Eastern tele-

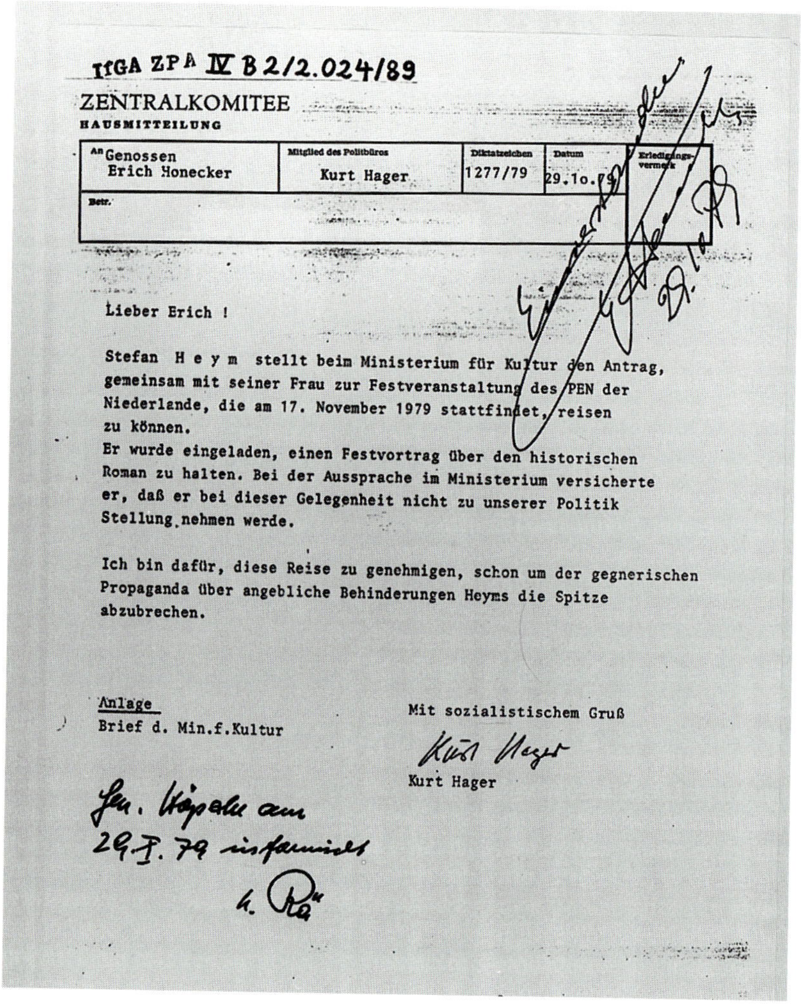

IfGA ZPA **IV** B 2/2.024/89

ZENTRALKOMITEE
HAUSMITTEILUNG

An Genossen Erich Honecker	Mitglied des Politbüros Kurt Hager	Diktatzeichen 1277/79	Datum 29.10.79	Erledigungs-vermerk
Betr.				

Lieber Erich !

Stefan H e y m stellt beim Ministerium für Kultur den Antrag, gemeinsam mit seiner Frau zur Festveranstaltung des PEN der Niederlande, die am 17. November 1979 stattfindet, reisen zu können.
Er wurde eingeladen, einen Festvortrag über den historischen Roman zu halten. Bei der Aussprache im Ministerium versicherte er, daß er bei dieser Gelegenheit nicht zu unserer Politik Stellung nehmen werde.

Ich bin dafür, diese Reise zu genehmigen, schon um der gegnerischen Propaganda über angebliche Behinderungen Heyms die Spitze abzubrechen.

Anlage
Brief d. Min.f.Kultur

Mit sozialistischem Gruß

Kurt Hager

157. A photocopy of an internal memo from the Politbüro, the effective 'cabinet' of the GDR. Kurt Hager, one of the most powerful members, reports Heym's request for a visa. Honecker's agreement ('Einverstanden. E. Honecker. 29.10.79') is featured in the top right.

vision. He therefore tried to cultivate the support of his fellow citizens by appearing as often as possible on Western television, usually making controversial statements about both German states. The Archive holds the tapes of all such appearances; it also contains numerous audio-tapes of readings, interviews and discussions from the fifties to the present day.

Heym was a great people's hero, much to the embarrassment of the leadership, not least because the writer was seen as a crucially important figure in socialist societies. One of Heym's novels, probably his best, makes this very point about the power of the writer. *The King David report*, published in 1972/3, is superficially concerned with how the biblical story of King David,

158. Heym normally used the typewriter for his outlines, but the parallel columns here demanded longhand. The division is into 'Organisation of chapter'; 'Method of telling'; 'Points covered'.

in the Books of Samuel and the Kings, came to be written. Who actually wrote it? What constraints was he working under? What compromises had to be made? This brilliant text, which illustrates the problems of any writer in a totalitarian state, is the most complex Heym ever wrote and Plate [158] shows some of his detailed planning. Plate [159] reveals a page of the translation into German. The original parodies the Authorized Version; the translation, Luther's Bible. The Archive contains thirteen separately bound volumes covering every aspect of the novel's composition and translation, as well as material relating to the successful rock opera which was based on it [160].

159. Heym's corrections show his constant striving for the right tone in this typical page of the translation from English into German.

DDR-Erstaufführung
Rock-Oper

nach Stefan Heym
von T. Miklós/G. Kemeny/T. Kocsák

Der König David Bericht

Volkstheater   Halberstadt

160. One of the few posters advertising Heym's work. *King David* was published (in a very small print run) during the 'thaw' following the election of Honecker. The rock opera based on the novel enjoyed considerable success in Hungary, but performance in the GDR was restricted.

Heym published his next novel, *Collin,* an attack on Party hacks, in the West – without obtaining GDR permission; for this he was fined and expelled from the Writers' Union. That meant he was stripped of his pension rights and the numerous privileges accorded to writers in the GDR. Following this, Heym spoke out fearlessly to Western journalists, and as a result of his comments a new law was hastily introduced into the GDR criminal code. It carried a penalty of up to five years' imprisonment for anyone who communicated to foreigners information which could be seen to 'damage' the GDR – a law promptly referred to in the West as the 'Lex Heym'. The key papers relating to this episode are all contained in the three large boxes in which the author placed prime items around which he constructed his autobiography, *Nachruf* (1988); much of this was also based on his diary entries [161].

Despite the difficulties constantly placed in his way Heym kept on fighting, and never more so than in the final days of the Republic. He was one of the first to recognize the power of Gorbachev's thinking, and he was a consistent supporter of moves to liberalization in the other countries of the communist bloc. In the last few months before the collapse of the Republic, at the age of seventy-six, he wrote some of the best articles of his career. Interestingly, they did not urge either the overthrow of the government or the unification of Germany: they preached the building of a truly socialist state in which all could develop freely. This was also the theme of his powerful speeches of the time, one of them delivered to a crowd of up to a million people in East Berlin. The Archive contains a very large number of cuttings from the international press covering every aspect of his political activities at this point. There are also numerous videos.

Heym's disappointment with the new united Germany resulted in his decision to place his archive, in December 1992, in Cambridge University Library, where he considered it would be safe and where no item would be suppressed. Personal contacts with Cambridge had convinced him that the Archive would be fully secure there and would be treated with respect. He continues to visit and to send material, and much of a political nature was added during and after his successful campaign to enter the German Parliament in 1994 (when he became 'Alterspräsident', Father of the House).

The above outline has been of necessity highly selective, but the actual size of the holdings can be gauged by the fact that, apart from several hundred hardback volumes, there are 281 boxes of literary manuscripts, 75 boxes of correspondence, 35 boxes of newspaper clippings, approximately 300 audio-cassettes and over 100 video-cassettes.[1] There are, obviously, very few gaps in what has been preserved of the rich inner and outer experience of a fearless intellectual, a writer, translator, journalist, and politician.

1. For a more precise listing of the holdings, see P. Hutchinson, 'The Stefan Heym Archive in Cambridge University Library', *German Life and Letters*, 46 (1993) 291–6. Thanks to the generosity of the Leverhulme Trust, a complete catalogue of the Archive was completed in 1997.

161. Diary entries, typed out and pasted onto separate sheets, as *aide-memoires* for Heym's autobiography. The entries make clear how regularly Heym was in contact with leading figures of the Republic.

```
GENERAL -  GDR CULTURE  - Saw Hoffmann - gave him Biermann
letter -   talked of cultural problems, the man agrees with
my viewpoints  mostly, asking  me to be discreet about his
Ketzereien - details see - July 16, 73
Plenzdorf dropped by - saw Held of cultural dept CC - Held
told him of two groupings in Politbureau - July 19

GENERAL GDR  - Honecker meeting - Werner of Min of Culture
- if I had time tomorrow 10 AM for meeting with Honecker -
alone.  Said I thought it was possible July 25, 73
Detailed report, July 26, 73
Honecker told  me that Ulbricht before his stroke had said
he once more wanted  to have  a  talk  with  me  (I  had
approached Lotte  about an interview with Ulbricht) - July
26, 73
```

Chapter 12

The Royal Commonwealth Society Library

John M. Mackenzie

O<small>F ALL THE</small> many great additions to the Cambridge University Library over the past few hundred years, the collection of the Royal Commonwealth Society (RCS) is both the largest and the most diverse. It is also the most recent, having been acquired only in 1993. In many respects it is indeed a 'collection' rather than a 'library' since its great strengths lie not only in books, but also in ephemera, official publications, rare newspapers, illustrations of all sorts, cuttings, photographs, private papers, diaries and even artefacts. Thus, as well as one of the greatest collections of books on European empires, its treasures include the magnificent Cobham Collection of materials on Cyprus, ranging from the earliest book in the Society's library to an assemblage of nineteenth-century pamphlets and ephemera; early gazettes and papers from West Indian and West African colonies of the late eighteenth and early nineteenth centuries; hand-written cyclo-styled newspapers from newly acquired territories in the era of the Scramble for Africa; panoramas of nineteenth-century India and no fewer than 70,000 photographs, including albums of royal visits to the Empire; as well as extraordinary artefacts such as a feather from the crown of the Zulu king Cetshwayo, an eighteenth-century pocket globe, a south Pacific musical instrument, a slave shackle, and even a statue of the Virgin Mary saved from the ruins of Saint-Pierre after the great 1902 eruption of Mount Pelée on the French Caribbean island of Martinique.

To comprehend how such a remarkable assemblage of materials came together, we need to understand both the history and objectives of the Society that spawned it and the interests and personalities of the librarians who stamped their dedication, individuality and scholarship upon it. Its unique value to the student of imperial history can be demonstrated by establishing a scholarly 'trail' in a specific region and period, while both illustrations and examples can reveal its diverse riches.

162. Title page from Fra Bianchi
Noe, *Viaggio da Venetia al S. Sepolcro…*
(Bassano, *c.* 1540), from the Cobham
Collection; the oldest book in the
RCS collections.

The Society, its library and librarians

The Royal Commonwealth Society Library truly takes the world as its oyster. The startling scale and chronological complexity of the British Empire from the sixteenth to the twentieth centuries ensures that such a great collection as this offers a major route into global studies. In any case, this library never concentrated solely on the British Empire and Commonwealth. Since its founders were principally interested in colonial 'intelligence', the comparative aspects of imperialism were as important to them as the national and patriotic. From its beginnings in the 1870s and 1880s, the era of the so-called 'New Imperialism', the library concerned itself with works of European exploration and expansion from the fifteenth century, as well as with the administration of rival empires, notably that of Germany. As imperial rule progressed to its nationalist fall, the library continued to add to its holdings in non-partisan ways.

Indeed, the identity of the Royal Commonwealth Society was inseparably bound up with its library. At a meeting on 26 June 1868, when it was proposed to found a Colonial Society, the Right Honourable Chichester Fortescue, who had been Parliamentary Under-Secretary for the colonies between 1859 and 1866, suggested that 'the formation of a colonial library, to which all interested in the welfare of the colonies should have access ... would be one of the most useful portions of your general scheme'.[1] By the end of 1868 the newly formed Society had secured promises from both the Colonial Secretary and the Secretary of State for India that colonial governors would donate books, official papers, newspapers and other materials relating to their territories.

The Colonial Society – which received its charter as the Royal Colonial Institute in 1882 and was subsequently re-named the Royal Empire Society in 1928 and the Royal Commonwealth Society in 1958 – was the first of a wave of patriotic and imperial societies founded in the second half of Queen Victoria's reign. Together, all of these heralded a quickening of interest in the economic, administrative, scientific and emigration potential of the British Empire. The objectives of the Colonial Society were to provide a meeting place for those gentlemen (women were not admitted until the early 1920s, but African and Asian Fellows were active from at least 1880) interested in colonial and Indian affairs, there to discuss and to listen to papers on imperial issues. Integral to this was the establishment of a 'Reading Room and Library, in which recent and authentic intelligence

1. *Proceedings of the Colonial Society*, 1 (1870) 6, quoted in Trevor R. Reese, *The history of the Royal Commonwealth Society 1868–1968* (London, 1968), p. 25. See also Donald H. Simpson, 'An internationally famous library', in *Royal Commonwealth Society centenary souvenir*, ed. Harry Miller (London, 1968), pp. 55–9.

2. Reese, *History of the RCS*,
Appendices A and B: the objects
of the Royal Colonial Institute,
and the supplemental charter of
the RCS, pp. 259–60.

upon Colonial and Indian subjects may be constantly available, and a Museum for the collection and exhibition of Colonial and Indian productions'. The latter function was largely taken over by the Imperial Institute, opened in 1892, but the Society continued to devote itself to undertaking 'scientific, literary, and statistical investigations'.[2]

These interests help to reflect why the word 'library' has always seemed rather restrictive in describing such a diverse assemblage illustrative of the relationship between Europe and the wider world. Yet when we use the word to mean a physical location, it is apparent that the growing society was very much influenced by the materials it collected. The first rooms of the Society, rented above a shirt shop in the Strand, were taken precisely to accommodate the library. When it was proposed in 1885 that the Society should move to its own extensive premises in Northumberland Avenue, the needs of the library were a prime consideration. When those premises were completely reconstructed to designs by Sir Herbert Baker between 1934 and 1936, yet again the library's requirements were at the forefront of the design. When a public appeal was launched in the 1930s, the library inspired a letter of support, 'some world-wide opinions and appreciations', from scores of scholars and educational figures in Europe, the United States and the Empire. This letter stressed that the Society offered totally free access, without charge, to all readers, regardless of their affiliations or origins. That remained the proud boast of the Society and its library throughout its history in Northumberland Avenue.

3. Royal Empire Society, *Appeal
brochure* (London, 1934), p. 5.

Yet the initial growth of the holdings had been slow. The first catalogue, charmingly hand-written in an exercise book in 1872, indicated that the library contained 273 items, not including official publications and its files of colonial newspapers. The first printed version, attached to the *Proceedings* in 1877, revealed that it had only doubled in the previous five years. By 1886, however, a much more sophisticated catalogue listed over 7,000 titles, including 4,700 volumes and 1,600 pamphlets. Its growth was now rapid, and substantial catalogues or supplements were issued in 1895, 1901, and, in four volumes, between 1930 and 1937: 'the most complete bibliography of the Overseas Empire yet published'.[3] When the library was packed and stored during the reconstruction of the headquarters in the 1930s, it was discovered to contain 244,000 items, weighing 130 tons and filling 36 pantechnicons. By the time the collection came to be moved to Cambridge in 1993 those statistics had well-nigh doubled.

Few libraries can have been more influenced by their librarians: only five of them have held the office between 1889 and the present. The riches of the library more than amply prove that all these librarians were adept at supplementing tiny book allocations by maintaining the initial tradition of securing major contributions from official sources and colonial governments, exchange arrangements with publishers and sister societies, as well as from members and other individuals.

The first full-time librarian, J. R. Boosé, handled a book budget of £100 *per annum* in the 1890s, rising to £200 by 1907. During his period the library grew seven-fold and had already established itself as a major scholarly resource by the end of his tenure.

Boosé's successor, P. Evans Lewin, held office for 37 years, from 1909 to 1946. He emerged as a major scholar and bibliographer in the field of imperial studies, devised the library's classification system, produced the multi-volume catalogue of the 1930s, and supervised the storage of the library and its transfer into the Baker building between 1934 and 1936. Under Lewin, the library expanded in a variety of ways. During the First World War, he wrote a report for the Foreign Office on the German administration in Africa and this interest was naturally reflected in the library's holdings. From 1927 the library issued a quarterly bulletin of all overseas official publications received, an invaluable compilation. The chairman of the Society's council, Sir William Clark, was influential in securing the gift of a collection of books on the Portuguese Empire when he spent some time in Lisbon during the Second World War. Indeed the manpower necessities of the war kept Lewin in office until the age of 70: he therefore had the sad task of rescuing the library after a German bomb passed through the Northumberland Avenue building on the night of 16–17 April 1941, destroying 35,000 volumes and 5,000 pamphlets and documents in the newspaper room and law library. Mercifully, the main library survived.

The librarian from 1946 to 1956, James Packman, continued the work of reconstruction, which included major repairs to the building, including the library itself. Sensibly, it was decided not to replace the law library in its original form. This post-war period also saw the revival of many of the projects which had placed the library at the forefront of imperial studies. The library and its librarians had been closely associated with the imperial studies committee of the University of London, with the imperial studies series of monographs founded in 1926 and with essay competitions on empire topics. All of these were now revived.

Such activities were to flourish under the second great librarian of the twentieth century, Donald Simpson, who had joined the library staff in 1945 and served as librarian from 1956 to 1987. He became a major scholar of the Empire and Commonwealth as well as a bibliographical and research adviser to many of the students and writers who used the collections. His *Library Notes* became essential reading, and information and enjoyment can now be gleaned from them in Cambridge University Library. He was influential in securing funding for the cataloguing of the photographic collection and he became particularly active both in the field of African exploration and in Canadian studies. His book, *Dark companions*, an account of the African contribution to nineteenth-century exploration, revealed the necessity of avoiding a purely European-centred approach. He also fought, with a quiet and dogged determination, the many battles which were required to maintain the library as a central aspect of the Society's activities.

By the time he retired and, in 1988, handed over to his successor, Terry Barringer, whom he himself had trained, the character of the Society was sadly changing beyond recognition. Throughout the twentieth century, many of its leading lights had feared that it would become merely a club; they had stressed that it was an intellectual institution or it was nothing, that the library was central to all its purposes. By the late 1980s, however, much of the older membership was dying out. The users of the library and the members of the Society were increasingly becoming two discrete groups. When major financial difficulties arose, club members began to see the library as a sort of giant cuckoo which could not be nurtured and sustained.

The succession of events that led to the transfer of the library to Cambridge has been chronicled by the present librarian elsewhere.[4] Somehow, through all these difficulties, she maintained the library's traditions: her publications on its resources, including a recent survey of the photographic collection, have been highly informative and valuable for all who work in the field.[5] Without her, and her comprehensive and detailed knowledge of the collections, the establishment of the library in Cambridge would have been a much less successful operation. Not the least of the treasures of the Royal Commonwealth Society Library have been its remarkable librarians.

4. T. Barringer, 'The rise, fall and rising again of the Royal Commonwealth Society Library', *African Research and Documentation, Journal of the Standing Conference on Library Material on Africa*, 64 (1994) 1–10.

5. T. Barringer, 'Images of Africa in the Royal Commonwealth Society collections', *African Research and Documentation*, 68 (1995) 85–91.

A scholarly 'trail'

The Royal Colonial Institute moved into its new premises in North-umberland Avenue in August 1885. It was a critical year in the history of European imperialism and of Africa. In Britain, politicians and public alike were agog at the events of the Partition of the so-called 'Dark Continent'. Bismarck's Berlin Conference had ended in February of that year; General Gordon had died in Khartoum; the Germans had unexpectedly appeared in east, west and south-west Africa; while events in southern Africa were poised for a major European push into the interior which would eventually lead to the foundation of the territories of Northern and Southern Rhodesia (Zambia and Zimbabwe), as well as Nyasaland (Malawi). Cecil Rhodes had secured his 'Suez Canal to the interior' through the British annexation of Bechuanaland, part of the modern Botswana. Concession-seekers and treaty-hawkers were congregating at the capital of King Lobengula of the Ndebele near the modern Bulawayo. Key concessions were secured in 1888 and acquired by Rhodes. His British South Africa Company was chartered by the British government in 1889, and in 1890 he sent a Pioneer Column into the interior to seek gold and found a white settlement on the Mashonaland plateau. The 1890s were to see this settle-ment pass through many vicissitudes: the gold was not forthcoming despite the presence of the ruins of Great Zimbabwe which were erroneously thought to confirm that this was indeed the biblical Land of Ophir. Africans resisted this intrusion with great vigour and the whites faced war and revolt which almost destroyed their relatively tenuous hold on the region.

The Library of the Royal Commonwealth Society offers an almost unri-valled opportunity to study these events. Official papers can of course be found in the Public Record Office; in the National Archives of Zimbabwe are rich deposits of private correspondence, together with oral materials relating to the period. For the student in Britain, however, the RCS Library has a greater diversity of published, official, ephemeral, manuscript and photographic material. Naturally, the library holds the published versions of the Portuguese records of the sixteenth and seventeenth centuries relat-ing to the area, as well as superb copies of all the books published on central Africa in the nineteenth century, including Livingstone's *Missionary travels and researches* of 1857 and the *Narrative of an expedition to the Zambezi and its tributaries* of 1865, the works of Karl Mauch, Frederick Courteney Selous and many others. The library also has the fine Oppenheimer series of publications dating from the 1940s, including the fascinating *Goldfield diaries* of Thomas Baines, artist, explorer and prospector, and the *Zambezi journal* of James Stewart, the associate of Livingstone who was so influential in the founding of missions in Nyasaland.

One might expect to find such works in any good library. Here, though, there are also manuscripts, for example the papers, folders and notebooks of the Reverend François Coillard of the Paris Evangelical Society who worked in Barotseland (in the upper Zambesi, the western region of the modern Zambia) from 1878. But perhaps the most remarkable attribute of the RCS collection is that the librarians created a unique chronological subject index from journal articles in a vast range of periodicals. This index is a treasure trove in itself, even before the materials which it accesses are summoned up. Moreover, nothing was beneath contempt: all forms of 'puffs', propaganda and travel accounts were grist to the mill of the librarians and the readers they served. This was far-sighted: historians, formerly so obsessed with official documents, have recently become much more interested in such sources, replete as they are with colourful insights into their age.

Rhodes's new territories – and therefore the history of Zimbabwe – are magnificently served by these materials. We find articles by A. Campbell on 'The land of the Matabele' from *Canadian Monthly* of 1876; by the Reverend John Mackenzie on Mashonaland and Matabeleland in the *Scottish Geographical Magazine* of 1887; and by Frederick Selous on 'Mashunaland and the Mashunas' in the *Fortnightly Review* of May 1889. Once the Pioneer Column had arrived in 1890, the journals were full of puffs for the new territory. We find ecstatic commentaries by E. A. Maund on 'Our new colony: Zambesia, Matabele- and Mashonalands' in the *Journal of the Tyne Geographical Society* for 1891; by F. Mandy on 'Golden Mashonaland' in *Scribner's Magazine* of 1892; by T. C. Collings on 'Mashonaland and Rhodesia as a field for the settler' in *Travel* of 1896 (he wrote in an unfortunate year, since, even as he was published, the Ndebele and Shona peoples were breaking out into revolt); by Colonel J. Y. F. Blake on 'Golden Rhodesia: a revelation' in the *National Review* of 1897; and by Selous again on 'The economic value of Rhodesia' in the *Scottish Geographical Magazine* of 1897.

If these titles give something of the flavour of an entire era, consider the pamphlets that appear in the same listings. We find F. O. Oates, *Matabeleland and the Victoria Falls: a naturalist's wanderings in the interior of South Africa* of 1881, strategically reprinted in 1889. More evocative are Eglinton and

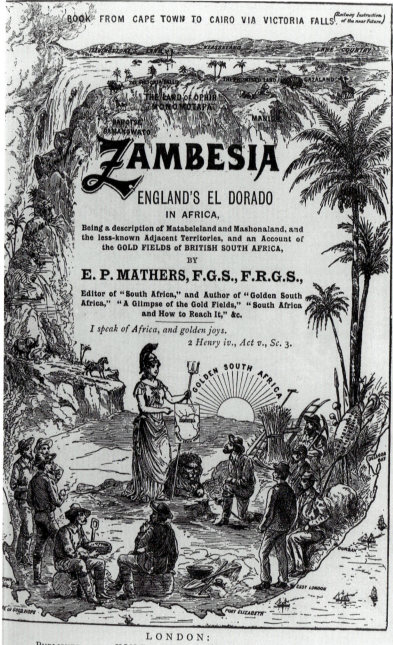

163. Title page from E. P. Mathers, *Zambesia: England's El Dorado in Africa* (London, 1891).

Company's *Handbook on Mashonaland, the country and how to reach it* of 1891–2; Sir J. P. Fitzpatrick's *Through Mashonaland with pick and pen* of 1892; the anonymous *From the Cape to Buluwayo; or how to travel to Rhodesia through British territory, by one who has done it*, 36 pages with maps, published in Vryburg in 1896 for 2 shillings.

This obsession with actually getting there is supplemented by the official publications of the British South Africa Company, including an early pamphlet entitled *General information of the country and press notices*: *information for intending settlers to Southern Rhodesia* of 1901; *A land of sunshine: Rhodesia 1909*; and (evidence of more settled conditions) *Rhodesia for tourists and sportsmen: an official handbook* of 1912; or *Splendid farming opportunities in Rhodesia: official illustrated handbook*, of the same year. Women were also active in this publishing bonanza. We find C. Cameron's *A woman's winter in Africa: a 26,000 mile journey*, and Mrs Tawse Jollie's articles on 'Back of beyond in Rhodesia' and 'Some humours of housekeeping in Rhodesia', respectively in *United Empire* and *Blackwood* in 1916. Other entries range from E. P. Mathers's rare 480-page book on *Zambesia: England's El Dorado in Africa*, of 1891, to H. B. Pope's 4-page *Life in Rhodesia: the Land of Ophir* of 1912, while the Reverend J. Springer beautifully combined God and Mammon in his *Heart of Central Africa: mineral wealth and missionary opportunity*, published in Cincinatti in 1909 [163].

Many of the settlers in Mashonaland, and, from late 1893 in Matabeleland as well, must have been blissfully unaware that they were the subjects of this major publishing event. They were battling against disappointing prospecting results (perhaps the land was not the El Dorado it was being depicted as), heavy rains, and, later, severe drought, agricultural failure, fierce resistance from Africans, incompetent administration and high prices, not to mention plagues of locusts and the cattle disease, rinderpest. As Albert, later Earl, Grey was to put it in 1896, all the plagues of Egypt were afflicting the nascent colony.

Cut off as they were in central Africa, what they craved was news. That craving was satisfied by a series of extraordinary newspapers, hand-written, often on lined ledger paper, and cyclostyled. These included the *Mashonaland Herald* and the *Zambesia Times*, the *Rhodesia Chronicle and Mashonaland Advertiser*, the *Mashonaland Times and Mining Chronicle*, the *Matabeleland News and Mining Record*, the *Umtali Advertiser*, the *Rhodesia Weekly Review*, the rather hopefully entitled *Nugget*, and the *Bulawayo Sketch*. The library has runs of all of these dating from as early as 1892: their

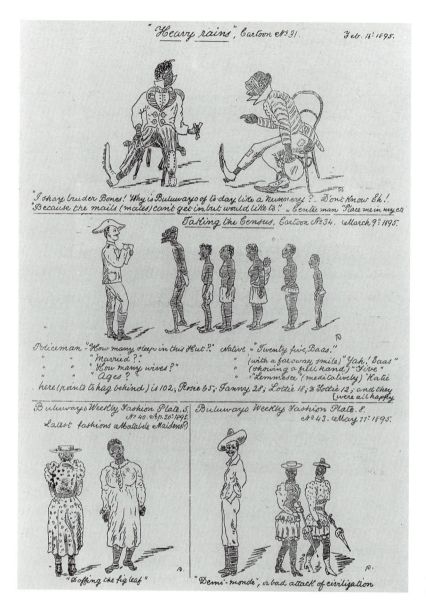

164. Cartoons from the *Bulawayo Sketch* of 1895.

advertisements, articles, leaders and snippets of world news provide more fascinating insights into the lives of the early settlers and their relationships with Africans than any number of official documents could provide [164].

The nature of their production meant that they could contain cartoons (some with racial content), but no photographs. The library, however, is not short of photographic evidence for the same period. The Reverend F.

165. One of W. Ellerton Fry's photographs of Mashonaland, around 1890, showing Chief Chibi (in white blanket, second from the right) and his followers, with two members of the Pioneer Column.

166. One of many pamphlets promoting the delights of Rhodesia for the settler and traveller, 1929.

Surridge, who had been chaplain to the Pioneer Column, presented photographs of Mashonaland and Matabeleland in 1891. They are captioned in fine copperplate and are presumed to be the originals of slides he used when he gave a talk to the Society in that year. The Column, indeed, had its own official photographer, W. Ellerton Fry, and the collection contains an album of superb high-quality photographs (148 prints in all) taken by him, one of fewer than 20 copies that survive [165].

The collection becomes even richer from Edwardian times and into the years between the First and Second World Wars. There are boxes of tourist brochures; emigration booklets; publications of the Rhodesia Resources Committee and of the Wembley Exhibition; and leaflets on the agricultural and mineral products of the country [166]. And, as evidence that the colony continued to be talked up in all sorts of unrealistic ways, we find Edna Boddington's *The call of Rhodesia: a Rhodesian romance*, printed in Salisbury and received in the Society in 1938. Accessions continued to reflect the central African dramas of federation, its dissolution, the UDI (Unilateral Declaration of Independence) of Ian Smith's government, and independence under Robert Mugabe in 1980, a mere ninety years – yet seemingly light years away in economic, political and social terms – from Rhodes's company and the early settlers, their photographs, newspapers and propagandist ephemera.

Other treasures

Such a 'trail' could equally be blazed for other territories in different continents and periods. Only a few further illustrations can be offered here. There are, for example, many other rare newspapers contained in the library. These range from the *Jamaica Gazette* of 1788, possibly unique, to the only known surviving copy of the *Royal Gold Coast Gazette* of 1822–4, a paper founded by Sir Charles McCarthy during his ill-fated governorship of the Gold Coast settlements, from March 1822 until his death in the fourth Ashanti War in January 1824; the *St Helena Herald* of 1854; the *Northern Rhodesia Journal* of 1909 (which contains a stirring call to settler independency); and the *Morogoro News*, the journal of the East African Expeditionary Force in 1916. Most valuably, there is an almost complete run of the *Mafeking Mail*, issued throughout the celebrated Boer War siege in 1899–1900. It was issued daily, 'shells permitting', on terms of one shilling per week, 'payable in advance'. The last one, number 150, contains a fascinating advertisement for the purchase of siege stamps from an eager philatelist with a remarkable eye for the main chance [167].

167. The *Mafeking Mail*: special siege edition of 1899.

The very first English-language newspaper in Cyprus was called, somewhat enigmatically, the *Owl*. The library obtained a set for the years 1888–96 in the outstanding Cobham Collection. Claude Delavel Cobham was Commissioner of the district of Larnaca for twenty-eight years, from 1879 to 1907. A man of independent means, he lived in the magnificent early eighteenth-century consulate of the English Levant Company and filled it with his collection of books and pamphlets on his beloved Cyprus. It was presented to the Royal Colonial Institute in 1913 and details of the rare sixteenth- and seventeenth-century books on the island appeared in *Library Notes* for December 1957. This collection is now being microfilmed in its entirety [168].

The British Association of Malaya collection has been heavily used since the move to Cambridge and is similarly a rich mine of photographs,

168. 'Youth and old age' from John Thomson's *Through Cyprus with a camera in the autumn of 1878* in the Cobham Collection. Thomson, best known for his photographs of China, took his camera to Cyprus within a few months of the island passing under British rule, following the Treaty of Berlin in June 1878.

unpublished memoirs and correspondence. Much of this has been micro-filmed for the Singapore National Archives, while the collection as a whole is being made much more accessible to scholars through online cataloguing. Further valuable photographic collections of Malaya have been added recently [169, 170].

The visual materials in the library range from the extremely valuable to the very humble. In the former category would come George French Angas's volume of sixty stunning coloured plates in *The New Zealanders illustrated*, while in the latter might be found a wonderful collection of early twentieth-century picture postcards of Zanzibar, Southern Rhodesia,

169. Tanjong Pagar Docks,
Singapore, c. 1892.

170. Beach Street, Penang,
in the 1890s.

171. Shipping cloves, Zanzibar; one of a series of monochrome postcards of Zanzibar scenes, published around 1925.

172. The Kullar Bridge, from an album of photographs recording the construction of the Nilgiri Railway, India, *c.* 1897 (acquired since the move of the RCS collection to Cambridge).

Nyasaland, the Seychelles and Mauritius. There are photographs taken by the Royal Engineers of the Suakin Field Force in the Sudan campaign of 1885; views of Freetown, Sierra Leone, dating from around 1847; an early sketch of Ottawa; and a spectacular panorama of Simla by Lady Elizabeth Tennant, 380 cm long and dating from the 1860s [171, **227–8**].

It is indeed precisely the idiosyncratic nature of this library which is its great strength. Anti-convict petitions, emigration pamphlets, materials relating to the many Imperial exhibitions, timetables for the Canadian Pacific Railway jostle with great illustrated travel works like William J. Burchell's *Travels in the interior of southern Africa* (2 vols, London, 1822 and 1824), purchased by the Society in June 1887, and invaluable manuscripts such as the letters of E. J. Harding, the secretary of the Dominions Royal Commission, on his tour of the Empire with the members of the Commission in 1913–16 [229].[6]

6. These were edited and published in *Dominions diary: the letters of E. J. Harding 1913–16*, ed. by Stephen Constantine (Halifax, 1992).

Nor is it a dead collection. Since the move to Cambridge University Library, accessions have proceeded apace, including a leather-bound album of photographs relating to the construction of the Nilgiri Railway in south India in the 1890s and an unpublished memoir on the history of the South African Labour Party from 1908 to 1958 [172–6, 230].

The Royal Commonwealth Society Library has survived bombing, fire, flood, theft, endemic financial crisis, and fears that it would be broken up and sold off in the early 1990s. Now that it is securely lodged in Cambridge University Library, it should survive for many more years as a vast and invaluable source for the study of European imperialism.

FIELD & RUSK'S CAMP. CHINESE CREEK. NO. 42.

173. Gold prospectors' camp in forest clearing, Demerara, British Guiana, 1880s.

174. Basket making, African Handicraft School, M'Sonneddi, Rhodesia, 1950s/1960s.

175. Jasper Avenue, Edmonton, Alberta, c. 1910.

176. Feather money: the price of
a girl bought as a teacher's wife,
Santa Cruz, Solomon Islands, 1892
(from an album of sixty photographs taken on a tour undertaken
by Bishop H. H. Montgomery in
the Melanesian mission ship,
Southern Cros

Chapter 13

But scientists are human: some insights into the progress of science

Alan Cook

177. Title-page of Galileo's *Dialogue* (Leiden, 1635) with the Latin form of the title.

1. I. B. Cohen, *Introduction to Newton's Principia* (Cambridge, 1971); D. T. Whiteside, *The mathematical papers of Isaac Newton*, 8 vols. (Cambridge, 1967–81); *The unpublished first version of Isaac Newton's Cambridge lectures on optics, 1670–1672: a facsimile of the autograph, now Cambridge University Library MS Add. 4002* (Cambridge, 1973); D. T. Whiteside, *The preliminary manuscripts for Isaac Newton's 1687 Principia 1684–1685* (Cambridge, 1989).

2. The Library's holdings include R. Descartes, *Discours de la méthode* (Leiden, 1637); P. Gassendi, *Mercurius in Sole visus* (Paris, 1632) and *Istituto Logica et Philosophiae Epicuri syntagma* (London, 1660); Galileo Galilei, *Siderius nuncius* (Venice, 1610) and *Dialogo supra i due massimi sistemi del mondo* (Leiden, 1635).

3. *The scientific letters and papers of James Clerk Maxwell*, ed. P. M. Harman, vols. I and II (Cambridge, 1990, 1995).

The progress of natural philosophy has owed a very great deal to the scholarship, hard work and imagination of members of the University of Cambridge, and the Library holds the works, papers and correspondence of some of the most distinguished and influential of them. Isaac Newton and Charles Darwin stand out among the rest, both for the effect each has had on natural knowledge and our concept of an autonomous world, and also because we have very full information about them. Darwin's papers, the most numerous and comprehensive of the Library's scientific manuscript holdings, are the subject of another chapter (see pages 118–35). Newton's papers in Cambridge are distributed between the Portsmouth Collection in the University Library, and the libraries of Trinity and King's colleges, along with others outside Cambridge, such as that of the Royal Society. They have been intensively studied, especially by I. B. Cohen and D. T. Whiteside, and facsimiles of some have been published for the Library.[1] Newton said that he saw further by standing on the shoulders of giants, and the works of some of those giants are in the Library, including many of the works of Kepler, the philosophies of Descartes and Gassendi, and above all the subversive essays of Galileo [177].[2]

Cambridge was also prominent in the physical sciences in the very fruitful years of the late nineteenth and early twentieth centuries when classical mathematical physics came to maturity and prepared the way for relativity and quantum mechanics. James Clerk Maxwell, the first Cavendish Professor of Experimental Physics, Lord Kelvin, and Sir George Gabriel Stokes are three of the most eminent mathematical physicists whose papers rest in the Library. Maxwell's papers are in the course of publication, as is the correspondence between Kelvin and Stokes.[3] Stokes's spectroscopic studies were a source of quantum physics, but most people will associate that with the discovery of the electron by J. J. Thompson and the many far-reaching investigations of Lord Rutherford into radioactivity and the nuclear structure of the atom. The papers of both these Cavendish professors are in the

Library, as is a further important archive, that of Sir Gerald Lenox-Conyngham, Surveyor-General of India, and the first Reader in Geodesy in the University. Stokes and Sir George Darwin had already done some very important work in mathematical geophysics when Lenox-Conyngham established the Department of Geodesy and Geophysics for observational work. From it there came, especially after the Second World War, profound discoveries and distinguished students who have become leaders in the study of the Earth, in this country and overseas. The physical study of the Earth goes back to the earliest days of Cambridge science, to 1600 when William Gilbert of St John's College, the physician to Queen Elizabeth I, published his *De magnete* and set out his model of the Earth as a great magnet.

The University Library thus holds sources for the study of two of the most crucial periods in the history of physics, but some may ask – do ask – why does the history of science matter? Is there any value in these holdings, other than a pious reverence for our intellectual forebears? Why not throw them away and make space for last week's electronic publications? There are at least four reasons for the study of the history of science. The study of natural science is one of the great human activities. We need to understand how it came to the state it is in now, just as much as we should study the history of economics, or warfare, or art, as aspects of the human condition. Many otherwise well-educated people see science as very mysterious; its history helps to dispel that mysticism and show that it is no less rational than other human pursuits. History also shows that scientific discoveries are not foreordained but are contingent, that the pursuit of science interacts with other human activities. Lastly, the history of science reveals how real scientists go about their studies, and shows especially the place of the untrammelled but prepared imagination in scientific discovery; and that science can be adventurous and fun.

In addition to the major deposits of the papers of individuals, the University Library holds many items, some unsuspected, that illuminate those more human aspects of science and scientists. I have chosen to illustrate that assertion with some material related to the life of Edmond Halley, the younger contemporary of Newton and, after him, the outstanding natural philosopher of the age, as well for the range as for the depth of his studies. Halley, a Londoner and an Oxford man, did not leave a personal archive like those of Newton and Darwin; and many of his papers are elsewhere – in the Royal Society, of which he was first Clerk and later a Secretary when Newton was President; and in the Public Record Office. The

178. A scribal ruling-board used by a student in medieval Cairo. (T-S K11.54)

179. Marcus Tullius Cicero, *De officiis*. The colophon of Johann Fust's and Peter Schoeffer's second edition dated 4 February 1466, with the purchase inscription of John Russell, 17 April 1467.

180. Marcus Tullius Cicero, *De officiis* (Mainz, Fust and Schoeffer, 1465). The first printed edition of a classical text. This copy on vellum was bequeathed by Samuel Sandars in 1894.

181. Bookcases were made in 1717–19 by John Austin to accommodate the Royal Library printed books in the West Room of the Old Schools; they are now on the first-floor galleries of the University Library. This illustration shows the royal arms from the door of one of the enclosures originally intended to hold manuscripts.

182a and 182b. 'Le gouvernement de corps domme' (MS Ii.5.11). Written in the early fifteenth century, the manuscript afterwards belonged to King Henry VII and Queen Elizabeth (of York).

folio 20v. Cupping to draw off blood: 'De ventouser'.

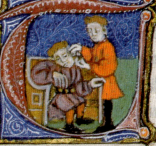

folio 41v. An ear inspection: 'Comment on garde les oreilles'.

PLINIO SECONDO TRADO
TINA PER CHRISTOPHOR
NO AL SERENISSIMO FERI

PREFATION

ITE
impo
narra
uella
lulti
ueriſ
diſſi
Catu
re qu
ſta ca
ſai m
piu c
fami

nai ſcriuerti:& āchora per che le noſtre choſe
mia audacia maxime dolédoti tu che pel paſ
procace epiſtola. Et accio che tutti glhuomin
uiua: Tu elquale hai triomphato & ſe ſtato

183. An illuminated initial from
the Royal Library copy of Pliny's
Historia naturalis in Italian
translation, printed at Venice
by Nicolas Jenson in 1476. The
volume is lavishly decorated by
Venetian or Paduan artists.

184. Christ enthroned amid the
seven candlesticks, from an
Apocalypse in French, part of a
large miscellany written in the
early fourteenth century, possibly
in East Anglia. (MS Gg.1.1)

185. The twelfth-century
Winchester Pontifical from St
Swithin's, showing the mass
for a bishop on the day of his
consecration. (MS Ee.2.3, Royal
Library)

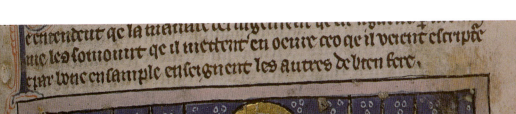

ectendeut qe la tcanuit de laugecence qe au ligne noz p̃ue t̃
qc les comoue qe il meue ẽt en oeure eco qe il ueient escripte
et par loue en sample enseign ent les autres de bien bere.

Eeo me recurual pur ueer la uoiz qe parla od moy e teo ui set
chaun delabres de oz. e entmij lu de set chaun delabres un qi re
semblote le fiz de la uirgine qi estoit uestu de aube deske a teire e

COLUMN OF TRAJAN.

186. 'Trajan's Column' from
J. Mérigot, *A select collection of views
and ruins in Rome and its vicinity*
(London, 1797–9). (John Harley-
Mason Collection)

CHEPSTOW CASTLE.

187. 'Chepstow Castle in
Monmouthshire', from *The
romantic and picturesque scenery of
England and Wales, from drawings by
P. J. de Loutherbourg* (London, 1805).
(John Harley-Mason Collection)

188. 'The Pump Room', from *Bath,*
illustrated by a series of views, from the
drawings of John Claude Nattes (London
and Bristol, 1806). Aquatint by J. Hill.
(John Harley-Mason Collection)

Aqua Roust del. from the original design of Capt.t Thos. Williamson. Shot from Rasala. R. Havll. sculp.

HUNTERS GOING OUT IN THE MORNING · · LES CHASSEURS SORTANT LE MATIN.

Published Jan.y 1.st 1805 by Edw.d Orme, Bookseller to His Majesty 59 Bond Street London.

189. 'Hunters going out in the
morning' from *Oriental field sports.
The whole taken from the manuscript
and designs of Captain Thomas
Williamson* (London, 1807).
(John Harley-Mason Collection)

following spread

190. 'The south side of Wawel
Cathedral in Cracow', from
Ludwik Letowski, *Katedra
Krakowska na Wawelu* (Cracow,
1859). Lithographic plate in two
tints by F. Stroobant. (Norman
Waddleton Collection)

191. 'Chechen and Lezghin
hunters', from T. de Pauly, *Description
ethnographique des peuples de la Russie*
(St Petersburg, 1862). Most of the
chromolithographic plates were
printed in Berlin, Munich and Paris.
(Norman Waddleton Collection)

192. 'The station at Orizaba', from
Album del ferrocarril mexicano.
Colección de vistas pintadas del natural
por Casimiro Castro (Mexico, 1877).
(Norman Waddleton Collection)

193. M. T. H. Perelaer, *Nederlandsch-Indie: de buitenbezittingen* (Leiden, 1883). Plates by J. C. Rappard. (Norman Waddleton Collection)

194. *Hyakumantō darani.* (Invocations of the million pagodas). Between the years AD 764 and 770 a very large number, possibly one million, of the Buddhist invocations known as dhāraṇī were printed in Nara after the empress Shotoku had crushed a rebellion. It was partly an act of religious appeasement but partly also a political act of patronage towards the Buddhist clerical establishment. The Library possesses four of these dhāraṇī, together with the miniature wooden pagodas in which they were originally placed. They are in Chinese, the international language of Buddhism in East Asia, and were probably printed with wood-blocks. They are undated, but many of the pagodas bear dates between the years 764 and 770. Apart from a single dhāraṇi found in Korea and printed about twenty years earlier, they are the oldest printed items in the world that can be dated.

妙法蓮華經藥草喩品第五
介時世尊告摩訶迦葉及諸大弟子善哉善
哉迦葉善說如來真實功德誠如所言如來
復有無量無邊阿僧祇功德汝等若於無量
億劫說不能盡迦葉當知如來是諸法之王
若有所說皆不虛也於一切法以智方便而
演說之其所說法皆悉到於一切智地如來
觀知一切諸法之所歸趣亦知一切眾生深
心所行通達無礙又於諸法究盡明了示諸
眾生一切智慧迦葉譬如三千大千世界山

195. *Myōhō rengekyō.* (The Lotus sūtra). The Lotus Sūtra was translated from Sanskrit into Chinese at the end of the seventh century by Kumārajīva, an Indian monk who worked as a translator in China, and it was extremely popular in Japan from the Heian period (794–1185) onwards. The Library has several copies: shown here is a luxury manuscript executed in gold on indigo paper probably some time in the twelfth century.

196. *Shakumakaenronsan gensho.* (Commentary on the 'Shakumakaenron'). This is a Buddhist exegetical work in Chinese but printed in Japan in 1288 at the Kongōbuji temple on the sacred Mt Kōya. The text is entirely in Chinese, but readers have punctuated the text by hand in red ink and have, in black, added some glosses in Japanese. The ownership seal impressed in red at the bottom of the page is that of Frank Hawley, who went to Japan to teach English in 1931 and assembled an outstanding collection of early Japanese books, all of which were confiscated by the Japanese government on the outbreak of war in 1941, although on his return in 1946 as a correspondent for *The Times* he was able to recover most of them.

197. *Taketori.* (The bamboo cutter). An illustrated manuscript of the *Tale of the bamboo cutter* executed early in the seventeenth century. The *Tale of the bamboo cutter* was probably written in the ninth or tenth century and it includes a number of folkloric elements of worldwide distribution. It is the story of Kaguyahime, the 'Shining Princess', a supernatural being found in a bamboo stem by a bamboo cutter who raises her as his own daughter. She grows up to be a beautiful young woman, but when urged to marry she either refuses or sets her suitors impossible tasks to perform. Finally, she admits that she is from the Palace of the Moon and, donning a robe of feathers, reluctantly leaves this world behind her. The scene shown depicts Kaguyahime and her father with one of the unlucky suitors.

界釋日次唱本論論日至俱成門釋日後作釋有
二初微細眷屬門有三初徵起論本日至則無境
就麁細異分作兩重論初門云何釋日後釋文有
有三初結指論此決擇中至眷屬門釋日次開章
論已訖至無明住地門釋日次眷屬無明住地門
畫報恩傳燈寺崇祿大夫守司空詮圓通法悟奉 勅撰
釋摩訶行論贊其玄跡卷第四

198. Deed of gift of the Acton Library by John Morley to the University of Cambridge, dated 6 February 1903. (University Archives)

199. The arms of Charles Emmanuel III, King of Sardinia and Savoy from 1730 to 1773, stamped in gold on the vellum binding of *Collezione di provvidenze pontificie* (Turin, 1770).

JOHANNES FLAMSTEEDIUS *Derbiensis*
Astronomiæ Professor Regius, Anno Ætatis 74. Obijt
Decem: 31 1719

EDMUNDUS HALLEIUS *R.S.S.*
Astronomus Regius et Geometric Professor Savilianus.

200. John Flamsteed, first
Astronomer Royal, on the title-
page of his *Historia coelestis
Britannica* (London, 1725).

201. Edmond Halley, second
Astronomer Royal, on the
title-page of *Edmundi Halleii
Astronomi dum viveret Regii tabulae
astronomicae accedunt de usu
tabularum praecepta* (London, 1749).

University Library does however hold the archives of the early Astronomers Royal at Greenwich, among them the first, John Flamsteed (of Jesus
College), and the second, Halley. In addition it has books and pamphlets
that display something of Halley's wide acquaintance and his eventful life.
His life was indeed eventful, and reflects the variety of his times, those of
the later Stuarts, at once exhilarating and hazardous.

Although the Library may not hold all the papers of Halley and his contemporaries, the range of its collections is a very great advantage in the
study of their lives and works. Along with some particular book or archive
there is likely to be found related material in a different collection, as well
as many bibliographical reference works. There can be few places in the
world where it is easier to pursue the history of science.

Edmond Halley

Even before he had taken his BA at Oxford, Edmond Halley set off to observe southern stars from the island of St Helena. He also viewed the transit of Mercury across the Sun as Gassendi had done in Avignon some forty-six years before [202]. When he returned he had become the most experienced of all his contemporaries in the novel use of telescopes to measure the positions of stars, and as such he was a welcome visitor to the doyen of astronomers, Johann Hevelius of Danzig. Hevelius did not use telescopes, and so got into bitter dispute with Robert Hooke, a dispute that Halley went out in the summer of 1679 to try to resolve. Hevelius had a wife, Elizabeth, who was thirty years younger than him but about fifteen years older than Halley. Elizabeth was herself a practical astronomer, as may be seen in the picture of her with Hevelius at his large sextant [203]. The picture is surely historic, for it must be the first representation of an actual woman engaged in some scientific activity. It is reproduced from the copy of the *Machina coelestis* that Hevelius presented to the University and that carries his inscription. Hevelius gave an account of the observations that they and others made in the course of Halley's visit in his *Annus climactericus* of 1685; the Library holds the copy that he presented to it [204]. On his return to London, Halley had a gown and petticoat made for Elizabeth at her request. They were very costly and took twenty yards of silk, a quantity that is rendered plausible by figure [203]. Many years later, some ill-disposed person put about the story that Halley and Elizabeth had an illicit affair in Danzig; but that was apparently just malicious Oxford gossip.[4] J. E. Olhoff published selections of Hevelius's correspondence during his lifetime, including letters to, from and about Halley. Again, the copy in the Library is the one Olhoff presented to the University and bears his inscription [205].

Some eighteen months after he returned to London from Danzig, Halley set off for France and Italy in company with his friend Robert Nelson. On the way to Paris from Calais they saw the great comet of 1680, as Halley told Newton, probably in early 1682, after he was back in London.[5] He visited

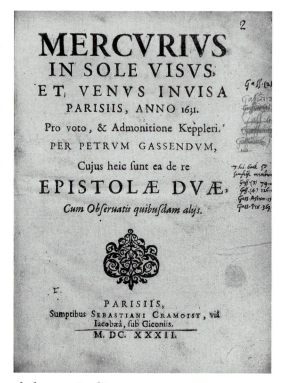

202. Title-page of P. Gassendi, *Mercurius in Sole visus* (Paris, 1632).

4. For Elizabeth Hevelius, see A. Cook, 'Ladies in the scientific revolution', *Notes and Records of the Royal Society of London*, 51 (1997) 1–12.
5. MS Add. 4004, ff. 97r, 99r, 101v.

the director of the new Observatoire in Paris, J.-D. Cassini, and observed the comet with him whenever possible until March 1681 [207].

Newton's aim in the third book of the *Philosophiae naturalis principia mathematica* was to show that mutual gravitational attraction could account for all the motions of the bodies of the solar system. He was successful in deriving Kepler's laws of planetary motion, as well as the polar flattening of the Earth and the precession of the equinoxes. As a result, the *Principia* was very influential in developing ideas of the Enlightenment, especially after Emilie du Châtellet, the vivacious mistress of Voltaire, had translated it into French [206]. Newton found comets, and even more the Moon, difficult to bring within the grasp of gravity. Newton had been interested in comets before he began on the *Principia*, and Halley had already brought him news of the comet of 1680, the study of which was to be prominent in Book III of the *Principia*. About 1695 Halley undertook the calculation of orbits of some twenty comets for Newton, and in doing so identified the comet of 1682 ('Halley's') as one that had appeared before and would return. David Gregory inserted Halley's account in later editions of his textbook of astronomy, *Astronomiae physicae et geometricae elementa*, and the University

203. Johann and Elizabeth Hevelius observing with the great sextant at Danzig (from fig. M of Hevelius, *Machina coelestis*, Pt I (Danzig, 1673)).

Library has a copy of the first edition of Gregory's book with a manuscript version of Halley's tract pasted in it, with a text that does not correspond to any of the printed versions. The book was at one time in a Scottish library, but the original owner is not known [208].

Newton's theory of the Moon has often been said to be a failure, and Halley's observations of the Moon over the twenty years when he was Astronomer Royal, even less satisfactory. That is not quite so. The motion of the Moon had long been known to be erratic and the young Cambridge astronomer, Jeremiah Horrocks, of Emmanuel College, had produced a description of it that Halley improved somewhat [209].

Halley married in 1682 and set up house in Islington, where he began systematic observations of the Moon, but continued them for no more than two years. All that was before Newton had started on the *Principia*. After Halley went to Greenwich in 1720 he observed the Moon systematically for almost twenty years. His records were on loose sheets that, after his death, his colleague John Bevis assembled in a

204. The title-page of Hevelius, *Annus climactericus* (Gedani, 1685), with his inscription presenting the copy to the University Library.

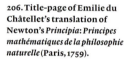

205. Title-page of J. E. Olhoff's selections of Hevelius's correspondence, with his inscription to the University.

206. Title-page of Emilie du Châtellet's translation of Newton's *Principia: Principes mathématiques de la philosophie naturelle* (Paris, 1759).

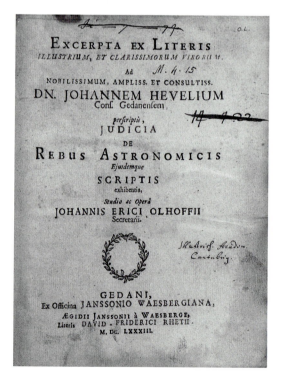

Auticus

Observationes de Cauda Cometæ prioris

Novemb 19 Cometa juxta spicam virginis existens caudam projicie-
bat ad usque caudam Leonis spectante judicio quodam
Postea caudam per meridiem versus occidentem proji-
ciebat longam satis & ad horizontem obliquam capita ... vel sub horizonte
vel pone ædificia delitescente vidit Hump. Bab. S.T.D.

De cauda Cometæ posterioris

Decemb 8 Stylormiteri Hallius noster tempore matutino Parisias
versus iter faciens prope Boloniam ante ortum solis Caudam
vidit Cometæ quasi perpendiculariter ex horizonte surgentem, at
ipse retulit in epistola quadam citante flamstedio. Unde Cometa
inquit flamstedius tunc borealem habebat latitudinem & cum sole
nondum conjunctus fuerat ...
♂ Decemb 10 ... post occasum solis, ibat cauda per medium
distantiæ inter caudam serpentis Ophiuchi et stellam (Bayero δ)
in ala austrina Aquilæ. Desinebat vero ad stellas tres exiguas
(Bayero A ω b) in ... Aquilæ juxta caudam, eductione caudæ
Aquilæ quidem, id est in linea jungente stellam ... secunda
magnitudinis in eductione colli Aquilæ, et stellam tertiæ quæ
penultima est in cauda ejus, & stellæ illi penultimæ [duplo
quidem] propior existebat quam in eductione colli. flamstedius
in Epistola ad nos datis. Desinebat igitur cauda in ♈ 19½ cum
lat. bor. 34¼ circiter
♄ Decemb 11 post occasum solis caudæ instar jubaris apparuit ab
horizonte erecti et lunæ latioris. Post crepusculi cessationem ex
tendebat ad usque stellas quartæ magnitudinis (Bayero α, β,) in capi-
te sagittæ (flamst. ib.) atque desinebat in ♈ 26 gr 43 cum lat
bor. 38 gr 34
☉ Decemb 12 Quamprimum nox obscura facta est, cauda transibat
per medium sagittæ, neque ultra medium longe extendebat. (flamst
ib.) Linquebat igitur stellas 5ta et 6ta magnitudinis, δ et 3 ½
triculo sagittæ quasi 40' ad occidentem, et ultra per 3 gra cir
citer vel forte & extendens desinabat in ... 4 cum lat bor
42½ circiter vel & 43 Desinebat utique e regione superiori
duarum informarum 4ta magnitudinis quæ supra sagittam ...
non et ultra extendebat. Nam cauda ensiformis nobis visa ...
sagittam longius superior quam flamstedio, in viam lacteam
nihil extendens et termino acuto paulatim languescens. Cæ...
in Astrolabio flamstedii, cauda hac nocte ... desinit accurate ...
stellas duas exiguas prædictas in tribule sagittæ
♂ Decemb 15 hor 5½ Lucida Aquila erat in medio caudæ ...
...cauda ...ocon iter austrinus ...Aquila erat...
partim ex circu... Erat autem cauda 50 grad longa ...
... apparitio probabile est.
♄ Decemb 18 Cauda linquebat stellas Delphini ad dextram ...
austrina Cygni quæ tertiæ magnitudinis et ...
...tenet per caudam quarta parte latitudinis ...
...Terminus ...
...distantiam ab horizonte ...
...Cygni Bayero dicto χ Decemb...
...stella stellula ...cauda incurvata...
♂ Dec...

ASTRONOMIÆ COMETICÆ SYNOPSIS

Autore EDMUNDO HALLEIO

apud OXONIENSES

GEOMETRIÆ PROFESSORE SAVILIANO.

Veteres Ægyptii et Chaldæi, si qua Fides Diodoro Siculo, longa observationum serie instructi, Cometarum æffectus prænunciare valuerunt. Cum autem iisdem artibus etiam Terræ motus ac tempestates, prævidisse ferantur, etiam dubium est Astrologæ potius ratrale subducto, quam Astronomiæ Motuum Theoriis, eorum de his rebus scientiam referendam esse. at de alia a Græcis utriusq populi victoribus reparta est apud eos doctrina; adeo ut eam quam nunc oeusq provehimus Astronomiam, Græcis ipsis, præsertim magno Hipparcho, ut Inventoribus, arreptam debeamus. Apud hos vero Aristotelis sententia, qui Cometas nihil aliud esse doluit quam ~~Cometas sublunares~~ Vapores sublunares vel etiam Meteora aerea, tantum obtinet, ut hæc Astronomiæ Inventus pars longe ~~nobilior~~ subtilissima, omnino neglecta manserit, cum nemini operæpretium visum fuerit, vagab et incertab fluctuantium in æthere vaporum semitas adnotare scriptisq mandare; unde factum ut ab aliis nihil fere de motu Cometarum ad nos transmissum reperiatur.

Sensta autem philosophus, perpensis duorum insignium seu temporib Cometarum Phænomenib, non dubitavit ista Loca inter corpora relicta assignare, Sydera esse rem mundo dirarura existimans, quanquam Motus eorum Legibus nondum compertis regi fatebatur. Tandemq vaticinio non irrito promittit aliquando futura secula, quibus hæc tam occulta deteges exhibet at longioris ævi diligentia: quibusq admirationi feret hæc Veteres nostræ potuisse, postquam demonstraverit aliquis Naturæ interpres, quibus Cæli partibus Cometæ oriri, ~~quanq~~ gradales sint. Ab hac autem Senetæ sententia in diversas partes abiit pene omnib Astronomorum Cohorb, at ipse Seneca, neq Phænomena Motus quibus opinionem hanc tueretur, æque tempora asternre dignatus est, quæ possunt ad hæc definienda usui forent. At absoluti pluribus Cometarum Historiib, nihil omnino indenus quod huic negotio inserviæ posse ante annum a Christo nato 1337, quo Nicephorus Gregoras historicus ac Astronomus Constantinopolitanum nobis Cometæ semitam inter fixas satis accuratæ descripsit. Tempora autem nimis sæpe confirmavit, ita ut non nisi quod obtinet quadringentis pene annis apparuere, Liberius et inconfirmavit, ut non nisi quod obtinet quadringentis pene annis apparuere. Adn Cometa anni 1472 omnium recte hic Cometa Catalogo quem damus insere mecabur. hic magnitudine ac velocitate ac terris proximus Regiomontanum habuit observatorem. hic magnitudine ac toma terribilis, unius diei spatio 40 gradus sub Circulo Cæli magno emensus est, ac omnium primus est de quo observata idonea ad nos pervenere. Quotquot autem Cometas conspexerunt usque ad tempora Tychonis Brahe magni illius Astronomiæ restauratoris, sub sublunares esse autumarunt adeoque parvi pendendos rispote pro Vaporibus habitos.

Anno autem ~~eod~~ 1577, Tychone jam studio Astronomiæ serio incumbente, comparatisq machinis ingentibus pro dimetiendis Cæli arcubus cum cura et rectitudine quam Veteribus hactenus fas erat: Emersit Cometa satis conspicuus, cui observando studium sese accinxit Tycho: multisq et fidis experimentis deprehendit, nulli eum sensibili parallaxi diurnæ obnoxium fuisse, adeoq non tantum non fuisse vaporem aerium, sed et etiam multo superiorem existere Lunâ: imo nihil obstare quin inter ipsos Planetas collocaretur; frustra interim contra obstrependibus Scholasticorum nonnullis.

Tychonis vero eximiam in observando industriam excepit Keplerus sagacissimum et pene divinum ingenium. hic Tychonis Laboribus fretus Systema Mundi verum ac physicum adinvenit, ac suo ingenium. Planetas omnes in plano per Solis centrum transeuntibus revolvi, curvasq ellipticas describere, eâ Lege, ut Areas Sectorum Ellptrorum, ad centrum Solis in Ellipsios foco constitui, temporibus quibus describantur æris semper proportionales sint. Invenit etiam distantias Planetarum a Sole esse in sesqui altera ratione temporum periodicorum, sive Cubos distantiarum esse ut Quadrata temporum. Ceterum autem artifici afflixere duo Cometæ, quorum alter maxime illustres. Ceterum observatis autem artifici afflixere duo Cometæ, quorum alter maxime illustres. Ceterum observationis Keplerus non uno parallaxi annua indice, Planetas inter Orbes planetarum his perlustrt Keplerus non uno parallaxi annua indice, Planetas inter Orbes planetarum liberrimum quaquaversum ferri, motu quidem non multum a rectilineo diverso, sed quem nondum definire licuit. At Hevelius, Tychonis æmulus, Kepleri vestigiis insistens, eandem hypothesin motus rectilinei amplexus est, ipse plurium Cometarum Observator perquam subtilis. Cæli tamen Calculum suum non penitus consentire gnarus est, viamq Cometarum versus Solem incurvari suboluit.

208. The first page of the manuscript version of Halley's *Astronomiae cometicae synopsis*, inserted in the University Library's copy of David Gregory, *Astronomiae physicae et geometricae elementa* (Oxford, 1702).

set of little books bound in vellum that are now in the archives of the Royal Observatory in the University Library.

By the time Halley went to Greenwich, Newton had taken the lunar theory as far as he would and Halley had calculated tables of the Moon's motion according to it. The tables were printed before 1720 but Halley did not publish them; that was left for John Bevis to do after Halley was dead.[6] However in 1731, half-way through his time at Greenwich, Halley published a paper in the *Philosophical Transactions* in which he claimed that Newton's theory was correct to within 2 min. of arc. People have always doubted that claim, but it is supported by further papers of Halley in the Observatory archives, the significance of which has only just become apparent. The further papers are loose sheets also bound up in vellum, and bearing calculations of the positions of the Moon at the times of Halley's observations, calculated according to the prescriptions in his published tables. In addition there are similar calculations for observations by Flamsteed, made thirty-six years earlier, at times when the differences from Newton's theory should have been the same as for the corresponding observations by Halley. Altogether there are, in a span of about three and a half years, more than a hundred of Halley's observations that can be paired with ones by Flamsteed, and the agreement within pairs is of the order of 1 min. of arc, while the difference of the mean of a pair from Newton's theory is indeed about 2 min. of arc standard deviation. Halley's claim in his paper of 1731 therefore seems justified. Halley himself noted a few pairs but the greater part have only now been identified. Newton's theory and Halley's observations are put in a far more favourable light, but were not known to be so in their own day, for they remained and remain unpublished.[7]

6. *Edmundi Halleii Astronomi dum viveret Regii tabulae astronomicae accedunt de usu tabularum praecepta*, ed. J. Bevis (London, 1749); translation: E. Halley, *Astronomical tables with precepts both in English and in Latin for computing the places of the Sun, Moon, &c.* (London, 1752).
7. See A. Cook, *Edmond Halley* (Oxford, 1998).

209. Title page of Jeremiah Horrocks's works, collected posthumously by John Wallis.
210. Title-page of Robert Ferguson's pamphlet of 1684.

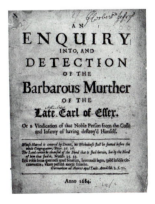

Aſſaſſionates had thus by a ſecond murder delivered themſelves from the apprehenſions they were in of being detected for the firſt; yet there aroſe an other perſon, who as he had better opportunity of knowing the whole Myſtery of the Lord of *Eſſex's* death, than *Meak* the Sentinel had; ſo from remorſe of Conſcience for what he had been acceſſory unto, and from an abhorrency of that bloody Fact, which he ſo well knew the Authors and Perpetrators of, he begun to diſcourſe and communicate it with ſhame and loathing to others. The perſon whom I mean was Mr. *Hawley*, a Warder of the Tower, living in *Wincheſter-ſtreet*, being a Perſon both for Reputation and Eſtate far above that *Hawley*, in whoſe houſe the Earl of *Eſſex* was then Priſoner when his Throat was cut, and therefore one without whoſe knowledge, conſent and contribution, it cannot be ſuppoſed to have been done. And by how much he was not only more capable than others to detect the whole villany of the Noble Man's death, and lay open the enormous crime in all the parts and branches of it, but was of better credit than the Sentinel, and more likely to obtain belief from the World in what he ſhould declare, by ſo much was he to be eſteemed for a moſt dangerous perſon to the Conſpirators, and to be treated as one from whom they might dread the moſt fatal miſchief to themſelves as well as their cauſe. Hence the intelligence was no ſooner conveyed to a *great Man* and the reſt of the *Juncto*, that *Hawly* had been talking ſuch things concerning the Earl of *Eſſex's* death, which it concerned them no leſs than both their Lives and Honours to have concealed; but they reſolved to deſtroy him, and thereby prevent his prating for the future, and being able to tell any tales. And being informed that he was inquiring where he might purchaſe an Eſtate, they employ one to tempt him out of Town, under pretence of his ſeeing a parcel of Land that was to be ſold. For they thought, that ſhould they cauſe him to be murdered in or about the City, it would fill all men with jealouſies of their being guilty of his death, eſpecially conſidering the Reports which went of them, and the ſuſpicions that they lay under of having cauſed *Meak* to be killed. And therefore in order to the getting him deſtroyed with the more ſecrecy, and the adminiſtring the leſs apprehenſion about the Authors of his death, they prevailed on him by the baite and temptation which I have mentioned, to take a journey into the Countrey. Whence having reſolved that he ſhould never return, they employed ſome to dogg, and others to way-lay and murder him. And with that Secrecy as well as Obedience, were their Orders and Decrees executed, that it was a conſiderable while after his Death, before he could be heard of, or his Body found. But when after long ſearch and enquiry after him; his *Corps* were at laſt found, there were all the marks and Symptoms of a moſt barbarous Aſ-

ſaſſina

211. An extract from Robert Ferguson's pamphlet of 1684, with the reference to the death of Halley's father. Halley's father, his name here spelt 'Hawley', lived in Winchester Street. The other Hawley was the gentleman porter of the Tower, who may or may not have been a relative of the astronomer.

About two years after Halley's marriage, his father, a rich citizen of London living in Winchester Street, just off Broad Street, was found dead, murdered undoubtedly, near Stroud in Kent. Pamphlets in the University Library connect his death with that of the Earl of Essex in the Tower of London some nine months earlier.[8] Like other well-to-do citizens, the father evaded duty in the City train bands by enrolling as a yeoman warder of the Tower. As such he was only required to attend when the sovereign was personally present there. Unhappily, as it turned out, he was on duty when the Earl of Essex was found dead in the house of the gentleman porter. Essex was one of three noblemen, the others being Lord Russell and Algernon Sidney, who were charged with treason after the discovery of the Rye House plot to assassinate Charles II and the Duke of York on their return from Newmarket in the spring of 1683. Russell was the first to go for trial in July 1683 and on the day he went from the Tower the king and the duke were most unusually there together. That morning Essex was found dead with his throat slit from ear to ear. It seems that he committed suicide, but it was put about that he had been murdered at the instigation of the Duke of York. Halley's father disappeared from his house in March 1684 and his damaged body was found in April, washed up on the shore of the Medway in the grounds of Temple Manor opposite Rochester. In a pamphlet written shortly after, and widely distributed in French and Dutch as well as English, Robert Ferguson, who was associated with the Rye House plotters, set out reasons for claiming that Essex had been murdered and supported his argument by, among other allegations, the assertion that Halley's father had been done away with at the behest of the Duke of York because he knew too much about the disreputable circumstances of the death of Essex [210, 211].

After the 'Glorious Revolution' of 1688, Laurence Braddon, also an associate of republicans, repeated the allegations in other pamphlets, in more lurid terms. Halley himself may have been in some way involved, for Robert Hooke reported him as being 'concerned' when the House of Lords reopened investigations into the death of Essex after the departure of James II in 1689. The family problems that followed the death of the father seem indirectly to have affected the timing of Halley's visit to Newton in Cambridge that set in train the composition of the *Principia*.

8. [R. Ferguson] *An inquiry into and detection of the barbarous murther of the late Earl of Essex* (1684): two issues in English, a French and a Dutch translation – the pamphlet is anonymous but generally assigned to Ferguson; L. Braddon, *Essex's innocency and honour vindicated. As proved before the Right Honourable (late) Committee of Lords, or ready to be disposed. In a letter to a friend, Lawrence Braddon of the Middle Temple* (Gent, 1690); L. Braddon, *Vindication of the Earl of Essex from Bp. Burnet's false charge of self-murder* (London, 1725).

The Royal Observatory

Halley was in at the very foundation of the Royal Observatory at Greenwich for, still an undergraduate, he was one of the party that went to view the site where it was to rise. After it came into use, Halley often collaborated with Flamsteed there, initially no doubt as an apprentice assistant, but later as an equal colleague. The records of that first agreeable period are in the Flamsteed papers of the Royal Observatory and in other Flamsteed papers, all now published.[9] Later, however, for reasons that are not entirely clear, Flamsteed became very hostile to Halley. Newton, after he became President of the Royal Society in 1704, obtained possession of Flamsteed's observations and the star catalogue Flamsteed had derived from them, and arranged for them to be edited and published without Flamsteed's consent. David Gregory was the first to be charged with the edition and after his death Halley took it on. The latter's version, with the observations up to 1690 and Flamsteed's catalogue as revised by Halley, was published in 1712, and enraged Flamsteed [212]. Flamsteed later prepared his own version, but it only appeared posthumously, in 1725. The result of the sorry story can be seen in the 1712 and 1725 editions, both in the University Library, and the course of the dispute can be followed in various preliminary manuscript versions of the catalogue that are now in the Library in the Flamsteed papers of the Royal Greenwich Observatory.

Edmond Halley has long awaited a comprehensive biography that would draw on unpublished material and would do justice to his varied accomplishments and the great influence he has had on the course of natural philosophy. While much material is not in Cambridge, and it would not be possible to write his biography without going outside Cambridge, it is also the case that the sources for some of the more bizarre aspects of his life are to be found here: for his father's death, for his relations with Flamsteed, and for his study of the Moon at Greenwich, begun when he was sixty-four and continued to the end of his life almost twenty years later. This chapter, written just as my biography of Halley has gone to press, may be some thanks for the privilege of having been able to call upon the resources of the University Library with its many treasures for study in the history of natural philosophy.[10]

212. Title-page of Flamsteed's observations, edited by Halley and published as *Historia coelestis libri duo.*

9. E. G. Forbes, L. Murdin, F. Willmoth, eds., *The correspondence of John Flamsteed, the first Astronomer Royal, vol. 1: 1666–1682* (Bristol, 1995).
10. A. Cook, *Edmond Halley* (Oxford, 1998); I am indebted to Nicola Thwaite and Adam Perkins for help in selecting material for illustrations, and to them and other members of the Rare Books and Manuscripts departments for invaluable courteous assistance in the past.

Chapter 14

The University Archives (what are they, anyway?)

Elisabeth Leedham-Green

Although there have been occasional centuries when they have been housed in close proximity to them, the University Archives must be counted as recent arrivals among the University Library's holdings, moving into the newly built extension from the Old Schools in 1972 and only fully integrated in 1977. The earliest document to survive among them dates from within fifty years of the probable genesis of the University and stands as the first of a large number of documents recording the University's struggle, first of all to survive within the town of Cambridge, and then quite soon to dominate it. Physically unimpressive, it takes the form of Letters Patent from Henry III, issued at Westminster on 7 February 1266, granting to the chancellor and masters the right to a quinquennial assessment, to be made by two masters and two burgesses of the town, of the rents of houses inhabited by scholars [213].

Far more significant for the establishment of the University as an enduring corporation had been three writs issued by Henry in 1231, of which the originals do not survive, having perhaps perished in the bonfire of University records which formed such a popular feature of the local celebrations of the Peasants' Revolt in 1381. This fire, merrily though it may have

213. Letters Patent of Henry III allowing a quinquennial assessment of rents in the town, to be conducted jointly by representatives of the University and of the town, 7 February 1266. The oldest surviving record in the University Archives.

blazed, nonetheless spared the great majority of the University's charters extant at that date. With a solitary exception, however, the documents surviving from before that date are indeed charters – assorted grants of privilege from the crown and the church – the University's muniments, or defences against a potentially hostile world. Very few of them are decorative – the University had no funds to spare for such frivolities – but a charter of Edward I, confirming the privileges accorded by his predecessors, was seen as meriting an illuminated initial showing two doctors of theology and one each of canon and of civil law gratefully receiving the charter from the king [231].

These grants of privilege, even if they seldom qualified for adornment, clearly claimed pride of place among the documents deemed worthy of preservation, but it is certain that other types of record were also kept: lists were kept, and prominent among them are not, as the romantic might assume, lists of graduates, but lists of the University's modest holdings of cash and other valuables. The treasurers of the University were the annually appointed proctors who, on resigning office, handed to their successors an authenticated list, in the form of an indenture, of the contents of the various University chests, consisting chiefly of expendable cash; cash provided by benevolent individuals as a source of student loans; plate or, more often, shabby and out-of-date texts, deposited as security by the borrowers; the University processional cross, along with some vestments; and, indeed, the University muniments. The earliest of these indentures dates from

215. William Rysley's list of the University muniments, 1420, showing, e.g. at the foot of the first section, above the first heading, some of the annotations ascribed to John Fisher and, on the right-hand side, new locations entered by Registraries Romilly and Luard.

214. Proctors' indenture accounting for the contents of the University Chest, 1362/3.

Inuentariu bonor mobiliu ad astam coem vniuisitatis Cantebrigg
ptin sub anno dni Millmo CCCC xx̄ & Henrici sexti &c
magistm Wilłm Pysley complatu

a Inptm Sigilliu de argento
b It bursa cois cu suis content
c It bursa magir Roberti tey cu ptinet &c It ex dono eiusd
d It bursa psbri cu ptinet tenata do trio vnuisitatis & de scot
— nute cunt ad ficas celebrari p aia magri do Thorneton

f litera extra ordine reperies inferius post D

☞ Indulta Regum

a Item **Henrici post conqum Anglie tercij** In pmus q̄d dom̄ scolariu p Duos Magros & Duos burgenses ad hoc deputatos tax̄ vnr potuit do quinqueniu in quinqueniu ‧ ‧ ‧ ‧ ‧ ‧ ‧ vol. I. 1.

b Item de Aldermanis adiunardis q̄dior : De teptacoe pistorib3 regrarijs vno refusa & fundacoe vicoꝝ &c ‧ vol. I. 2

c It q̄d vic mundab canc ad refinem cuiussŏ cu suis refinis ‧

d It q̄d no fiat torneamenta p quinq milliaria in circuitu ‧

a **Edwardi primi** In pmus vna magna carta confirmacois quar puileg p patrom suu pris concessoꝝ ‧ Drawe I. 1

b It cofirmacio carte de refurendo vic in defctu inditie ‧

c It q̄d ad refuiscone q̄ agroꝝ vic faciat pclamari & refistat no fiant torneamenta p quinq milliaria ‧ vol. I. 12

d It vna concessio du placet q̄d scolares potint laicos conuinc coram canc̄ & causis psonalib3 ‧ vol. I. 11

e It q̄d vicenalia vegtarioꝝ forstca assiguntr hospit sci Johis ‧ vol. I. 8

a **Edwardi sdi** In pmus magna carta cofirmacois puuileg a suis pgenitorib3 pruis concessoꝝ ‧ habetur sub E littera

b It q̄d vic faciat pclamari no fiat Baschbria ‧

c It cofirmacio q̄d vic capiat malefactores ad psisuoꝝ canc̄ ‧ vol. I. 13

d It q̄d vicenalia forstca assiguntr hospitali sci Joh ‧ Drawe I. 3

e It vna ptectio p tuicoe scolariu & suoꝝ ‧

f It alia carta magna afirmacois puileg p ꝓ cessa ‧ vol. I. 17

1362/3. It would appear to be the survivor of an early exercise in records management by virtue of having been filed, by some person of less than perfect palaeographical skills, under the year 1462/3, and so escaped the destruction of all others prior to 1430 [214].

It is at about this time, early in the fifteenth century, that we see signs of the University, or at least of some of its officers, first distinguishing their muniments from their other valuables. It was probably not spin-off from any celebrations of the University's bicentenary but rather a reflection of a sense of growing self-confidence and, indeed, of spaciousness related to the completion in about 1400 of the new Divinity Schools with the new chapel above the Regent House, equipped with a small vestry in which the records were stored from, we may surmise, about 1420. There were thirteen boxes of these records; one William Rysley, probably a proctor, made a list of them [215].[1]

1. The list, in the 'Liber rerum memorabilium' (University Archives (henceforth UA): Collect. Admin. 5) has been transcribed and admirably presented by C. P. Hall in 'William Rysley's catalogue of the University muniments, compiled in 1420', *Transactions of the Cambridge Bibliographical Society*, 4 (1965) 85–99.

216(a) and 216(b). A gauging manual, with instructions on checking wet and dry measures, apparently purchased for, rather than compiled by, the taxors, to assist them in their supervision of weights and measures used in the town (1617).

The items listed by Rysley comprise somewhere between 130 and 140 documents of which the majority (89) are royal or papal grants, listed under their respective reigns. To these have been appended lists of documents relating to the acquisition of the land for the University Schools, to assizes, to exequies, to commissions of the peace, to colleges, to the composition with Barnwell Priory for Midsummer Fair, and a variety of other matters. Later proctors, the latest perhaps John Fisher himself, Senior Proctor in 1494, have annotated and augmented the list, as they used it in their annual check on the contents of the University chest, referring, no doubt, to the instructions on how to locate particular items. The fifteenth-century additions, however, are of a kind with the items listed by Rysley, almost all of them grants of privilege or of exemption, the essential bulwarks of the University's defences; only a tiny fraction refer to the University's internal deliberations or legislation.

Much the same is true of the next surviving list of the 'Scripta et munimenta reperta in Archivis Academiae' compiled by Matthew Wren, then President of Pembroke, in 1622. Wren's list is apparently based on Rysley's, and is entered in the same book. After the royal and papal grants it lists some sixty deeds of title relating to University property in the town and to Burwell rectory. It records also the foundation deeds of the Lady Margaret professorship and preachership, and of the Rede lecturers (originally three of them, to be appointed annually and to lecture in the Schools on humanity, logic and philosophy). The final section – 'Acta aliaque scripta ipsius Universitatis' – documents largely, once again, the University's dealings with outside bodies and individuals.

There is very little among the archives listed here that reflects the day-to-day life of the University, although notable exceptions are the magnificently detailed contract, still surviving, for the construction in 1466 of the timber roof of what is now the University Combination Room,[2] and the proctors' indentures for the contents of the University chests. Neither the contract nor the indentures, by this time, served any useful purpose – there could be no possibility of redress; and we cannot tell whether their retention is evidence of nascent antiquarianism or of bad housekeeping.

Between 1420 and 1622 many of the more substantial series, central to the University's history, had sprung into being: the University Grace Books, starting from 1454, registered – in addition to the formal decisions of the regents – the earliest annual audits (an invaluable source for the as-yet-unwritten histories of the University fire-engine, the activities of the

2. UA: Luard 128; discussed and largely transcribed in R. Willis and J. W. Clark, *The architectural history of the University of Cambridge and the colleges of Cambridge and Eton*, 4 vols. (Cambridge, 1886, vols. I–III reprinted 1988) vol. I, pp. 13–14; vol. III, pp. 92–6.

University scavenger, and other essential features of University life) and, from 1465, fees paid on admission to degrees. From the 1480s, letters sent by the University were copied into a book; probate records were methodically kept from shortly after 1500, soon to be followed by continuous records of matriculation. From the second half of the sixteenth century, the Vice-Chancellor's and the Commissary's courts, both in their regular weekly sessions and in their jurisdiction at Sturbridge and Midsummer Fairs, spawned both bound volumes and loose documents in profusion, pregnant with salacious allegations. None of these feature in Wren's list. Such things were clearly not seen as 'archives'. The University finances were still the business of the Vice-Chancellor and the proctors, most of the rest of the documents were the working records of the Registrary.

The office of Registrary was created in 1506 and his function was to keep the University's records – 'keep' in the sense rather of compiling than of preserving – and for the next 400 years it was to be the energy of individual registraries, and the balance each struck between recording and preserving – and, it must be said, between industry and indolence – which were to dictate the nature of the surviving evidence for most of the activities of the University.

Meanwhile there would continue to be very significant documents which were neither *in archivis* nor in the custody of the Registrary. From

218. Elizabethan statutes of 1570 with great seal, with the Queen's signature at the head, and place and date of the grant entered by Lord Burleigh at the foot. The Elizabethan statutes, enhancing the authority of the Vice-Chancellor and Heads of Houses, remained in force, in theory at least, until the revision of the 1850s.

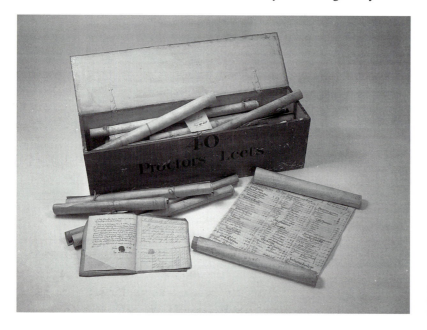

217. Proctors' leet box: an archival container of, probably, the eighteenth century.

Elizabeth dei gra Anglie Fraunc & Hibnie
Regina fidei defensor &c Dilecto nobis Cancellario magistris et scholaribus
vniuersitatis Cantabrigien Salutem Quanta verum vestrarum tura nos
perpetuo solicitos dum Artibus Academie vestre studium non tam priuilegia et
nra benignitate, vobis concessa quam legum ac statutorum vigorem nova quedam
dispositio manifeste declarauit. Quorum alleuo minus obsisteue, amicosq studio
vestris memoribus alleuo concordie, vestreq reipublice vestre gubernationi
consulere possitis De illo abunde, satis a nobis esse prouisum ssub eiisdem
licet tum diu a nobis inchoata esse non ignorimus. vt leges intueri expetendas
vobis deberimus. vna tamen atque experientia optima efficerit verum, magis sua
edeis animaduertimus, in alio aliqua te correctione digna Eiusue vos sentie
homine inuicta ianuaq scientia aliquando, nobis prouidens esse adiiciendam diguis
Negotia tam quod nouis euenerut, nouo meliore augilio suscile recurrens Anne vero
cum ista oma annuate et speramus sint absoluta. et presenta. ea a vobis oculis
cum ea quadeus obedientia. atque animi alacritate accipiens sunt Leges igitur
as futura hac libello conscripta. atque sumi nri regia autheritate sanciens
vobis in vestrum remedu misimus ac promulgamus diligenter. atque fideliter
a vobis obseruandi quepomun Quod dum feceritis illicet et oportet ex vimo
parrentio, non solum a deo optimo maximo. et a nobis laudem et premin
expetabitis. verum etiam vna tum pietate atque optimarum artium non medio
incremento omes gradus ad Academie, in pulchernimo ordinem addecnte, illuss suaue
atque dignitatis optime prouidentes florentissimam efficiete Et tandem quod
apud nos non minimi est momenti exemplo vos sanguis in omni conatu et mente
postris reliqui populi nim ad consimilem legum nostram obseruaram et ad pacem
concordiam deuamq obedientiam tragerus. atque inducus digni regni fauore digni
prouisus ac literarum premio Sed quoniam echoctari liberum exercis, voluntate
mandatum necessitatem facit. Nec vero priuatis animus se penses pene mein
ad leges custodiendas reginum, omnibus igitur Artibus, mor studio in har pte
competat, maxim q vobis qui potestatem publicam Academie exercetis vel
singulorum collegiorum gubernacula tenetis Mandamus vt et vos ipsi statutis sua
Academie ad vos pertinent obseruetis et si reliqui omnibus diligentiam in
eisdem obseruandis expiatis illarumq executioni solo vmbus memoriam Si
vero (quod absit) fauore gratia lenitate vel meroru sua tes contemn negligi
reu non obseruari aliquando contigerit vos qumbo illam executioni demandata
est, quiq aliorum gubernationem suscepistis Huic transgressionis vos
indicabimus atq a vobis exactam rationem illme vel ex post remit domina
Thesino. et volumtatem in vobis has leges suscipiendi bona, qr literis
probateniq discendi et facultatem eisdem ad vestris scholarum exercendi
et exequendi concedas. Dat apud Manerium nrm de Regina 25 septembris.
anno Regni Nostri Duodecimo. et ano xrixti 1570 In cuius rei testi
monium has litras nostras manu nostra signatas merito sigillo nostre Anglie
muniri fecimus Die et ano suprabid

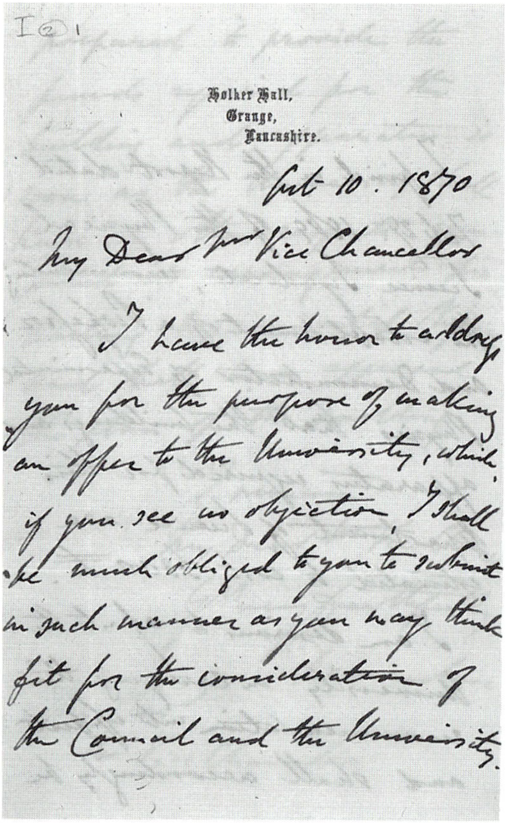

I ⓒ 1

Holker Hall,
Grange,
Lancashire.

Oct 10. 1870

My Dear Mr Vice Chancellor

I have the honor to address you for the purpose of making an offer to the University, which, if you see no objection, I shall be much obliged to you to submit in such manner as you may think fit for the consideration of the Council and the University.

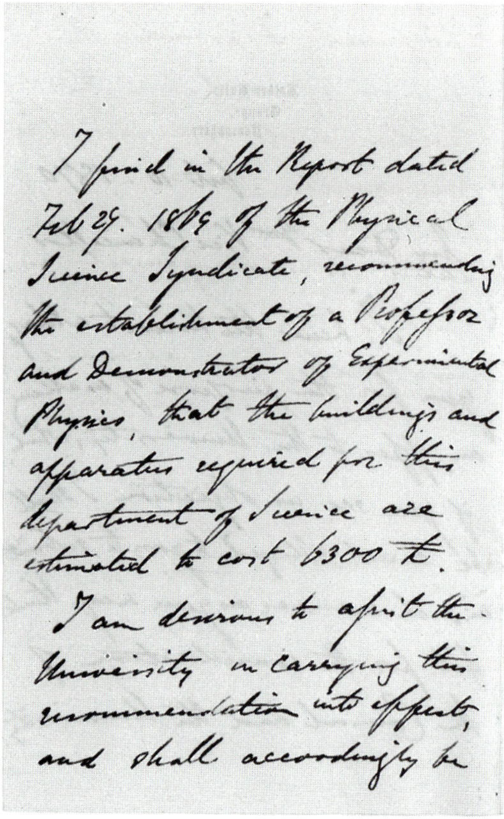

I find in the Report dated Feb 29. 1869 of the Physical Science Syndicate, recommending the establishment of a Professor and Demonstrator of Experimental Physics, that the buildings and apparatus required for this department of Science are estimated to cost 6300 £.

I am desirous to assist the University in carrying this recommendation into effect, and shall accordingly be prepared to provide the funds required for the building and apparatus, so soon as the University shall have in other respects completed its arrangements for teaching Experimental Physics, and shall have approved the plan of the building.

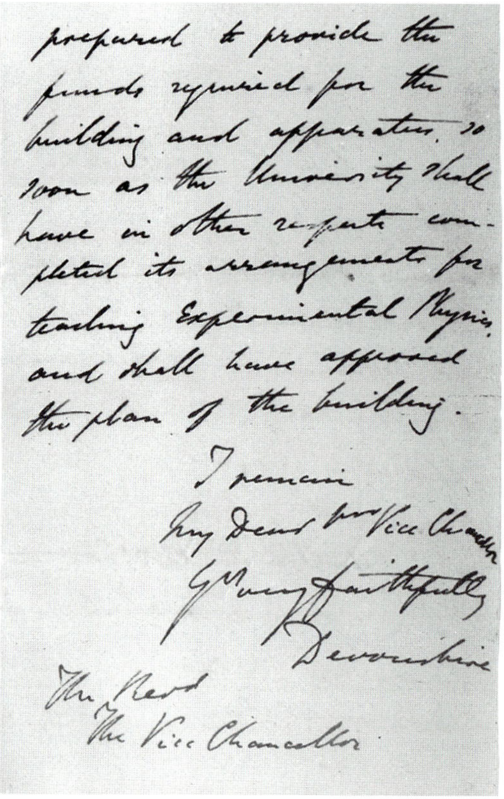

I remain
My dear Mr Vice Chancellor
Yours faithfully
Devonshire

The Revd
The Vice Chancellor

219. Letter to the Vice-Chancellor from the Duke of Devonshire, 10 October 1870, offering to pay the £6,300 required to construct and equip a building for experimental physics – realized as the Cavendish Laboratory, named in his honour.

1570 the status of the Vice-Chancellor as chief executive officer of the University was much enhanced. The University provided him, for the term of his office, with a few works of reference, notably a copy of the statutes, but not with premises from which to conduct his business, or with clerical assistance. His burden of correspondence, both with other officers and with external authorities, was often heavy. At the end of his term he might have amassed a large quantity of paper. This he customarily destroyed. Very occasionally Vice-Chancellors' papers survive in their colleges. The rare survivals in the University Archives – the letter-books of John Jegon, Vice-Chancellor 1596–8 and 1600–1,[3] and of James Cartmell (1849–50 and 1865–7)[4] and the loose correspondence of James Power (1870–1 and 1878–9) [219][5] – and the six volumes of the correspondence of Edward Atkinson (1862–3, 1868–70, 1876–8) preserved in the University Library's Manuscripts Department[6] give us a tantalizing glimpse of what we have lost. It could have been worse: books of precedents compiled for the use of successive Vice-Chancellors – notable among them the 'Great Black Parchment Book' (Collect. Admin. 9), listed in early copies of the 'tradita' along with keys to the University chest, and the like, as things to be passed from the outgoing to the incoming incumbent – are known to have languished, stranded in one college or another, sometimes for centuries, before being restored to light and to public usefulness.

Meanwhile, the University's most vital documents, the sole copies of the statutes, dating from the thirteenth century, in copies made mostly from the late fifteenth century, with later enactments, interpretations by the Vice-Chancellor and Heads of Houses, forms of oaths, and a mass of other vital information, were routinely carried about the streets, especially when the streets were riotous. The statutes, and their observance, were the business of the proctors, the maintainers both of discipline and of the democratic rights of the regent masters, and their books were their badges of office as well as their manuals.[7] Their books were, accordingly, fortified as much, no doubt, to enhance their value as offensive weapons as for their own protection [220]. It may be, indeed, that the Junior Proctor's Book is the only murder weapon held by the Library, given that, in 1523, the aptly named John

3. UA: Misc. Collect. 7, 8.
4. UA: Misc. Collect. 46–7.
5. UA: VCCorr. I–VI.
6. MSS Add. 6580–5.
7. UA: Collect. Admin. 1–2; an earlier Proctor's Book, partly cannibalized to make Collect. Admin. 2, survives as Collect. Admin. 3.

220. Junior Proctor's Book, showing studs and carrying chain.

Bryganden of St John's, Junior Proctor, was indicted for homicide, an indictment dismissed by the University as inspired by the 'unmitigated malice of the townsmen'. My goodness me, why should they complain of mere homicide?

Not until after 1785, when the University statutes were first printed in their entirety, were these heroic volumes committed to the safe-keeping of the Registry and the proctors equipped with less cumbrous and less lethal tomes.

Nor was it much clearer which of the records held by the early registraries were to be regarded as the property of the University. When John Mere, Registrary effectively from 1531 and officially from 1543, died in 1558, he left to the University not only his house in Bene't Street but also eleven volumes and two bundles of records 'made by him *and bought*' (my italics). Nothing that survives can be identified with anything that Mere could possibly have purchased, and although it is possible that he had built up a small reference library, since lost, the more likely implication is that a number of volumes which we now regard as central to the University records were regarded by Mere as his private property and that he had paid for their raw materials. Not that he was unmindful of posterity: he entered in spaces in Grace Book A a day-by-day account of the Henrician visitation of 1533/4 and, in manuscripts now in the library of Corpus Christi College (whither he blithely allowed his friend Matthew Parker to carry off many items from the University's records), accounts of the doings of the Visitors of Edward VI and of Mary, all sent to assess the University's performance as a nursery of orthodox clergy.[8] Files coming in today present remarkable parallels.

It would be possible, but too demanding of space – to say nothing of patient readers – to trace step by step, and to plot one against the other, the fortunes and contents of the Archives and the role of the Registrary as it evolved from that of recording angel to that, after the First World War, of executive archangel, at which point active concern with non-current files became more than could be expected of him, except, perhaps, when it came to their destruction. Very few Registry files survive for the years 1910 to 1924, virtually none for the years from 1924 to 1947.

Some of the highlights in registrarial concern for the records can be briefly sketched with reference, once more, to major undertakings by way of listing. In the mid eighteenth century, Registrary Lynford Caryl compiled an 'Index' of the records comprising two substantial volumes [**233**].[9]

8. The first diary is transcribed in the printed edition of *Grace Book A*, ed. Stanley Leathes (Cambridge, 1897), pp. 221–30, the two later ones in J. Lamb, *A collection of letters, statutes, and other documents from the MS Library of Corpus Christi College, illustrative of the history of the University of Cambridge during the period of the Reformation from A.D. MD to A.D. MDLXXII* (London, 1838), pp. 109–20, 184–236.

9. UA: In. 1–2.

Fortunately he also provided an index to his index, as the lists themselves make it plain that what confronted Caryl was a vast mass of loose documents thrust haphazard into a variety of boxes and drawers, like found with like only by too infrequent chance. Each item was individually numbered and entered in his books, books which were to serve, and to be augmented by, his successors, notably by Joseph Romilly a century or so later when he set about the task of reducing this chaos to order, an order based often on subject matter rather than on the origins or functions of the documents.[10] As Romilly sorted and rehoused the collection he compiled a new index, also in two volumes, while punctiliously marking each item in Caryl's list with its new location.[11] Romilly too provided an index to his index, rendering it too a tool still serviceable.

The process was completed by Romilly's successor, Henry Richards Luard, Registrary from 1862 to 1891, who, when not overwhelmed by his duties as Perpetual Curate of Great St Mary's, took the loose documents, drawer by drawer, and had them bound up into the familiar brown 'Cambridge University Registry' guard books, topic by topic, and had copies of the list of contents of each guard book bound up into three impressive volumes which, regrettably, he failed to persuade the University Press to publish.[12] Further volumes were compiled, along similar lines, under Luard's successor, J. W. Clark, largely by a simple process of cannibalizing the University *Reporter*.

In this form the University's records up to the First World War present themselves as neither more nor less than the working library of the Registrary, each of the lists, until Luard's, containing a section called 'Books', with a mixture of records and reference works shelved indiscriminately, syndicate minutes and the *Valor ecclesiasticus* cheek by jowl. No wonder: not only was it his duty to 'keep' the records, in both senses of the term, but the Registrary was also, with the obvious exceptions of the Librarian and, later, the Director of the Fitzwilliam Museum, the only administrative officer of the University provided with premises in which to exercise his office.

In a decentralized university, the doubt – as to whether this or that item is 'mine' or the University's – which has deprived us of the mass of Vice-Chancellors' correspondence inevitably persists. Even now it sometimes comes as a surprise to the secretaries of committees, of syndicates, even of Faculty Boards, to learn that such things are the stuff of the University Archives. Not only syndicates, but whole departments have come and gone, leaving no trace behind them but sparse mention in the *Reporter*, or in the

10. D. M. Owen's *Cambridge University Archives: a classified list* (Cambridge, 1988) endeavours to restore these *disjecta membra*, at least on paper, to their original files.
11. UA: In. 3–4.

12. UA: In. 5–7.

Students' Handbook or the *Calendar*, now defunct. Some have vanished, to our shame, in very recent years and yet since their move into the University Library in 1972 the holdings of the University Archives have increased some four-hundredfold, thanks largely to vast deposits by the central offices but also to very substantial accessions from Cambridge University Press, the Botanic Garden, the Careers Service, the Board of Continuing Education and other enlightened institutions and departments within the University. Our lists now have little of the aesthetic appeal of Rysley's, of Caryl's or of Romilly's: the computer has deprived them of any glamour they might otherwise have had, but offers glorious scope for sorting and for searching – and for not having to re-type the lot every time collections are re-shelved [222–4].

221. Samuel Taylor Coleridge's Greek Ode, awarded a Browne medal in 1792, from a volume containing the successful submissions for the medal. The subject set was a topical one: the wretched lot of the slaves in the West Indies – *Sors misera servorum in insulis Indiae occidentalis*.

****

222. One of three cases in the Library holding modern files deposited by the General Board.

13. Private papers of members of the University, including notes for lectures, are rather the preserve of the University Library's Manuscripts Department, while the colleges each maintain their own archives – archives far likelier to contain biographical material than are the routine records of the University itself.

223. Cambridge University Press invoices, 1920–2, pasted into a grotesquely vast volume.

In 1885, Registrary Luard found himself in captious mood when required by the Commissioners to describe his duties. He listed them under nineteen heads, of which the first four describe his archival functions. Item 15 is also relevant:

> Correspondence: This, which is an important part of the Registrary's duties, has largely increased of late years. It consists of letters (a) asking for information respecting persons who have studied or graduated here or on points of University history, which can only be given by the Registrary; (b) asking for information which the Registrary can give more easily than anyone else; (c) asking for information which can be quite as well ascertained from the *Cambridge Calendar*; (d) and of foolish and ignorant questions of all kinds, from all quarters of the world.

The last category is, of course, quite unknown to the Registrary's archival successors, and, were it not so, to cite examples would be actionable! Otherwise little has changed. In quantity, enquiries about ancestors, or applicants for jobs, most of whom are not and never have been members of the University, are probably the most common. On the other hand, life is much enlivened by researchers, including Ph.D. students, investigating the records, be they thirteenth- or twentieth-century records, or anything in-between, in new and interesting ways. Basically, however, the University Archives still constitute the Registrary's working library, limited as they are to the papers generated in the administration of the University and all its constituent parts,[13] and it is the University's administrators who have first call upon them. Usually their enquiries require consultation of documents less than a hundred years old, frequently less than two years old, but in recent years, when the question of college bar licences was much at issue, Richard II's charters, issued in the aftermath of the Peasants' Revolt, were once more extracted *ex archivis* to serve as weapons in the University's armoury.

1949.

May 6th   Machine in operation for first time. Printed table of squares (0 - 99), time for programme 2 mins. 35 sec. Four tanks of battery 1 in operation.

May 7th   Machine still operating, — table of squares several times. Table of primes attempted — programme incorrect. Necessity for another amplifier in Distributing Unit 3. (Panel 37) noted. Coder 3 (Panel 68) finished.

May 9th   Still operating — corrected programme for table of primes tried successfully — machine operating for 1 hour 58 min during which primes up to 1500 were calculated and printed [Programme included no short cuts and employed subtraction only] No faults and still operating in afternoon. Primes up to 4759 calculated in 40 mins.

May 10th   Still operating. Battery 1 began to be tested and wired up. 3 Panels 1 giving trouble. In afternoon using short cut programme Primes up to 5711 calculated in 60 mins. "Banda" duplicating system tried on Teleprinter, machine calculating and printing primes up to 1000. 50 copies being made of results.

May 11th   Modifications to machine started. Extra amplifier in Distributing Unit 3. and relays for Print Check order [F] mounted and wired. Initial Input modified to supply resetting and start pulses, also to short out Order Tank during Initial. Machine "cleaned up."

May 12th   Minor clearing corrected. "Cleaning up" completed. Check Print order (F) relays completed. Machine tried. Phantastron dividers giving trouble — circuit modified to more stable form.

May 13th   Modifications continued.

May 14th   Modifications continued.

May 16th   Modifications Continued.

224. EDSAC log, recording the first successful run of the first university computer, 6 May 1949.

Chapter 15

The University Library and its buildings

Christopher Brooke

ONE OF THE characters in Thomas More's *Utopia,* observing the fields and villages that had been laid down to pasture in the late Middle Ages, declared that 'your sheep, which were wont to be so meek and tame ... now ... be become so great devourers ... that they eat up and swallow down the very men themselves'. It is the same with books. Once let into a building, they spread and grow until they have filled every corner of it. At both Oxford and Cambridge fine buildings were constructed in the late Middle Ages and early modern times for University meetings and disputations; for faculties; for lectures; and for libraries. In due course the libraries crept into the lecture rooms and meeting rooms, and the lecturers and faculties had to go elsewhere. But there was this difference: the Oxford library was altogether greater and grander from the fifteenth century on; and after Sir Thomas Bodley had restored and greatly extended the whole complex, it became one of the wonders of the academic world. After Bodley, Cambridge never had so many books as Oxford; to a considerable extent the University Library was overshadowed by the greatness of the college libraries. Yet it grew inexorably too, spread throughout the Old Schools buildings and spilled, in the nineteenth century, into what had once been the early buildings of King's College behind and about it. By 1900 both the Bodleian and the Cambridge University Library had filled their ancient sites; and one of the greatest questions ever debated in either university lay before each: should they burrow underground, seek makeshift solutions, while preserving their ancient core – or should they seek a new site and a new building? Oxford followed the first course, Cambridge the second.

The ancient constitution of Cambridge – however modified and streamlined in recent decades – still preserves some of the lineaments of its medieval origin; it is relatively slow-moving and cumbersome, and has often been berated by impatient bureaucrats for its failure to make rapid decisions. Had it not been so slow, and often so indecisive, the University Library as we know it could never have existed. The Old Schools might have been transformed into a palace of learning, but it could never have been the vast open-access library which has helped to make Cambridge so attractive to scholars of innumerable disciplines. For this a new site and a fresh start were needed.

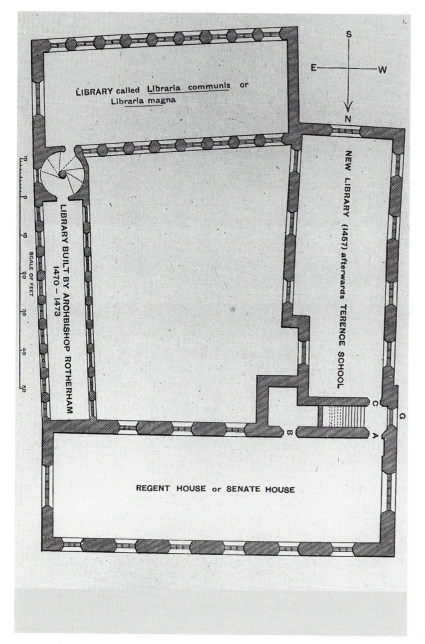

225. The ground-plan of the old University Library, from R. Willis and J. W. Clark, *Architectural history of the University of Cambridge* (1886).

The Library in the Old Schools

Modest as it now seems, the University Library had already, by 1500, occupied two sides of the original quadrangle of the Old Schools [**50**, 225, 226]. It began in the west in a modest room of four bays, then moved into the more extensive south wing; and in the 1470s Thomas Rotherham, Chancellor of England and of Cambridge and Archbishop of York, built the east wing to house his own gift of books. Thereafter the library suffered many vicissitudes, and envious eyes were cast on Oxford in the age of Bodley, in the early seventeenth century. Slowly the books advanced. A medieval university or college library was a long room, well lit by windows on either hand, with lecterns set at right angles to the walls running between them, on which books could be laid, and, if need be, chained. In the sixteenth and seventeenth centuries, most college libraries saw bookshelves rise to engulf the lecterns, although at Trinity Hall the enchanting old-fashioned library of the end of the sixteenth century still preserves the character and light of many medieval predecessors. The seventeenth-century college libraries of Cambridge not only allowed more space for books than readers; some of them were also monumental. The Library of St John's is a monument to Bishop John Williams, more spectacular than either of the libraries his great rival, Archbishop Laud, gave to St John's College, Oxford; the Library at Trinity reflects the image devised by its first patron, Isaac Barrow the Master, and by its architect, Christopher Wren. It was complete by 1690, and remains a unique monument to seventeenth-century ideals of human learning. It outshone the University Library much as King's Chapel outshone Great St Mary's, the church of the whole University.

In 1715 the advent of the Royal Library – trebling the University's collection by a single gift – spread panic in the Senate. First, the south-west corner of the quadrangle, actually a part of King's, was taken over and built up into the dome room which forms the background in Rowlandson's portrayal of the old Library in its heyday [**234**]. Then the western range was fitted out once more for books, and they spread rapidly towards the Regent House, the northern wing, the most substantial space so far unconquered. At this point James Burrough of Caius, at the opening of a distinguished career as an amateur architect, proposed an immense extension to the Schools, facing towards Great St Mary's, with one wing for the Senate House, another for the University offices. In the event, only the Senate House was built, under an alliance between Burrough and James Gibbs – but the books could take over the Regent House.

The nineteenth century saw a proliferation even more daunting. Once again a vast new scheme was mooted, of which only one range came to pass: the magnificent neo-Grecian Cockerell Building of 1837–42. It was built where the old hall of King's had stood. The remains of King's early buildings around and behind the Old Schools were acquired by the University in the 1820s in time for this development – and for further building for the Library and the University offices later in the century. The Cockerell Building provided space for books and museums for a time; and a monumental upper library to rival Wren's at Trinity. One might almost suppose that it was designed to house the final expansion of learning. If so, it was based on an illusion. Gradually, inexorably, every nook and cranny in the Old Schools was absorbed and filled; the arrival of Lord Acton's great

226. The Schools quadrangle and old Library, c. 1690, from David Loggan, *Cantabrigia illustrata*.

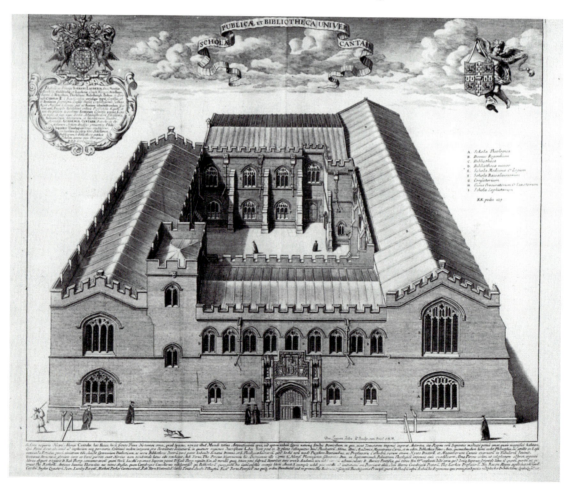

1. On the old Library, see R. Willis and J. W. Clark, *The architectural history of the University of Cambridge and the colleges of Cambridge and Eton*, 4 vols. (Cambridge, 1886, vols I–III reprinted 1988) especially vol. III, chapters 1–5; as well as J. C. T. Oates, *Cambridge University Library; a history. From the beginnings to the Copyright Act of Queen Anne* (Cambridge, 1986); and David McKitterick, *Cambridge University Library; a history. The eighteenth and nineteenth centuries* (Cambridge, 1986).

library in 1902 was the *coup de grâce*: it brought expansion once again to the point of crisis.[1]

The debate

In Oxford, about 1900, it was commonly supposed that the possession of Greats and the tradition of classical, historical and philosophical learning had given Oxford the predominance in humanist studies. It was seriously argued in Oxford that science should be left to Cambridge, and that Oxford should become a university of the humanities alone; and this sort of view was not confined to Oxford. Yet in the generation which followed, Oxford became a great scientific university – without losing Greats or its humanist eminence – and Cambridge has become a powerful rival to it in the humanities. The provision of what, for the 1930s, was (and perhaps still is) the best research library in Europe – by which I mean the library not with the largest resources but with *open access* to the largest number of books useful to a scholar – fundamentally altered the place of Cambridge in the arts. There are many other elements in the story. Thus, in the last decade of the nineteenth century and till 1906, Cambridge contained, in Frederic William Maitland, one of the very few nineteenth-century English medievalists on whose books no dust has gathered, who can be read with the excitement of new discovery as freshly now as when his books were published. One could multiply such examples.

On 7 May 1921 the Senate of the University of Cambridge agreed, by a modest vote of 121 to 73, that a new site be sought for the University Library. Few more important decisions have been made by that body in its long and chequered history. It was by no means the end of the debate: the anxious University Librarian, A. F. Scholfield, felt obliged in March 1924 to provide an elaborate defence of the decision, since many voices were being heard to question it. Nor did anyone know how it was to be financed. Yet it came to pass. The central figure of my story is Sir Hugh Anderson, Master of Caius from 1912 to 1928, University Commissioner in the 1920s and a sort of super-vice-chancellor who interpreted the findings of the Commission and helped the new model of the University to come to life – and who was deeply committed to the plans for a new Library.[2] In 1926 officials of the Rockefeller Foundation visited Anderson to discuss their liberal plans for financing the biological sciences – and went away half-committed to

2. The reminiscences of Maisie Anderson, Sir Hugh Anderson's daughter, 'Time to the sound of bells', now in the Gonville and Caius College Archives, publ. in the *Caian* (1988–93).

financing a new Library. When Anderson died in 1928 Giles Gilbert Scott had produced plans for the Library, the site had been chosen, and half the cost promised by the Rockefeller Foundation. In 1931 the first piles were driven and in 1934 King George V opened the new Library. In the years leading to 1972 it was enlarged, and in the early 1990s it has been extended again; yet more additions are currently under construction. The University Library is the centre of study and research in Cambridge, the main key to its work and reputation in many fields – and in its galleries and tea room much ardent learned discussion has taken place, and many marriages have been formed; its saga continues unabated. The central events in its creation, however, belong to the years 1920 to 1934.

Over the previous generation there had been countless schemes to improve the old University Library and enlarge it. Its role as a legal-deposit library, and the vast expansion of learning of the late nineteenth and early twentieth centuries, meant that it was flooded with books, and the readers were driven into smaller and smaller corners. The Bodleian faced the crisis first, and began to burrow. In Cambridge there were schemes for modest new buildings, and for providing a roof over the eastern court – the main court of the original Old Schools. In 1901 the old Registrary, John Willis Clark, was actively canvassing support for this plan. Eventually it was put to the vote and Clark 'was intensely vexed when the Syndicate's proposals were *non-placeted* by nineteen votes'. He regarded it as a major victory for the forces of darkness in Cambridge; but he battled on. If the obscurantists had not won; if these schemes had matured; if the First World War had not given a long pause for reflection; the vote of 1921 might well have gone another way, and Cambridge might have struggled on with its hopelessly inadequate old Library. In Oxford the same debate took place over the first thirty years of the twentieth century. The Bodleian started with an enormous advantage which it never relinquished; and very naturally and properly there attached to Duke Humfrey and Bodley's splendid quadrangle a sentiment which could never quite attach itself to the Cambridge Library. So Oxford rejected all schemes for a new site or the provision of a major library elsewhere; and the 1930s saw the same Giles Gilbert Scott build the modest extension, the New Bodleian, which has helped to bind this great library to its ancient ways – while Cambridge, which lost every battle except the last, has perhaps the finest working library in Europe.

In 1902 an 'Extension Subsyndicate' had been formed to seek other means of enlarging the Library. Anderson enjoyed a first view of the Library

Syndicate and the Extension Subsyndicate from 1909 to 1912, when he was already Master of Caius. By then Anderson had evidently a deeply planted interest in the problem of the Library, which was to bear remarkable fruit. The First World War prevented any action; but eventually, in 1918, the Subsyndicate produced a final report, recommending a whole series of daring measures – underground stores, a new bookstore on the west court, a reading room in the east court, and so forth. It seems to have been immediately recognized that these measures would prove immensely costly for a relatively modest return. So in 1920 the Library Syndicate itself suggested to the University that a new building be set up on the south side of the Senate House yard. This did not find favour, and it was increasingly evident that a full and serious investigation of alternative buildings or alternative sites was needed. On 22 June 1920 a new Syndicate 'to consider the needs of the Library for further accommodation and the means of satisfying them' was set up, including the most strenuous opponents of the previous half-measures, but also Hugh Anderson, F. J. H. Jenkinson – the Librarian – and A. F. Scholfield – shortly to succeed as Librarian.

At their first meeting in July 1920 the Syndics prepared for bold measures. They readily agreed to minute their disapproval of all schemes for putting more buildings on the old site; and they agreed unanimously that it was 'desirable to secure a site for either an extension of the Library or a new home eventually for the whole Library'. Dr Pearce, Master of Corpus, and Dr Anderson and two others were set to work to consider possible sites. They briefly pondered an earlier idea for a building in front of King's, which was readily seen to be inadequate and unacceptable. They dismissed the Pitt Press and a site in Jesus Lane. Then they fastened on the Corpus cricket ground by Sidgwick Avenue, where the Sidgwick Site, the new humanities complex of the 1960s and 1970s, was eventually to lie, a space comprising three acres, which could be increased to four and a half if the college garden was thrown in.

When the discussion opened on 24 February 1921 Sir William Ridgeway, the Disney Professor of Archaeology and a Fellow of Caius, rose to his feet; and a tremor might well have passed through the proponents of the report, for he was the prince of the *non-placeters*, a man who had led the opposition to every scheme for improving the lot of women in Cambridge and previous plans for the Library. His speech was so comparatively urbane as to make one suspect that he and Anderson had been in conclave. He did indeed condemn earlier proposals in his most eloquent manner, observing that a building on the south side of Senate House yard 'would have destroyed for ever the finest academic view, not only in this country but in Europe'. But he went on to say that 'they had before them a fine, statesman-like scheme'. He did not quite agree that the proposed site was the best that could be chosen. What he did want to emphasize was that the principle of the scheme was the true one. 'Once for all let the University make up its mind not to interfere with the ancient University [the Old Schools], where everything that was good, and perhaps some things that were bad, had taken place from the thirteenth century . . . The question now was whether the site proposed on the Corpus ground was the best available for the purpose. He had looked round anxiously, and he was sorry to say he could only see one other site – the playing field of King's and Clare which had been used for the First Eastern Hospital. If there was any chance of the University being able to acquire that in the near future, he believed that they would all urge strongly that that would be the more appropriate place, much more convenient, much more acceptable than the proposed site at Newnham.'

On the plot he had named, the University Library now stands. No doubt its merits were less obvious to those who viewed it in the early 1920s than they are today, since it had been covered with a hutted hospital, later converted to temporary housing; but to those who knew west Cambridge well it could not fail to commend itself, and to Ridgeway goes the credit for this crucial proposal.

Ridgeway was followed by an eloquent plea from Dr Cranage, later Dean of Norwich, not to remove the Library from its old centre; he spoke heatedly of the inconvenience of moving the Library to 'the suburbs'. He was answered by Mr Forster Cooper of Trinity, a member of the Syndicate, who cited the experience of Harvard, where the decision had been made to bring the library into a single new building; a new building might take a very long time to complete, but they must plan for it. The debate was wound up by Anderson. The Senate had to plan for a secure long-term future, not just for the twenty or thirty years which was all that they could foresee on the present site; although 'he shared the feeling that it would be a great loss to lose the central site', there was gain too, for the University would recover its old buildings and have a centre for offices and 'dignified rooms for receiving guests, and other associations with past centuries'. The Syndicate had looked for a more central site and had not found it; hence its report which he hoped the Senate would accept.[3]

3. My account of the making of the new University Library is largely based on C. N. L. Brooke, *A history of the University of Cambridge, Vol. 4: 1870–1990* (Cambridge, 1993), chapter 12, with detailed references. The main sources are the Archives of the University Library, the University Archives, and the Archives of the Rockefeller Foundation, for which see Brooke, p. 381 n. 30. For Sir Gilbert Scott's archives and plans, now in the RIBA Library and Archives, see the useful summary of plans, sources and literature by G. Fisher *et al.*, *Catalogue of the Drawings Collection of the Royal Institute of British Architects, The Scott family* (Amersham, 1981), p. 169, Scott G. G., no. 28. There is also a fascinating small notebook, Cambridge University Library, MS Add. 9247, which has notes and sketches reflecting his earliest ideas. Of the RIBA archives, I have consulted, from ScG Boxes 42–56, nos. 42–4, 49, 51–6; the description by Scott is in ScG 42/4/291; a modified version brought up to date to 1933–4 is in 49/4. In later descriptions Scott came increasingly to emphasize his own initiatives in design, to which he attributed the differences between the Clare building and the Library. Nothing is said of Mr Rockefeller; and it was probably true that the tower was Scott's own inspiration – it may even be that he had been toying with some such idea before he heard of the benefactor's views – but there can be no doubt that it was the Librarian's letter quoted above which was the catalyst which changed the colour and shape of the façade. For appreciation by an architectural historian, see Gavin Stamp in *RIBA Drawings Collection: The Scott family*, pp. 166–7, 169.

227. Volcano of Tongariro; one of sixty coloured plates from George French Angas's *The New Zealanders illustrated* (1847).

**228. Part of Lady Elizabeth
Tennant's panorama of Simla, 1860s.**

229. Portrait of a Bushman from
William J. Burchell's *Travels in the
interior of southern Africa* (1822).

230. Part of Lieutenant Thomas
Wingate's panorama of Bombay
of about 1840.

231. Letters Patent of Edward I, 6 February 1291/2, confirming privileges granted to the University by his predecessors: initial 'E' showing the king presenting the charter to a Doctor of Canon Law (standing, left) in a *cappa clausa*, with two slits for his arms, a Doctor of Civil Law (standing, right) in a *cappa manicata* [with sleeves] and two kneeling Doctors of Divinity, also wearing the *cappa clausa*.

DWARD⁹

eius noio primus Henrici
terij regis filius pmogeni
tus et in regno successor,
pre decedente in tra scla
ront Saracenos milita
bat. Absens tamen ysl die
Nouembr ano dni 1272. et
etatis sue ano xxxvmi regni
declarat⁹. Et tandem cu
e ibi vulnere ab assasino inslicto convaluisset in
priani xe lxxsue ministerio Roberti Kilewardeby
Cantuarien archiepi Westmonasterij in templo
S. petri sacrat⁹. Hic Scotos mastix, dicis est,
contra quos militans morte correptus apud Burgu
super arena transmetat⁹ vij die Julij ano dni 1307
prope septuagenariud occubuit cu regnasset anos
xxxvmi mense scd vij dies Vni et Westmonasterij
sepultus est. Cantebrigienses autem tm scholares
qm oppidani texta privilegia huic prlaro regi attribu
terre debent quoz nonulla desiderant⁹. Nos autem
tenorem eoz que in artio reperire potuimus statim
subijciemus.

Mandatu Baronibz Sctrij de quinqz ndeio fribz
pdicatoribz Cantebr allocand.

E dwardus dei gratia
rex Anglie, dns Hibn et dux Aquitan
Baronibz suis de Scario saltm. Al
locate Roberto del Esex vicecomiti no
Cantebrig et Huntingdon in exitibz eiusdem Comi
tatus, quinqz ndeio quas rex preptd liberavit
fribz pdicatoribz Cantebrig ad expensas suas sac
tas tenend mcp geidale capituld sud ap Cantebr
acquietand. Dat per manu W. de Merton can
cellij apud scm Martinu magnu Lond quinto die
Octobr ano regni mi primo

Ex Rotulo liberat
Scutellie de ano
pmo regis Edw
pmi menbr. 2.
In Turr London.

232. Title-page for charters and
other grants of privilege from
Edward I, from the two-volume
'Liber privilegiorum et libertatum
alme universitatis Cantabrigiensis'
presented to the University by
Robert Hare, Clerk of the Pells, in
1587. This illuminated copy may
possibly date from shortly after
Hare's time. It contains tran-
scriptions of many charters of
which the originals do not survive
in the University Archives. The
two working copies – one held by
the Registrary, the other (which
contains also transcripts of the
town's charters) often held by the
Vice-Chancellor – therefore still
serve as useful tools.

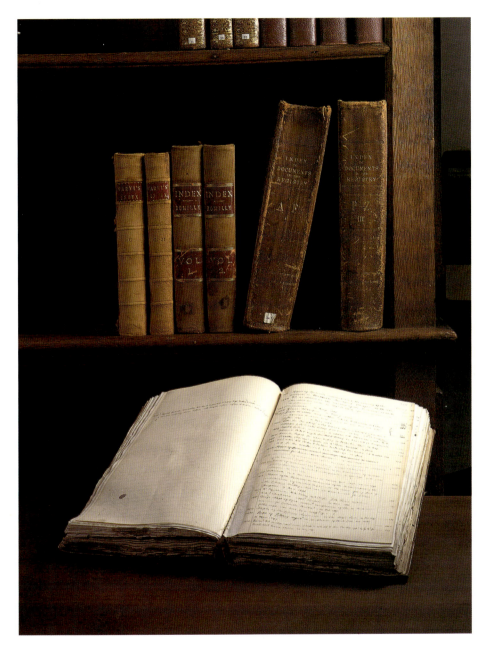

233. Indexes to the University
Archives compiled by Registraries
Caryl, Romilly and Luard, with
Luard's second volume open.

234. The old Library in the late
eighteenth century, as portrayed
by Rowlandson.

The vote was taken and the report approved. Within a few weeks it became apparent that Ridgeway's comments had borne fruit: King's and Clare put their heads together and let it be known that they were open to negotiation. In May 1922 the University was asked to endorse the decision.

Designing the Library

Meanwhile the Syndicate on Library Needs were quietly engaged in seeking an architect. They compiled a list of possible architects in June 1922, with Giles Gilbert Scott, who was already building the Memorial Court for Clare on the west side of Queen's Road, in front of the Library site, at its head; but they also proposed a competition. Plans were still going forward to this end, when Sir Hugh Anderson (as he now was) mentioned that Lord Esher had visited the site, and the Vice-Chancellor put before the Syndics a letter sent by Lord Esher to the Duke of Devonshire, which transports us for a moment into the world of the Whig grandees of the eighteenth century. Esher was a Cambridge graduate but had no special connection with the project or the University; he was simply a great man – a former head of the Office of Works – with much experience of building and fund-raising. The search for funds doubtless explains his involvement. On 10 May 1923, he wrote to Devonshire, who was High Steward of the University:

> I went down to Cambridge yesterday, inspected the site, examined certain sketch plans, and talked the whole matter over with the Vice-Chancellor, the Master of Caius, and others. The site is an excellent one, immediately behind the new buildings of Clare. The sketch plans are by a man called Mitchell … They will not do and would appeal to no one. We discussed the method of procedure, and it was resolved to ask you to join with all of us in approving the selection of [Giles] Gilbert Scott to make a plan and a design for the new Library. We were all of us opposed to a competition. The choice of Scott was decided by the fact that he was the architect of the new buildings at Clare.

The duke lent his approval to the selection of Gilbert Scott to make sketch plans, adding, 'I wish we could light on a substantial benefactor, but I think the idea will appeal to Cambridge men.' This proceeding, which seems to a modern reader, used to orderly competitions and more open government, remarkably high-handed, commended itself to the Syndicate; and they were also much impressed by the need for the new Library to live with the new Clare buildings.

On 28 September 1923 Scott visited the Library and had his first recorded discussion with members of the Syndicate. By such means the first consultation with Scott grew into an assumption in their minds that he was to be the architect; and although it was a while yet before the competition was formally abandoned, from this point on Anderson and some of his colleagues were quietly working to make Scott's plans acceptable. Doubtless they had interested Esher and the duke in their ideas with a view to an appeal; but not long after, the wind was to blow from a new quarter.

Scott produced his first design in 1923–4; and of this some plans and charming sketches survive. The new Clare building has a gateway and entrance, with a modest touch of classical Georgian after the Adam mode, in the shape of two pillars and an architrave, and the building is of blue-grey bricks. The first sketches of the Library show a long façade with a classical feature in the centre, an entrance with four pillars and an architrave, and with wings reminiscent of the orangeries of eighteenth-century mansions, the whole of blue-grey brick. It was similar in concept to the Clare building, but larger and more stately [235].

Scott's first briefing in the autumn of 1923 was evidently an oral briefing by the Librarian and members of the Syndicate, and no record survives of what passed between them. There is indeed a formal typed brief, evidently

235. Gilbert Scott's original design for the new University Library. Water-colour by Cyril A. Farley, 1924.

Scholfield's work, though not signed; but it presupposes earlier discussions, and very largely consists of details of shelf length and the special needs of manuscripts and other reserved books. None the less, the essence of what Scott was told – or of what emerged from those first discussions – is not far to seek. The building itself – in the design of bookstacks, gallery, Catalogue Room and Reading Room – has much to tell us, and this can be confirmed by the first of the several general descriptions Scott himself provided.

'In many respects this library offers to the architect an entirely new problem in library planning, the most important and dominating characteristic being the system of "open access", which admits the reader to the book-stacks for the purpose of obtaining any book he may require.' He could look for little help elsewhere, since, for a library on this scale, Cambridge was 'in many respects unique'. In much later years the Rockefeller Foundation organized a tour of major American university libraries for Scott and the Syndicate. From this, it seems, he learned comparatively little: the original inspiration is as clear in the building of 1934 as in the designs and manifesto of ten years earlier; it had been adapted by long reflection and study; it had in outward semblance been greatly altered. But the basic conception of bookstacks, gallery and Reading Room survived.

> At Cambridge the architectural treatment of the book-stack has to be boldly faced, as these features form the bulk of the building. The peculiar fenestration of a book-stack, with its very long narrow windows gives, however, to the exterior of these features a distinctive character, and depends for its effect [within] upon its general proportions and the contrast of the coloured ceiling with the plain plastered walls.

Design and statement both show the most careful attention to how the readers would search for their books, in a setting as light as glass and decoration can make it, and read them close to the stacks or in the Reading Room, which must be reached by comfortable and accessible corridors: the close link of Catalogue Room and Reading Room was part of the Librarian's brief. The other features of design on which Scott laid emphasis were the simple character, with modestly ornate ceilings and doors, of the great Reading Room and the main Gallery – and the breadth of the Gallery to allow space for the original book-cases of the Royal Library, with their books in them [**181**, 236–8]. This feature, in which the old and the new Libraries were marvellously woven together, was ruined in the 1950s when a vandal

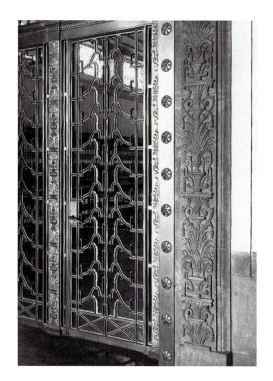

236. (top left) The gallery on
the first floor, showing the
eighteenth-century cases of the
Royal Library and their books.
(*Country Life*)
237. (bottom) The Reading
Room, 1997.
238. (top right) The entrance to the
Catalogue Room showing Scott's
ornamental stone and metalwork.

damaged a number of the books: they had to be put into reserved cases and works of less value and beauty set in their place. I confess that I would dearly like to see the original books restored to their homes – protected by modern electronic devices – so that this most inspired feature of Scott's design can once again be properly appreciated.

Financing the Library

In the years which followed, Scott made only two major changes in his design, both at the behest of John D. Rockefeller, Junior.

In the early 1920s, Mr Rockefeller had inaugurated an imaginative and beneficent scheme to endow and revivify the study of the biological and medical sciences, including agriculture, in a variety of centres scattered over western Europe; in 1922–3, Richard M. Pearce visited Europe specifically to discuss the development of medical research at a number of centres, and in October 1923 he came to Cambridge and stayed in the Master's Lodge at Caius. The outcome was a substantial endowment for pathology; and Anderson soon emerged as the chief negotiator for Cambridge. When further emissaries from Rockefeller came to plan aid for other biological sciences in the summer of 1926, it was doubtless Anderson to whom they primarily looked for guidance. The visit is ill recorded, but it is evident that, in the warm, beguiling company of Anderson, they were inspired with the idea of helping fund a new University Library. The chief negotiator in 1926 was Mr R. B. Fosdick, a central figure in the Foundation over many years; but he came on behalf of the International Educational Board – a limb of the Rockefeller Foundation specifically concerned with medical and biological sciences – and he evidently advised that negotiations carry on at a higher level. The outcome was that he carried back to New York a letter from the Chancellor of the University, Lord Balfour, to Mr Rockefeller, Junior, in person, dated 6 August 1926. 'Mr Rockefeller's reply was cordial, but non-committal.' He feared aid for one library might lead to other similar demands, and he did not care for Scott's plans. 'By the way', he wrote to Fosdick, 'the design for the library seems to me atrocious. I would hate to be a party to the erection of such a building in so beautiful a surrounding, but then that is a detail.' None the less, over the two years which followed, there somehow came to be a growing confidence that Rockefeller aid would come.

Meanwhile, on 27 April 1927, Scholfield the Librarian wrote to Scott a letter of consummate tact. Referring to the criticism of a major would-be benefactor, he wrote:

> One may say generally that the façade was thought not to be sufficiently imposing...Not that there is a want of dignity, but it is self-effacing, austere, and with no trace of richness. And it was partly its modesty, so to speak, partly its austerity that made it appear to our critics that this new Library was alien in spirit to the rest of the aggregate of buildings that make up the University of Cambridge. Partly too the grey brick and dark red tiles looked discrepant and cold to eyes accustomed to the red brick and green slates of St John's, of Jesus, of Magdalene, or the mellow stone of King's and of Trinity...A fresh design for the façade was asked for.

Scott replied at once, saying that he would think the matter over carefully; and by early June he was in Cambridge with new designs, foreshadowing a

239. April 1932: pile-driving for the new University Library.

building in reddish brick with a tower. Thus was accomplished the transformation from a practical library with modest classical features to the Assyrian palace which confronts us today. Throughout 1927 and 1928 the plans for the new Library, the negotiations with the Rockefeller Foundation, and with the Government and other bodies, to provide the rest of the money needed went steadily forward. On 30 October 1928, the University discussed the formal offer from Rockefeller, and with only one dissentient voice – a physicist disappointed to see so much money go to biology – it was greeted with a chorus of approval, and of thanks to the Master of Caius. At this moment of triumph, Anderson was dangerously ill; he died on 2 November.

In 1929 the final plans and estimates came before the University, and after brief discussion were approved. The Library was to cost £500,000: £320,000 for the building, the rest for maintenance, removal and essential endowment. The Rockefeller Foundation gave £250,000 to the Library; the

240. An artist's impression of the new University Library to be, by J. D. M. Harvey, 1931.

Ministry of Agriculture and Fisheries and the Empire Marketing Board each gave £50,000; Lord Melchett (who chaired the appeal) and Mr Robert Mond gave £10,000 each; and when these and other lesser sums had been added together, the University made up what was lacking from its own resources.

On 29 September 1931 the first of 1,200 ferro-concrete piles was driven into the ground [239]. Over the piles a raft was laid and over the raft the Library grew; and on 22 October 1934, King George V came to open the new Library [240]. Meanwhile, a mighty operation had been planned and executed to prepare the books for their removal and carry them across the Backs. In June and July 1934, over a period of eight weeks, 689 horse-drawn loads carried 23,725 boxes of books – excluding bound copies of newspapers and large elephant folios, which required separate treatment.[241]

Epilogue

Since 1934 the books, like the sheep of More's *Utopia*, have devoured every available space at an alarming speed. The Library was extended in the early 1970s to the designs of Gollins Melville and Ward in the style of the day; in the 1990s, Harry Faulkner-Brown has added further to it, in direct imitation of Scott. New workshops and a new tea room have enabled some of its essential functions to continue. More extensions are under construction,

241. The horse and wagon moving books from the old to the new Library – emerging from the old Library, now the Old Schools.

4. In my earlier writings I was much indebted to the help of Nigel Hancock, Elisabeth Leedham-Green and Patrick Zutshi; more recently I have also had particular help from Mr Harry Faulkner-Brown, Dr David McKitterick, and from the staff of the RIBA Library and Archives, especially Mrs Angela Mace, Archivist.

and the Library has to face the immense problems of an era of very rapid change in the nature and use of libraries, and especially the growth of modern technology. For those who seek ready access to large numbers of books, however, and who welcome some exercise in the pursuit of their quarry, it is incomparably the best library I have encountered; and for fifty years – to me as a scholar – it has been a paradise.[4]

Index

Acknowledgements

Plate [15] reproduced by gracious permission of Her Majesty The Queen; [16] by permission of the Controller of Her Majesty's Stationery Office; [20] by permission of Professor The Earl Russell; [44] Beth Hatefutsoth-Visual Documentation Center, Tel Aviv; [109] by permission of Professor H. B. Barlow; [115] by permission of Sir Rupert Hart-Davies; [228] Country Life Picture Library.